Uncertainties, Mysteries,

What is it to listen? How do we hear? How do we allow meanings to emerge between each other?

This book is about what Freud called 'freely' or 'evenly suspended attention', a form of listening, a kind of receptive incomprehension, which is fundamental and mandatory for the practice of psychoanalysis and psychotherapy. The author steps outside the usual parameters of psychoanalytic writing and explores how works of art and literature which elicit and require such listening began to appear in Europe, in abundance, from the late eighteenth century onwards.

Uncertainties, Mysteries, Doubts is a timely reminder, in the present era of audit and manualisation, of some of psychoanalysis's deep and living cultural roots. It hopes – by immersing the reader in the emotional, critical and contextual worlds of some artists and poets of Romanticism – to help psychotherapists, psychoanalysts and counsellors in the endless challenge of staying open to their clients and patients, faced as we all are, therapists and clients alike, with multiple pressures to knowledgeable closure.

Robert Snell is an analytic psychotherapist, a member of the London Centre for Psychotherapy, and an Honorary Senior Research Fellow in the Centre for Therapeutic Education at Roehampton University. He has a doctorate in art history from the Courtauld Institute. He is the co-author, with Del Loewenthal, of *Post-Modernism for Psychotherapists* (2003).

Uncertainties, Mysteries, Doubts

Romanticism and the analytic attitude

Robert Snell

 Routledge
Taylor & Francis Group

LONDON AND NEW YORK

First published 2013
by Routledge
27 Church Road, Hove, East Sussex BN3 2FA

Simultaneously published in the USA and Canada
by Routledge
711 Third Avenue, New York, NY 10017

Routledge is an imprint of the Taylor & Francis Group, an informa business

British Library Cataloguing in Publication Data
A catalogue record for this book is available from the British Library

Library of Congress Cataloging in Publication Data
Snell, Robert, 1951–.
  Uncertainties, mysteries, doubts: Romanticism and the analytic
  attitude/authored by Robert Snell.
    p. cm.
  Includes bibliographical references.
  1. Psychoanalysis and the arts. 2. Romanticism.
  3. Psychoanalysis – Philosophy. I. Title.
  NX180.P7S56 2012
  700'.4145—dc23
  2012008512

ISBN: 978-0-415-54385-9 (hbk)
ISBN: 978-0-415-54386-6 (pbk)
ISBN: 978-0-203-09417-4 (ebk)

Typeset in Times New Roman
by Florence Production Ltd, Stoodleigh, Devon

MIX
Paper from
responsible sources
FSC
www.fsc.org   FSC® C004839   Printed and bound in Great Britain by the MPG Books Group

Jacques. 'If you keep asking questions, we'll have circled the entire globe before we get to the finish of the tale of my love-life.' Master. 'What's it matter provided you go on talking and I go on listening? They are the two most important things, aren't they?'

(Diderot 1999 [1796]: 35)

The psychoanalytic cure, as innovative as it may be in the history of inter-human relations, can have neither sense nor results unless it encounters and enters into relation with something pre-existent and fundamental in human existence and its movement of temporalisation . . .

(Laplanche 1992: 171)

Contents

List of figures

Acknowledgements

Thank you to Graham Alexander, Roger Bacon, Dennis Creffield, Frank Gray, Rod Harman, Brett Kahr, Percival Mars, Richard Morgan-Jones, Ann Scott, my sister Sarah Snell, Sarah Soutar, Robert Stone, Lawrence Suss, Anne Tyndale and Marcus West, for conversations that have contributed, directly and indirectly, to the thinking behind this book. Warm thanks are also due to my travelling companions from the London Centre for Psychotherapy year of 1993, Sylvia Douglas, who read draft sections of the book, Mark Fletcher, Andrew Kilburn, Doula Nicolson and Valerie Scott; to Sharon Keating and Katayoun Medhat, enspiriting friends and readers; and to Del Loewenthal and the students and staff of the MSc and Doctoral programmes in Therapeutic Education at the University of Surrey and latterly Roehampton University, who have been such lively sources of learning over the years. Thank you, too, to Florángel Lambor for her untiring assistance in obtaining permissions, to Brook Barbieri and Ginevra de Bellis, and to Kate Hawes and Camilla Barnard at Routledge for their patience and editorial support. None of the above, of course, bears any responsibility for the book's slips, errors and shortcomings.

I am grateful to the University of Sussex, Psychological and Counselling Services, for a valuable period of leave to work on the book. Versions of Chapters 2, 3 and 5 were given as talks at Surrey and Roehampton Universities, under the umbrella of the Surrey Association for Psychotherapy and Counselling. Versions of Chapter 3, on Goya, were offered as lectures/seminars to the Brighton Association of Analytic Psychotherapists (now Psychotherapy Sussex), at the London Centre for Psychotherapy, at Canterbury Christchurch University, to postgraduate painting students, and at the 2006 Tavistock 'Creativity and the Unconscious' conference.

The extract from Diderot's *Jacques the Fatalist*, which opens the book, appears by permission of Oxford University Press, and the sentence from a lecture given by Jean Laplanche at the University of Kent in 1990 by permission of the Institute of Contemporary Arts, London. Goethe's poem *Wandrers Nachtlied II, The Wayfarer's Night Song II*, with a prose translation by David Luke, is reproduced by permission of Penguin Books Ltd from *Goethe. Selected Verse. With plain prose translations of each poem,*

Penguin Classics, London, 1964, p. 50. Copyright © David Luke, 1964. Extracts from Hölderlin's *The Journey*, *Bonaparte*, *The Sanctimonious Poets*, *Hyperion's Song of Fate*, *The Neckar*, *The Course of Life*, *Ganymede*, *Bread and Wine*, *Half of Life*, *As on a Holiday* . . . and *The Ister* are taken from *Friedrich Hölderlin: Poems and Fragments*, translated by Michael Hamburger, fourth edition published by Anvil Press Poetry in 2004 and reprinted by Penguin in 2007. Translations from French are my own, unless otherwise referenced.

'Re-read Stendhal in your middle age, you will find him a powerful consolation', advised Dr Anita Brookner, my tutor and supervisor at the Courtauld Institute. Her teaching is an important part of the background to this book, and it is a pleasure, from my now middle-aged perspective, to be able to acknowledge my gratitude here.

Last, and very far from least, thank you to Kim, Alex and Hannah, for putting up with me during the book's gestation, and for your collective encouragement throughout. It would never have happened without you.

Introduction

In 1805, writing in his notebook, the poet Samuel Taylor Coleridge coined the word 'psycho-analytical', pre-dating Freud by ninety-one years. Coleridge was wondering at how the classical, pagan gods had survived as living presences in medieval Christian minds. He concluded that the modern reader would need 'a strong imagination as well as an accurate psycho-analytical understanding' in order to get a real sense of this; it was an 'anonymous hidden life', active 'in the ordinary unchecked stream of Thought' of the times like a kind of 'Contraband' (Coleridge 1961: para 2670).[1] A 'psycho-analytical understanding' would have to proceed, like one of Coleridge's own wandering but wonderfully sure-footed sentences, tangentially, indirectly (Eng 1984: 463). Interest such as Coleridge's in medieval and chivalric 'romances' was also key to the naming and development of Romanticism: Romanticism and psychoanalysis are bound together from their beginnings.

What follows is about this undirected but somehow actively receptive state of mind, and its central importance in psychotherapy. It is generally referred to, conveniently but far too concretely, as the 'analytic attitude'. Freud called it 'free-floating' or 'evenly suspended attention' (Freud, S. 1912: 110). It is a kind of 'free' listening, the counterpart to the free association that psychoanalysts encourage in their patients, through which the unconscious, like contraband in the ordinary unchecked stream of thought, might have a chance of declaring itself. It is an emotional orientation in the therapist, a commitment, founded in respect, to maintaining a radically open-minded stance: a suspended state somewhere between passivity and readiness for emotional and verbal activity. W.R. Bion called it 'reverie', which he likened to the Romantic poet Keats's 'negative capability', a capacity for staying in 'uncertainties, Mysteries, doubts' and deferring attempts at logical or discursive sense-making (Bion 1984b [1970]: 125; 1990: 45, 47). It involves an attempt to bracket off judgements and preconceptions; it requires a moratorium on claims to understand, often in the face of tremendous pressure from within the listener, from her interlocutor, from the surrounding culture, or from all of these together, to seek relief from the unknowns of the unconscious and of the other person in supposed knowledge or certainty.

It is a state informed by 'benevolent neutrality'. It is also an insistently reflexive kind of listening which, implicitly and explicitly, the therapist invites the patient to engage in too: it allows room for both hearer and speaker to attend to their emotional and associative responses, voiced or unvoiced, to what each hears, in themselves and each other, so that the patient might make contact with more and more aspects of his unknown (repressed, disavowed, projected . . .) self. Jacques Lacan spoke of the 'analyst's desire' (Fink 1997: 6–7): to maintain a position constituted not by a 'so-called analytic neutrality' in which 'the analyst is in a stupor', but by a wish to introduce the subject to the primary 'language of his desire . . . which – beyond what he tells us of himself – he is already speaking to us unbeknown to himself' (Lacan 2007: 242–3).

Imagination must indeed play its part: the listener must try to stay alive to possibilities as yet unrealised or undreamed in the speaker(s). Imagination is needed in order to keep open a hospitable mental and emotional space – D. W. Winnicott thought in terms of the 'potential space' of the analytic setting as a whole, for creative play and cultural experience (Winnicott 1985 [1971]: 126 ff.) – which the patient might, in time, of their own accord, come to occupy and shape.

It is what Coleridge, evoking the poetic imagination, called 'a hospitable freedom or playfulness of mind, rather than a fixed and perhaps premature intellectual judgement' (Holmes 1999: 130n1). Far from the distanced, objectifying standpoint that it might at first seem to suggest, the phrase 'analytic attitude' returns the word 'analysis' to its ancient Greek roots: analysis as loosening up, unbinding, in order to make room for something else. The process thus set in motion continues, potentially, into the lives of *both* participants well after the end of therapy.

Without such a frame of mind there could be no psychoanalysis nor analytic psychotherapy. It is the indispensable foundation of a working therapeutic alliance. It is fundamental among the broad principles – working in the transference, attention to childhood, sexuality, dreams and the drives – underlying and constituting classical psychoanalytic practice, and it is mandatory for analytic work in *all* its forms, from individual psychoanalysis to the analytic group to time-sensitive psychodynamic counselling to analytically informed organisational consultancy. Well maintained, it can be therapeutic in itself, and this should never be underestimated. Yet it is not the whole of psychoanalysis or therapy: interpretation and 'technique', informed by theory, are also necessary. The analytic attitude is always, inevitably, in uneasy tension with them. For the gap between theory and doing is a 'slippery liminal space' in which the most basic assumptions behind theory can find themselves challenged (Cotton and Loewenthal 2011: 87). If theory and technique are not the focus of this book, the importance of trying to stay in this difficult, interesting space is.

The book is also about a field of critically important cultural precedence for this attitude, an area of historical underpinning, without which it is hard to see how it could have developed as a therapeutic resource. Radical open-mindedness and a Coleridgian 'suspension of disbelief' (Holmes 1999: 130) were responses to massive social and political crisis, and a consequent, widely felt loss of bearings, in the years around the French Revolution. This period, from which stems so much else that characterises modernity and post-modernity, witnessed a foundational crisis of sense-making. Contemporaries, particularly the young, had to rise to a task more urgent than anything their parents or grandparents had faced: how to respond to and find meaning in the rapidly changing emotional and social landscape in which they found themselves? What to say about it? How to negotiate its highs and lows, or feel they could shape it, and how to know what they wanted or what they were doing? Former discursive, rational approaches no longer seemed adequate; classical Enlightenment could indeed seem part of the problem. They had to find their own means and directions, and it was a task that could be as destabilising as it was liberating. Behind Coleridge's or Keats's exhilarated evocations of creativity and imagination there was thus something more pressing.

Roots and precedents for the analytic attitude are not only to be sought in evocations of this kind, suggestive as they are. They can also be found in ways in which artists and writers, at this time of immense uncertainty and unforeseeable possibility, found themselves inviting spectators and readers to join them and actively engage with their work. The book suggests that it was, above all, the Romantic work of art itself that laid the foundation for analytic receptiveness, through the listening, responsive, 'not-knowing' state it could invite and require in the reader or viewer (and, in so far as it did this, constitute itself as 'Romantic'). Works of art and literature that elicited and demanded a kind of 'receptive misunderstanding' (Hildesheimer 1982: 41) began to appear in abundance in late eighteenth- and early nineteenth-century Europe. Such works do (and did) not so much reward attempts to explain them as require us to feel, react, and try to find ways to describe and reflect upon the experience. They set up new, dynamic and 'dialogic' relationships between themselves and the spectator/reader.

Typically, confrontation with art of the Romantic era demands an emotional stance, a mental and emotional availability, which contemporary analytic psychotherapists might recognise: an openness, through a readiness to day-dream and free associate, to ambiguities and multiple meanings, to enigmas and encodings, to the indeterminate; to the unrepeatable quality of the present moment, as well as to the allure of the past; to feeling, to the fleeting, fragmentary and subliminal, to dream, desire and terror, the erotic and the life of the body. The Romantic work of art can open us as it did contemporaries to the contingent, the unexpected and unforeseen, the phenomenology of the everyday. It can help connect us to experiences that lie beyond our immediate experience, to irreducible *otherness*, to the inalienable mystery of self and other.

It might be argued, of course, that any art can do this, in that it asks us to accept and respond to it the way it is; in refusing closure and resisting definitive interpretation the art of the Romantics is like all great art. Romanticism, however, brings this refusal and resistance to a new pitch and intensity; it can vigorously invite, and just as vigorously repel. It requires us to face ourselves as the fallible and unsure creatures we all fundamentally are: the work of art, as Lacanians say, is 'in the place of the analyst' (Brousse 2007).

One might argue further, as for example the literary historian and critic Joel Faflak has (Faflak 2008), that Romanticism constituted a, if not the, crucial founding moment of psychoanalysis; that in an important sense Romanticism *was* psychoanalysis, *avant la lettre*. In its concern with self-exploration, relationship, eros, anxiety, terror and mystery (see Coleridge, Friedrich, Novalis or Byron, for example) Romanticism was more than just one precedent or adumbration of psychoanalysis among others. It was also a hermeneutics; this was the first time in modern history that a widely experienced cultural phenomenon could make such a claim. It was founded in a respect for the elusiveness of meanings and for 'the hermeneutic principle according to which mystery and incomprehensibility foster understanding' (Calhoon 1992: 15). Acceptance of nonsense and a determination *not* to understand are the foundations of psychoanalytic meta-psychology. 'In his bid to make apparently anomalous human behaviour intelligible', wrote Hugh Haughton,

> Freud was led to construct a theory that places unintelligibility at the heart of mental processes . . . in an astonishing transformation of the Cartesian project, it made self-unintelligibility the paradoxical cornerstone of psychic identity . . . psychoanalysis greatly extends the domain of intelligibility, but it does so by rendering more and more areas of psychic life elusive or unintelligible, or presenting it as a drive towards unintelligibility, disguise, secrecy, and self-subversion . . . As Lionel Trilling said . . . 'of all mental systems, the Freudian psychology is the one which makes poetry indigenous to the very condition of mind'.
>
> (Haughton 2003: ix–x)

By the same token, Romantic criticism of Enlightenment was in opposition to 'the destimulation that the removal of mystery entails' (Calhoon 1992: 19). Romanticism was a challenge to what Theodor Adorno and Max Horkheimer (1989 [1944]) called the Enlightenment compulsion to repeat, in which 'every occurrence is a recurrence' and the unprecedented is reduced to the already known (Calhoon 1992: 33, 41). Undoubtedly, Freud's 'fundamental rule' of free association has philosophical roots in the Enlightenment, in seventeenth- and eighteenth-century associationism, deriving from the philosophy of John Locke; but free association could hardly have emerged as a foundational practice for psychoanalysis without that openness to surprise and the unknown which was central to Romanticism and the Romantic imagination.

Imagination, in turn, is key to the analyst's ability to come from somewhere else. For that great beacon of Romanticism, William Blake, we are all artists, creatures of divine imagination; this for Blake is why we were put on earth. Mental anguish results from all that stands in the way of our becoming artists: false rationality, narrow religion and the infliction of cruelty. From this perspective, Freud's main stroke of genius one hundred years later was to devise a physical and emotional setting in which people might be able to hear more clearly from their creative/destructive selves; the non-interfering quality of the analyst's attentiveness, and the analyst's ability to be a surprise to the patient, are central.

Lingering with works of the Romantic period may thus also be a way in which, as practitioners, we can help hold ourselves to an 'analytic' openness. In some (but only some) respects we in the 'developed' world inhabit more sheltered times than a Blake, Coleridge or Keats. We are, for example, free of most of the diseases that cut lives short two hundred years ago. Understandably, we accord the scientific and medical methods that brought this about tremendous prestige. As practitioners, we also have a large and rich body of psychoanalytic experience and theory of our own to draw upon. For all these reasons, we can delude ourselves the more easily that we somehow do know what we are talking about, what to say in advance, what would be a 'correct' response to the person who comes to us in search of something. In an age in which psychotherapy is ever more manualised and subjected to all kinds of reductive auditing, a reminder of psychoanalysis's Romantic roots and affinities may be timely.

Romanticism, as Roger Bacon has written of psychoanalysis, 'operates on the limits of what it is to make sense and thus engenders the anxiety of senselessness, the destruction of . . . assumptions about how to (and what) makes sense' (Bacon 2006: 13). Chapter 1 offers a short introduction to Romanticism, and develops some ideas on its relatedness to psychoanalysis.

Chapter 2 documents some salient and representative statements of the analytic attitude from Freud onwards, and aims to convey a sense of the nuanced multiplicity of ways in which analytic listening has been evoked and problematised.

What restless movement between openness and claims to understanding or knowledge does the work of art instigate in the viewer/reader/listener? The next three chapters take this question up in explorations of works by the Spanish painter Francisco Goya (1746–1828), the German poets Friedrich Hölderlin (1770–1843) and Novalis (Friedrich von Hardenberg, 1772–1801), and the French poet Charles Baudelaire (1821–67).

In the final chapter, the French poet, novelist and dramatist Alfred de Vigny (1797–1863), the American poet and short-story writer Edgar Allan Poe (1809–49), and the English poet John Keats (1795–1821) add their own reflections on how an analytic attitude might be conceptualised and embodied.

These particular figures were chosen to represent a cross-European and transatlantic range, for an analytic/Romantic orientation or state of mind was evoked and sustained in viewers and readers across (often contested) borders. There are others on whom I might have focused – Blake, Wordsworth, Coleridge, Shelley, Turner, Hoffmann, Büchner, Heine or Nerval, for example; the French painter Théodore Géricault, whose paintings of the early 1820s of inmates of Paris asylums are among the most challenging and mind-opening portraits in the history of Western art, will, I hope, be the subject of a separate publication. Each was selected because he is a major figure, capable of generating seemingly inexhaustible possibilities of meaning and interpretation, and this in turn is what qualifies him as Romantic. The reputation of each has grown over time precisely because of the degree of emotional intensity, indeterminacy and suggestiveness of what he produced. If each is a representative Romantic, it is also, above all, because he connects us to untamable, Dionysian aspects of the unconscious.[2]

Each of these figures too illuminates a different aspect of a living commitment to 'analytic' openness, and/or a different area of resistance to it. Goya struggled and invites us to struggle with the lures of rationality, the 'great dream' of reason. What *is* that fearful thing, he insistently asks, on the margins of our awareness? No contemporary artist articulated the crisis in European Enlightenment with Goya's trenchancy, and he did this not as a philosopher but as a painter; he lived and embodied it.

Hölderlin, too, wrestling with the limitations and imperatives of language, lived and embodied his struggle. Novalis tapped language's unstoppable resources; both poets require a confrontation with unknowability, unpredictability and indeterminacy.

Baudelaire's verse and prose drew on an earlier Romanticism and herald modernism. They bring into focus the unrepresented and voiceless, who become metaphors for internal states; by inviting reverie, his work can invoke such states, often with a frisson of horror, in the reader. He opens us to an awareness of the gulf between the alienated individuals of the city, in the first flush of a capitalism whose legacy therapist and patient continue to negotiate.

Vigny and Poe offer fictional portraits of proto-analysts, a poet–philosopher doctor and a poet–philosopher detective. Keats too illuminates a proto-analytic mentality, not through fiction but in his very being as a poet; he can connect us simultaneously with joy, sociability and a chronic sense of defeat, with all that this can imply for therapeutic practice. If negative capability is always compromised, threatened by closures that themselves operate unconsciously, is there hope for us yet?

Romantic art, for the Romantics, was simply art that can speak to us and move us in the conditions in which we live today (Stendhal 1970: 71). Viewed in this way, Romanticism has no end date. Romanticism and, at its best, psychoanalysis stand for values, meanings and ethics, which oppose attempts to reduce the human subject to smooth-running, atemporal, apolitical mechanism; we shall encounter a chilling adumbration of this reductionism in a story of 1877 by Villiers de l'Isle Adam (1838–89). The book aims to help sustain the living, reflexive and thinking aspects of psychoanalysis, as an animator of creative and potentially subversive activity, not an anodyne servant of 'well-being' (see Rizq 2011). For we need, in the words of André Green, to

> revise the frontiers that an arrogant and dominating mode of thinking has tried to establish between health and illness . . . [which] also means accepting that one cannot be fully alive and fully human by escaping the difficulties of existing, desiring and thinking . . .
>
> (Green 2005 [2002]: 28–9)

I have quoted freely throughout the book. While this might risk making for tedious reading, I hope it may work to strengthen the case for a deep affinity between a Romantic and an analytic stance rather more than if I had only relied (although I also do rely) on my own partial, tendentious readings and responses. In a sense, this is an anti-Romantic procedure. Romanticism repeatedly asserted the artist's and the viewer's right to trust his or her own senses and judgements, and in this it bequeathed something of importance for the working analyst. Extensive use of quotation has, on the other hand, its own impeccable progenitor: Walter Benjamin envisaged a whole book that would be an album of quotations, and this came into being in his great *Arcades* project (Benjamin 1999 [1982]), on which I have drawn particularly in the chapter on Baudelaire. It is an approach that hints at the multiplicity of possible responses to the works of art and literature under discussion; it might help underline their 'Romantic' openness to interpretation and reinterpretation, and, at the same time, draw attention to the particular style of the interpreter's act of interpretation, whether it is the analytic attitude itself, a painting, print or poem that is being discussed. It is also to acknowledge one of the Romantic period's discoveries and, thanks to Bakhtin and post-structuralism, our own period's rediscovery: the extent to which any text, however apparently coherent, is traversed by many voices and is the product of them.

For what else does the working therapist do but listen to the multiple voices of the person who comes to them, what else is the analytic setting designed for than to create a space, an ambience, in which it may be possible for both analyst and patient to listen for these voices, in their particularity and otherness? At the same time, both these approaches, the Romantic and that which takes courage from Benjamin, are antidotes, consciously so, to the thrall of dead, unquestioned, received ideas. Both are on the side of the interminability of the conversation with the other and the unconscious.

Chapter 1

Psychoanalysis and Romanticism

Crisis, mourning and the mysteries of the ordinary

Romanticism was not so much a movement, an -ism, a cultural or artistic programme, as a state of mind, a form of engagement. Examinations of psychoanalysis's Romantic roots have been wide and various. Pre-Freudian intuitions of the unconscious and earlier medico-philosophical 'discoveries' of the unconscious have been unearthed and explored (Whyte 1960; Ellenberger 1970). The great German dramatist Schiller's role in the origins of the talking cure has been recognised (Dewhurst and Reeves 1978), and a German cultural tradition in psychology in the eighteenth and nineteenth centuries has been mapped (Bell 2005). Templates for a psychoanalytic model of mind have been discerned in English Romantic poetry (Williams and Waddell 1991). It has long been acknowledged that Romanticism was an integral part of Freud's own cultural and linguistic heritage. It was so much in the air he breathed that its influence on him is not easy to quantify, and he himself did not always see any need explicitly to acknowledge it. He did allude to Romanticism as part of the prehistory of psychoanalysis (Freud, S. 1924), and biographers have noted his profound familiarity with Romantic literature and philosophy, with Schiller and Goethe, whom he could quote at length, Heine, a particular favourite, and Schopenhauer (Gay 1988: 128; Jones 1953: 312 ff.). Hearing Goethe's 'Essay on Nature' read aloud at school, Freud wrote, was what decided him to study medicine (Jones 1955, 1957: I, 31). He drew on a vast breadth of reading (he read English, French and Spanish), from Sophocles to Shakespeare, Cervantes and Dickens. Biographers, however, have not always sufficiently acknowledged the extent to which, within this culture and reading, Romanticism, and not only German Romanticism, was responsible for lending his work a particular vitality, a driving sense of excitement.

Early in his career Freud had been impressed by Flaubert's *Les Tentations de Saint-Antoine*, which, he wrote in a letter to his future wife Martha in 1883,

> calls up not only the great problems of knowledge, but the real riddles of life, all the conflicts of feelings and impulses; and it confirms the awareness of our perplexity in the mysteriousness that reigns everywhere. These questions . . . are always there, and one should always be thinking

of them, for they can take us by surprise and 'assail' and rob us of our 'composure and spirits'.

(cited in Symington 1986a: 77; see also
Jones 1953: 191–2)

Freud admired the Romantic Ludwig Börne's essay of 1823, 'The Art of Becoming an Original Writer in Three Days', which advocated free association and the creativity of a mind roaming free of constraint, to which images and thoughts might present themselves unbidden. He had been given the book containing this essay when he was 14, and it was, by his own account, the only book from his boyhood that he had kept (Freud 1920: 265; Symington 1986a: 82; Jones 1953: 270–1). Did he also know Heinrich von Kleist's essay, of the early 1800s, 'On the Gradual Production of Thoughts While Speaking' (Kleist 2004)?

The French psychoanalysts Madeleine and Henri Vermorel have surveyed Freud's Romantic roots in some detail. They noted that German Romantic writers are less frequently quoted in his collected works than the classics, from Sophocles to Shakespeare; references to Romantics are nevertheless plentiful, from E.T.A. Hoffmann, whose fantastic tale 'The Sandman' was the starting point for Freud's most 'Romantic' work, *The Uncanny*, to the novelist Jean-Paul (Richter), the Grimm brothers, Friedrich Wilhelm Schelling, the father of the philosophy of Nature, Gothilf Heinrich von Schubert, author of an influential book called *Symbolism of Dreams* (1814),[1] and the theologian and philosopher Friedrich Schleiermacher. Other poets and thinkers, Uhland, Rückert, Lenau, Chamisso, Tieck and Bettina Brentano, are also represented, as are Schlegel and Novalis, albeit sparsely (Vermorel and Vermorel 1986: 2–3). Freud's Romanticism shows itself in the very direction of his researches: into dreams (Novalis, von Schubert, Schleiermacher), chaos, the unconscious and repression, jokes and aesthetics (Jean-Paul, Hoffmann, Heine). Among his actual teachers at least one, a Frenchman, Jean-Martin Charcot, might in some respects qualify as a latter-day Romantic.

The legacy of Romantic biology and medicine can be felt throughout psychoanalysis: a view of symptoms as symbols of an overall situation in which something is wrong, thus of therapy as the cure of souls, and the consequent centrality for treatment of the physician's empathy (see also Bell 2005). Origins of drive theory can be discerned in the late eighteenth-century concept of *Reiz*, or excitability, deriving from the Scottish physician John Brown[2] (Vermorel and Vermorel 1986: 8–9). Romantic predeliction for the fragment, and emphasis on the tension between extremes, find their echoes in the open-endedness and dynamic, conflict-focused nature of Freudian psychoanalysis (Vermorel and Vermorel 1986: 10). Freud's approach to dreams as riddles, popular forms that everyone responds to, may have felt as freeing to him as the discovery of the democratic vitality of folk songs did to Herder, Goethe and the Wordsworths.

The new value that the Romantics placed on childhood was also an essential precondition, from Blake's *Songs of Innocence* and Wordsworth's 'The Child is father of the Man' (Wordsworth 2000: 246), to Baudelaire's idea that 'Genius is childhood regained at will' (Baudelaire 1975–76: II, 684). So were attitudes to madness, which the Romantics tended to regard not just as the breakdown of rational thought but also as 'an alternative, which promised not only different insights but also a different mode of reasoning' (Rosen 1998: 115). Nor would psychoanalysis have been conceivable without the Romantics' emphasis on the 'modern man' (Sachs 2010: 56–7), the emancipated individual and his and increasingly her development. This was evident in the popularity, around the turn of the nineteenth century, of the *Bildungsroman*, the novel of the unique formation of a character: Goethe's *Wilhelm Meister's Apprenticeship* (1795–96), for example, or Novalis's *Heinrich von Ofterdingen* (1802) (Vermorel and Vermorel 1986: 9). Roots for psychoanalysis can be discerned in solitary Romantic self-analysis, as advocated by Börne, for example: 'The true act of self-education lies in making oneself unwitting' (Jones 1953: 271). They are also to be found in the sociable, co-creative style of Romantic working methods, for which Friedrich Schlegel coined the terms *Symphilosophie* and *Sympoesie*. The groupings, friendships and *cénacles* of the Romantics, with their love affairs and disputes, were echoed a century later in the congresses, societies and gatherings of psychoanalysts, with all their passions and schisms.

At the same time, and perhaps this is a generally more familiar account, Freud was an heir of the eighteenth-century Enlightenment, with its commitment to Reason as something inherent to Nature and Nature's immutable, post-Newtonian laws: he was a builder of master theories and universal explanations, most prominent among them infantile sexuality and the Oedipus complex. For psychoanalysis has also tended to consider itself a continuation and extension of Enlightenment, a project to extend the explanatory reaches of Reason to the phenomena of the irrational and reclaim them from religion and metaphysics. Freud indeed repeatedly acknowledged his debt to Enlightenment (Gay 1995: xviii–xx; Habermas 1972). He was a 'biologist of the mind' (Sulloway 1979) in a more modern sense too, the product of Darwinism, the rationalist and positivist teaching of Meynert and Brücke, and the materialism of the physiologist Helmholz, with its roots in the Enlightenment and Descartes. Freud saw himself the founder of a science, whose practitioners to this day hold 'scientific meetings'.

Another widely accepted view among analysts and historians of psychoanalysis is that Freud's genius stemmed from his 'dual identity' (Vermorel and Vermorel 1986: 15): psychoanalysis is a marriage of Enlightenment and Romanticism. In this view Freud developed a body of theory and practice that held two human poles in tension, a wish for stability, order and general, reliable principles, with an openness to flux, the undecidable and the unforeseeable; a pull towards certainties and universal truths on the one hand,

and on the other an acknowledgement and celebration of transience and doubt (a polarity manifest, of course, in the cultural battle between Classic and Romantic in Europe around the turn of the eighteenth and nineteenth centuries). On one hand, the Enlightenment ambition for a world whose workings were transparent to and ordered by Reason, and, on the other, the Romantic rediscovery of the power of that which is outside Reason's domain: dreams, the uncanny, and all the slippages and displacements of meaning between individuals and groups, what Freud called the great gaps in the data of consciousness (Freud, S. 1915: 166). In an elegant formulation Thomas Mann described psychoanalysis in 1929 as 'a Romanticism which has become scientific', in which 'libido theory [is] stripped of all mysticism'. Psycho-analysis was 'the form of modern irrationalism which' – in Mann's view unlike Romanticism – 'unequivocally resists every reactionary abuse to which it is subjected' (Mann 1970 [1929], cited in Vermorel and Vermorel 1986: 17). 'Science and Romanticism', wrote Neville Symington, 'came together in psychoanalysis' (Symington 1986a: 83).

Yet if psychoanalysis is such a marriage, none of the in-laws has ever been very happy about it. For, as Symington continued, 'psychoanalysis to this day remains a scandal to the natural scientist as it also is to the Romantic' (Symington 1986a: 83). Psychoanalysis's anti-credentials as a pseudo-science, typically linked to allegations of Freud's mendacity and moral failures, have been so frequently rehearsed as hardly to need recalling here: from Jeffrey Masson (1984, 1989) and Frederick Crews (1995) to a recent French publication entitled *Le livre noir de la psychanalyse* – The Black Book of Psychoanalysis (Van Rillaer etc. 2005, and see Snell 2007).

From the point of view of the Romantic, psychoanalysis errs far too closely on the side of a normalising, Enlightenment rationalism. Here is a great French historian of Romanticism, Albert Béguin, for whom psychoanalysis seemed

> to rely on a metaphysic which is closer to the eighteenth century than to Romanticism. Conscious and unconscious exchange certain of their contents, but the cycle which these two parts of ourselves constitute is a closed, purely individual cycle (even if you add in, as second-phase Freudianism wants to, the survival of ancestral images). In contrast, the Romantics all accept that the life of darkness is in ceaseless com-munication with another, vaster reality, which is anterior and superior to individual life. It is the same with the end that psychoanalysis has in view, it aims to restore the person afflicted with neurosis to sound behaviour and sociability. Romanticism, indifferent to this kind of health, looks out for images, even morbid ones, which will point the way to unknown regions of the soul: not out of curiosity, not in order to clean them up and make them more productive vis-à-vis our lives on earth, but in order to find there the secret of all that which, in time and space, extends us beyond ourselves and makes our present existence merely a point on the

line of an infinite destiny. This opposition, which separates psychoanalysis from mysticism as it does from Romanticism, closes it against any real understanding of that which could only be, from its point of view, a clear-cut case of psychosis.[3]

(Béguin 1938: xvi)

Béguin went on to deplore psychoanalysis's attempts to understand works of art, which would, for example, stretch to speaking of 'Baudelaire's failure' (a reference to a book of 1932 by René Laforgue, with the provocative title *The Defeat of Baudelaire*) (Béguin 1938: xv–xvi).

Others too have argued, from a broadly Romantic perspective, that in seeking to establish psychoanalysis as a science Freud diminished the way we account for the richness and mystery of human existence and experience. The philosopher François Roustang, for example, has complained:

To want to reduce humanity, human anguish, the infinite richness and complexity of human relations, to a certain number of elements which one can master and hold in the palm of one's hand, seems to me to be both genius, and pernicious. If you analyse Freud's work you cannot admire his stroke of genius without being frightened by what he did.

(Roustang 2006 [2001]: 22–3)

If psychoanalysis is a marriage, it is a compromised and unstable one, in frequent need of professional help. One need only consider its endemic history of splits and controversies, which continue today in spite of a growing acceptance of the value of theoretical pluralism. The marriage metaphor, moreover, seems to depend on a naive, descriptive, non-dynamic understanding of Romanticism: Romanticism as simple opposition to Enlightenment rather than in complex, dynamic and shifting tension with it, questioning it, problematising it. Sophisticated commentators such as Thomas Mann or Lou Andreas-Salomé have seen psychoanalysis as a significant step *beyond* Romanticism, a process of 'getting to know dark forces all the better for not merging with them' (Vermorel and Vermorel 1986: 17); but this is to take things even further than Béguin and caricature Romanticism as a mere wish for oblivious, unreflective merger with the darkness. The premises of a discourse based on bipolar Enlightenment/science/reason – Romanticism/art/unreason distinctions are questionable historically; both were embraced within what Richard Holmes (2008) has characterised as 'a sense of wonder'. As well as a poet and dramatist, Goethe was a 'natural philosopher' who wrote about biology, evolution, mineralogy, mining, economics, horticulture, geology and optics, and made a major contribution to the theory of colour. Coleridge studied his friend Humphrey Davy's discoveries in chemistry and the action of electricity. Novalis, a surveyor of mines, drew on optics and the chemistry of Lavoisier precisely to undermine a mechanistic and dualistic account of the universe:

'Doesn't life also, like light, break up into colours? . . . All effecting is transformation. In chemistry one observes things changing into one another.
But that is not so in that which one terms mechanical influence' (Novalis 1989:
71 [no. 248]). In the 1820s the painter John Constable had no difficulty
considering himself a natural scientist (Thornes 1999).[4] Symington and others
do not take into account the extent to which the science–art split was itself a
later nineteenth-century phenomenon. The use of the word 'science' to
describe methodical enquiry into the natural world does not seem to become
current, in Britain at least, until around the 1840s (Williams 1976: 232–5).
The Romantic period saw an explosion in experimental activity of many kinds;
'scientific' discovery was an integral part of Romantic questioning.[5]

In one way, of course, Romanticism *was* a rejection of Enlightenment,
particularly Enlightenment's belief in universal calculability, its commitment
to a rule of 'equivalence' in which 'the dissimilar [is made] comparable by
reducing it to abstract quantities . . . [and] that which does not reduce to
numbers . . . becomes illusion'. In this way, wrote Adorno and Horkheimer,
the 'destruction of gods and qualities alike is insisted upon' (Adorno and
Horkheimer 1989 [1944]: 7–8). Or, to put it another way, as Baudelaire did,
'Voltaire, like all lazy people, hated mystery' (Baudelaire 1975–76: I, 688).
At the same time Romanticism worked to reinvigorate Enlightenment and
older pre-revolutionary forms and assumptions. Coleridge's musing on the
survival of paganism in the Middle Ages needs to be understood in this context
– how to reconnect with former sources of vitality? For Hölderlin, and, a
decade or so later, Keats and Shelley, the sense of a classical, Greek ideal that
was longed for but now out of reach, the withdrawal or death of the ancient
gods, was a generative force. The naked male body based on classical Greek
and Roman protoypes had been the visual language of late Enlightenment: in
the hands of the neoclassical painter Jacques-Louis David it became the basis
of the French revolutionary republic's visual propaganda and the official
language of the academy. Yet Géricault, for one, adapted and made powerful
use of it in his great painting 'The Raft of the Medusa' (1819), in a radical
extension and repotentialising of critical Enlightenment (Eitner 1972). Stendhal
cast *De l'amour*, his idiosyncratic meditation on the revolutionary effects of
love, in the form of an eighteenth-century philosophical treatise. Baudelaire
injected Parisian slang into the classical French verse form, the alexandrine.

'Classics' such as Sophocles (translated by Hölderlin, among others),
Shakespeare, Calderón or Milton (consider Blake's great homage) were
themselves partly Romantic rediscoveries; Romanticism set the seal on their
modern 'classic' status. Romanticism's interest in the details of individual
lives was a development of Enlightenment: the novel exploring the singular
experiences of interacting individuals was an eighteenth-century invention
(Richardson, Fielding). Jean-Jacques Rousseau's elevation of the 'Natural',
represented by the child and the Noble Savage, which he set against the
corrupting influence of civilisation, is a 'Romantic' trope at the heart
of Enlightenment. The Kantian 'sublime', which enshrines a pleasurable

recognition that Reason can legislate over the most forceful sense impressions (Audi 1999: 886), is also an acknowledgement of the mind's awesome power. Romantics as well as Freud drew on the associationist psychology of the eighteenth century. Radical doubt was also part of the Enlightenment project.[6] Freud was, like Goethe, 'an internationalist who retained his links with . . . Enlightenment' (Vermorel and Vermorel 1986: 16), but it was Kant's subversive Enlightenment, the seed-bed of Romanticism. Freud stated this in his paper 'The Unconscious' of 1915:

> The psycho-analytic assumption of unconscious mental activity appears to us . . . as an extension of the corrections undertaken by Kant of our views on external perception. Just as Kant warned us not to overlook the fact that our perceptions are subjectively conditioned and must not be regarded as identical with what is perceived though unknowable, so psycho-analysis warns us not to equate perceptions by means of consciousness with the unconscious mental processes which are their object. Like the physical, the psychical is not necessarily in reality what it appears to us to be.
>
> (Freud, S. 1915: 166 ff.)

He never failed to register the sheer strangeness of the encounter with the other, external and internal (Laplanche and Pontalis 1988: 456).

Psychoanalysis's current claims to respectability, in much of the world, rest on its self-definition as a science (albeit one requiring artful practitioners). Attempts have been made to fit it to the model of science developed by Thomas Kuhn. In Kuhn's process-based understanding of scientific progress and (r)evolution, different phases of enquiry give rise to different problems, and thus to disagreements and controversies, out of which a new paradigm or theory is established, developed and consolidated, then destabilised by the discovery of ever more anomalies, until it is modified or dissolved in favour of a new paradigm (Kuhn 1962; Britton 1994: 4). This is an account that would locate psychoanalysis as a science of observation and theory, a member of the family of the natural sciences. It is an account which embodies an idea of periodic crisis, and implies a teleology ('one day science will discover a cure').

Looked at from another perspective, however, that of the experience of psychoanalysis in practice, an account with a different emphasis may be called for: psychoanalysis not so much as a body of knowledge, evolving towards some final goal through periodic destabilisation and revision, as a state of permanent revolution. An acceptance that resolution is never possible, only unending upheaval, is inherent to psychoanalysis; it requires a capacity for a different kind of reflexiveness.

*   *   *

Crisis, tension and revolution are inscribed in the very beginnings and at the very heart both of Romanticism and, one hundred years later, of psychoanalysis: the ego is no longer master in its own house. The era of the philosophers of Nature cited in *The Interpretation of Dreams* was that of the political, social and cultural traumata of the French and the Industrial Revolutions. Late eighteenth- and early nineteenth-century contemporaries were obliged to suspend their disbelief, and the role of a category of people, artists, which was itself undergoing transformation within the same ferment, evolved new forms of response that might begin to be adequate to the barely comprehensible experience of the times. As a character in Penelope Fitzgerald's 1995 novel *The Blue Flower* expresses it, the French Revolution was the event to end all events, something altogether beyond interpretation. Another character, poring over a newspaper report of the execution of Louis XVI in 1793, is able to read the words but utterly unable to make sense of them (Fitzgerald 2002 [1995]: 34). At the end of the next century Freud and Breuer found themselves facing a similar crisis of comprehension: in Toril Moi's words, they had 'to let the madwoman speak, to consider *her* discourse as one ruled by its own logic, to accept the logic of another scene' (Moi 1989: 197).

The very word Romanticism, as a historical term, describes a prolonged moment of intensified energy: Romanticism was the expression of a state of mind-in-crisis. The 1789 Revolution in France was in many respects the product of the eighteenth-century's faith in the transformative power of Reason. Many in Europe greeted it with enthusiasm, as if they were assisting at a new birth: such was the 'Bliss . . . in that dawn to be alive' expressed by the young William Wordsworth in *The Prelude*, the sense of new possibility, and of things coming to fruition in fulfilment of Reason's dream (Wordsworth 2000: 550). Wordsworth and Coleridge's *Lyrical Ballads*, the first edition of which was published in 1798, aimed to effect a parallel revolution in, and through, poetry. 'Nothing was dreamt of but the regeneration of the human race', recalled the poet Robert Southey in his Tory middle age. 'Few who were young in 1789 ever freed themselves from the experience, whatever their later revulsion from the consequences' (Hughes 1979: 7). Other contemporaries, like those fictionalised in Fitzgerald's novel, experienced revulsion from the outset; the French Revolution was also that which defied and nullified Reason, the end point of speech and meaning.

The crisis that exploded in Paris in 1789 and unfolded in the 1790s shook European societies to their foundations. The execution of Louis XVI, Marie-Antoinette and most of the royal family, and the mass killings of aristocrats, priests, nuns and others during the Terror, cast every assumption about the stability of Western thought and feeling into doubt. The proclamation that 'the day has arrived . . . the advancements in human reason have prepared this great revolution' could have a profoundly disturbing and disjointing effect, falling as it did from the lips of Robespierre, the Terror's chief architect (Kuzniar 1987: 17–18). The fact that massacre could be unleashed in France of all countries and Paris of all cities, home of civility, Enlightenment and the *philosophes*, threw the whole idea of social order and human self-regulation into question – irreversibly (Bonnefoy 2006: 49–50).

The crisis could manifest in personal breakdown. It can be found, for example, in the work and life of Goya, the subject of Chapter 3; works of the most radical ambiguity, expressive of a shattering loss of certainty, followed a breakdown in the mid-1790s. It registered in the life and work of Heinrich von Kleist, a child of the Enlightenment whose reading of Kant around 1801 contributed to his doubt and despair about the very knowability of people, things and events; at the same time it was, in the years before his suicide in 1811, that which spurred him into writing (Luke and Reeves 1978).

This sense of a constantly unfurling crisis was acutely and widely felt and expressed; alongside new freedoms was 'a new angst, as people searched for a framework within which to lead their lives' (MacCarthy 2003: 158). Between the execution of the French Bourbon king and the battle of Waterloo were two decades of almost uninterrupted European warfare, from the revolutionary wars of the 1790s to the astonishing triumphs of Napoleon right across the continent, from Italy to Prussia; French armies invaded Spain and Russia, and without Nelson's victory at Trafalgar might have crossed the Channel too. Napoleon was the product of revolution which by the late 1790s could neither be reversed nor advanced, but, as he saw it, only taken in another direction through his own daring intervention; the *tricolore* of the Republic must be exported. Napoleon was the embodiment of the unprecedented. For his enemies, especially after he had himself proclaimed Emperor in 1804, he was crisis and hubris personified, an anti-Christ on the loose; his admirers ranged from an ambivalent Goethe or Beethoven to Byron who, along with many other contemporary and later Romantics, wholeheartedly identified himself with him. After 1815, in the period known as the Restoration, there was an attempt, orchestrated from Vienna by the Austrian Prince Metternich, to re-establish former social hierarchies. Monarchies, generally repressive and reactionary, reinstated themselves across Europe, in an attempt to turn the clock back to the *ancien régime*, the pre-revolutionary days of Catholic, Bourbon, legitimacy. In France, a further revolution in 1830 reconfigured this project, and was accompanied by a new wave of (now self-consciously 'Romantic') artistic activity (its prime mover, Victor Hugo, invoked Napoleon). At the same time, northern Europe was beginning to experience the seismic socio-economic upheavals of the Industrial Revolution: a shift away from agriculture towards economies based in factories and cities, the movement of whole populations, the numerical expansion both of a working and a middle class, and the accretion of greater and greater political and financial power to the latter. Eric Hobsbawm has described it as 'the greatest transformation in human history'. He was writing of England in particular, where no violent political revolution took place but where 'private profit and economic development' were the 'supreme objects' of successive Tory governments (Hobsbawm 1988: 13, 46, cited in Motion 1997: 11).

If this was in many respects a brutal period, the years between 1789 and the mid-nineteenth century were extraordinarily fertile in terms of literature, music, philosophy, science and art. A list of key figures, even if not all of them lived to see their contributions widely celebrated, would include Paine, Burke, Priestley, Franklin, Faraday, Herschel, Wollstonecraft, Blake, Coleridge, Wordsworth, Byron, Burns, Keats, Shelley, Mary Shelley, Austen, Kant, Goethe, Mozart, Goya, Beethoven, Schiller, Schelling, the Schlegel brothers, Hegel, Hölderlin, Novalis, Kleist, Büchner, Rossini, Weber, Schubert, Pushkin, Lermontov, Gogol, Manzoni, Leopardi, Friedrich, Turner, Constable, de Sade, de Staël, Stendhal, Géricault, Delacroix, Lamartine, Hugo, Balzac, Vigny, Musset, Gautier, Nerval, Poe, Baudelaire.

'Romantic' was a generic term used by contemporaries to describe certain art of their own and some preceding eras; 'Romanticism' is shot through with paradox and difficulty. The word can be taken to refer to the complex tensions and contradictions to which it was a response. In 1797, Friedrich Schlegel, the first great critic and theorist of Romanticism in Germany, where the idea of a Romantic 'movement' was born, wrote to his brother August Wilhelm that he would not be sending him his promised definition of the word 'Romantic' after all, since it was 125 pages long (Hughes 1979: 52). As a typological word, 'Romantic' is 'a whiff of grapeshot in an argument about human attitudes' (Hughes 1979:1).[7] As a historical phenomenon, it has been variously periodised (for an excellent discussion, see Butler 1981: 1–10). It developed and manifested itself in parallel but idiosyncratic and not always concurrent ways in Germany, Britain, Italy, Spain, or Russia (see Eichner 1972); it only found wide currency in France, for example, in the 1820s.

Its protagonists and adherents tended to be young, and if they lived into middle or old age they continued (with a few exceptions – Wordsworth, for example) to value youthfulness. In its energy and libido, internal conflicts, spirit of revolt, and claims to self-evident clarity of vision, it has something in common with what the second half of the twentieth century came to call adolescence. If it was rebellious and oppositional, its perceived opponents varied according to time and place: Enlightenment; neoclassicism; academicism; industrialisation; the bourgeoisie; political and religious oppression; politics itself; narrow morality; sexual hypocrisy; constraints in general; uniformity and conformity; ready-made opinions and received ideas . . . Romanticism was protean and multi-voiced. It could be politically progressive or, especially in some of its later nineteenth- and twentieth-century avatars, reactionary. It might or might not be nationalistic, or might or might not be liberal; it was linked with the anti-slavery movement, and with national liberation struggles from Poland, Italy and Greece to Latin and South America (Byron christened the yacht he bought in Venice in 1822 the *Bolivar* (MacCarthy 2003: 410)).

Faced with the failure of older norms Romanticism prized 'the holiness of the Heart's affections', in Keats's famous phrase (Keats 1958: I, 184). It prioritised feeling over rules and precepts. Take a man off the street and throw him into prison, suggested Stendhal in 1824, and tell him he will be free again once he can draw a naked figure in the correct, neoclassical manner of the school of David. He will be out after a couple of years. But ask him to paint 'some human emotion or spiritual impulse' – a lover's joy, for example – and he will be inside for life. For 'the emotions are not an exact science'; to be able to paint them 'you must have seen and felt their devouring flames' (Stendhal 1973: 100–1).

Romanticism allowed expression to whole new areas of feeling. It also re-examined and problematised the relations of the present to the past and future. It made previous eras and their aesthetic forms available to carry new meanings, while at the same time using them to satisfy a vague nostalgia and a need for a sense of continuity, as, for example, in the massively popular historical novels of Walter Scott, or the long-lived Gothic revival in architecture and design. Romanticism freed artists and writers from former obligations to emulate the (classical) best, but this still left a pressing task: how to reconcile a wish to make enduring artistic statements adequate to the present, with an intuition that the most valid response to the anxious, fragmented, fickle and fleeting nature of the times might be a mere sketch or fragment? In a late extension of Romantic thinking on this question, Baudelaire, in his essay 'The Painter of Modern Life' of 1861, reiterated an idea that art has two aspects, the transient and the eternal; the tension between the two helped make up the condition that he was among the first to call modernity (Baudelaire 1975–76: II, 685). Yet this is arguably not the most original or profound of Baudelaire's critical insights; it was an attempt to come to terms with sheer transience and contradiction, with the sense of living in a historical moment in which, as he wrote, the old was dead and the new not yet born (Baudelaire 1975–76: II, 493).

'It is not hard to see that our age is a time of gestation and transition to a new period', Hegel had written around half a century earlier (cited in Laplanche 1961: 130, n2); in *Phenomenology of Spirit* Hegel put contradiction at the very heart of identity. For Karl Marx, by the mid-nineteenth century, contradiction, tension and chaos were permanent, constitutive features of modernity. 'On the one hand', Marx said in a speech in London in 1856, the year of Freud's birth,

> there have started into life industrial and scientific forces, which no epoch of the former human history had ever suspected. On the other hand, there exist symptoms of decay, far surpassing the horrors recorded of the latter times of the Roman Empire. In our days, everything seems pregnant with its contrary: machinery, gifted with the wonderful power of shortening and fructifying human labour, we behold starving and overworking it; the newfangled sources of wealth, by some strange weird spell, are turned into sources of want . . .

> (Tucker 1978: 577–8)

In Marx's account, the ruling class had a vested interest in continual disruption; he characterised the dialectical, confrontational condition of modernity as 'uninterrupted disturbance, everlasting uncertainty and agitation' (Boyd Whyte 2010: 66).

By the mid- and later nineteenth century, even as Baudelaire was finding new life in it, a view was developing of Romanticism as 'romantic', that is, not so much a complex of lived responses grounded in experience as a wistful or defeated turning away from the world. It is a view encapsulated, perhaps, in the phrase 'the spirit of Romanticism', or in the high Victorian image of a languishing, other-worldly Keats. If Romanticism did enshrine, particularly in its early forms in Germany, powerful intuitions of the absolute and infinite, they were always felt to be in tension with the particularities of embodied experience; for Hegel, as Lacan noted, universal could never be separated from particular (Lacan 2007: 242). Romantic awareness of the necessarily fragmented and discontinuous nature of experience, together with the struggle with words and forms required to register and re-register it, constitute Romanticism as a 'permanent revolution'. Its legacy, or continuation, has been manifest, in art, in the restless and continuing search for means of expression that has characterised Western modernity. Disequilibrium and instability, indeed, in the age of globalisation, remain 'the rule rather than the exception' (Streeck 2011: 5).

*   *   *

Romanticism intuited and developed its response to crisis above all by means of literature, painting and music themselves, through its own art and previous art. The earlier literature that was the object of its discoveries and rediscoveries – Dante, Cervantes, Calderón, and Shakespeare above all (this was the era of the great Shakespearian actors and actor managers, Kemble, Kean, and Macready) – seemed to call a particular a state of mind into being and legitimise it. This had been heralded in the late Enlightenment: Dr Johnson, for example, was not entirely disapproving when he registered 'refusals of the protocols of sense' in Milton (Orgel and Goldberg 2004: xxx–xxxi). This state of mind received two of its most famous, fully fledged Romantic elaborations in the hands of English poets; both were prompted by the experience of Shakespeare. '*Negative Capability*, that is when man is capable of being in uncertainties, Mysteries, doubts, without any irritable reaching after fact & reason . . .' (Keats 1958: I,193), was the ineffable quality which Keats ascribed to Shakespeare in order to try to account for his impact, and which for W.R. Bion a century later was at the heart of what is required of the analyst.[8]

Keats's 'Negative Capability', which will be put in further context in Chapter 6, had had a recent precedent in Coleridge's 'negative belief', which Coleridge also characterised as a 'suspension of disbelief', or, in a double-edged political metaphor referring to curtailments of civil liberties, a suspension of the 'Act of Comparison' (Holmes 1999: 130). Coleridge too underlined that what he had to say was formulated as a result of an experience of literature. Part of the power of Coleridge's 'negative belief' lies in the description of imaginative activity which we have already heard: 'a hospitable freedom or playfulness of mind, rather than a fixed and perhaps premature intellectual judgement' (Holmes 1999: 130, n1). Later, as his biographer Richard Holmes points out, Coleridge emphasised the active, symbol-making capacity of the mind in reverie, as opposed to its passive, associative functions in dream-sleep (Holmes 1999: 230). Coleridge's breathtaking late summation of poetic activity and the power of imagination, in his *Biographia Literaria* of 1815, describes a form of mental and emotional work at its most exacting:

> This power, first put into action by the will and understanding, and retained under their irremissive, though gentle and unnoticed control reveals itself in the balance or reconciliation of opposite or discordant qualities: of sameness, with difference; or the general, with the concrete; the idea, with the image; the individual, with the representative; the sense of novelty and freshness, with old and familiar objects; a more than usual state of emotion, with more than usual order; judgement ever awake and steady self-possession, with enthusiasm and feeling profound and vehement . . .
>
> (Coleridge (1983) [1815]: II, 15–17, cited in
> Holmes 1999: 388)

What Coleridge describes is a capacity simultaneously to hold in mind several kinds of binary opposition; this requires both receptiveness and activity. His prose rocks the reader back and forth as if in echo of the tension and movement between the two. It is among the most powerful and precise Romantic adumbrations of an analytic attitude.

Cultivation of poetic imagination through reverie had, thanks partly to Jean-Jacques Rousseau (through his posthumously published *Rêveries du promeneur solitaire*, for example), become a self-conscious pursuit from the mid-eighteenth century, something divorced from explicitly religious contemplation; it both privileged and decentred the individual. Goethe's novel *The Sorrows of Young Werther* of 1774, which became a spectacular cult, brought reverie, sexual yearning and death into conjunction. In painting, in the hands of Girodet or Gérard, even the stoical neoclassical school of David could produce images of languid, sexually ambivalent other-worldliness. 'I have spent my life in reverie', wrote the former Napoleonic soldier Stendhal (1973 [1890]). A Romantic suspicion of exclusively discursive ways of trying to make sense led to a shift from a predominantly masculine towards a feminine mode of discourse. Women had played a foundational role in the French Revolution, notably in the great march on Versailles in October 1789. Mary Wollstonecraft, Ann Radcliffe, Jane Austen and the Brontë sisters, among many other woman writers, generated as well as responded to a grow-ing female readership and helped shape the *mentalité* of the period. The protagonists of this book are male; all, however, tend in their various ways to subvert gender expectations, to embody 'feminine' qualities and attributes historically seen as female: openness to other voices and the multiple projected desires of an audience, receptivity, even the attribute of having a body. A gender-sensitive account of Romanticism would always be 'attentive to the gender politics of both male and female writers' (Johns-Putra 2011: 106); Romanticism's tolerance or encouragement of gender and sexual ambigu-ities is evident in its interest in a polymorphous, sexually ambiguous Hamlet, or in Byron, whose bisexuality was no secret to contemporaries but which biographers long suppressed; it can be felt in Keats's 'effeminacy', and Baudelaire's enthusiastically complex identifications. The question of a non-discursive, feminine *voice* is in play: the 'excessive', flowing, musical, elusive and allusive voice heard by Hélène Cixous in Romantic writers such as Kleist, Hoffmann and Poe (Cixous 1976; see also Loewenthal and Snell 2003: 135–41).

Dreaming, swooning and half-waking states of nervous or erotic suscept-ibility were in the process of commodification. The patients and audiences of Franz Anton Mesmer and Amand Puységur were drawn into trance-like states both for entertainment and therapy (Ellenberger 1970: 53 ff.); Mesmer's 'animal magnetism' and his 'magnetic cures' attracted crowds as well as official censure.[9] Dreamy 'Gothick' thrills were stimulated by artists such as Fuseli (*The Nightmare*, 1781; see Myrone 2006). From the 1790s the 'phantasmagoria', commonly considered by historians to be a precursor to cinema, was a popular form of entertainment, with its hallucinatory, smoky effects and spine-tingling illusions of movement (the first phantasmagoria performance was probably in Paris in 1798 and invoked a spectral, vengeful Marat). Coleridge's one successful play, *Remorse*, owed its impact to phantas-magoric stage effects; it caught the edgy, 'introspective, self-questioning mood' of its London audience in 1813 (Holmes 1999: 336).

Interest in states of unconsciousness and semi-consciousness could be directed towards critical or epiphanic clarity. The laudanum or hashish-fuelled experiments and travails of Coleridge (*Kubla Khan* was written in 1797), De Quincey, Gautier and Baudelaire have been well documented (Hayter 1971 [1968]). Byron's companion Polidori made a study of somnambulism (MacCarthy 2003: 285), which was part of Mary Shelley's inspiration for *Frankenstein* in 1818. Sleep, dream, drugs and madness continued to intrigue the literary and artistic avant-garde well into the century and beyond; sensationalism and philosophical enquiry were intertwined.

Goya's series of etchings *Los Caprichos*, published in Madrid in 1799, was probably partly inspired by the phantasmagoria (Bird 2004). There was another kind of dream, too, to which, like William Blake, Goya alerted people, the great dream of post-Cartesian Reason itself. 'Copiers of nature [are] incorrect while Copiers of Imagination are Correct', wrote Blake (Blake 1988: 575). Blake's friends gathered around him so that he could interpret their dreams; Goya's *Caprichos*, and the so-called Black Paintings of two decades later, extended a preoccupation with dream and nightmare into territory hitherto unexplored in the history of Western art. Here, as in contemporary German idealism, were dream and madness not as escape or titillation, but as critique and a reaching towards a sense of something more securely grounded, an alternative form of order.

'Dream is a second life', wrote Gérard de Nerval in his novel *Aurélia* of 1855 (Nerval 1972: 131), an account of his hallucinations and arrest as insane (Nerval 1972:131). Boundaries between sanity and insanity, health and sickness, might be experienced as excitingly porous. The idea and the experience of madness and illness could be enlisted to conjure up exceptionally receptive states of mind. The convalescent who sits behind a café window watching the passers-by in Baudelaire's essay 'The Painter of Modern Life' exemplifies this (Baudelaire 1995 [1861]). Illness was part of the spectrum of life which the artist was obliged to face head on. Tuberculosis, syphilis, cholera and typhus were never far away; the treatments were often worse than the illnesses. One historian has even argued a case for 'the medical wellsprings of . . . despair': disease and its contemporary remedies were primarily responsible for Romantic openness to the 'horror of life' (Williams 1980: xiii). Much later in the century, Edmond and Jules de Goncourt turned illness into a kind of cult, in which extreme sensibility and tautened nerve-ends were put in the service of aesthetic pleasure, and, finally, brought to bear in a dispassionate chronicle of Jules's terrible passage though the last stages of syphilis (Brookner 2001).

Romantic artists evoked a parallel receptiveness in the viewers and readers of their own works. For a post-Romantic poet like Paul Valéry, such a refusal to allow interpretative closure would be characteristic of all real art. 'We recognise a work of art by the fact that no idea it inspires in us, no mode of behaviour it suggest we adopt could exhaust or dispose of it,' he wrote (Valéry, cited in Benjamin 1983 [1955 etc.]: 146); it is hard, however, to imagine such a critical view being held prior to Romanticism. Romantics were not concerned with insisting on how spectators or readers should respond, merely that they should, in one way or another, feel moved and involved; works of Romantic art depart from a classical paradigm in which clarity, legibility and coherence are privileged, which, in a word coined by Roland Barthes, are merely *lisible* (literally, legible), and lecture us. The best response to a picture, wrote Baudelaire, might be a poem (Baudelaire 1975–76: II, 418); Romanticism was a flowering of what Barthes christened the *scriptible. Scriptible* texts are generative: they stimulate imaginative participation and encourage the production of further texts rather than just passive consumption (Barthes 1970: 10 ff.). They can involve us, as their makers involved themselves, in complex plays of identifications, in meetings (or non-meetings) with ourselves as divided creatures: shifting, disturbing encounters that point to no final or definitive readings, only provisional ones. Sometimes their mysteries and opacities might be accounted for, as occasionally in Goya for example, by the need to encode for *samizdat* purposes; in post-restoration Vienna music in coffee houses functioned to muffle political conversations from the ears of Prince Metternich's agents. At the same time they work to engage us as the 'hypocrite readers' which Baudelaire recognised us to be, full of moral complexities and duplicities. Stendhal's investigations into self and memory, for example, are 'scandals to the reading self', as the novelist Adam Thirlwell has put it; if his novels are autobiographies they are the reader's as much as the novelist's (Thirlwell 2008). Such works ask of us, as Nietzsche demanded at the other end of the nineteenth century, responsiveness with no easy consolations, meaning-making with no recourse to an outside arbiter.

The nature of the text is, in the final analysis, inseparable from the nature of the audience. From around the mid-eighteenth century or earlier a new public was coming into being. The *philosophe* Denis Diderot's novels were initially intended for limited circulation among a small, international group of like-minded friends, but the sense of intimacy and of a knowing, personal involvement they set up was soon to appeal to a larger readership. Diderot's *Jacques le fataliste*, written in the 1760s, is full of playful authorial interventions and unpredicatable digressions that disturb the reader's intellectual comfort; much admired by Goethe, *Jacques le fataliste* was produced 'in a climate of jubilation' (Vernière 1970: 19) which suffuses its pages over two centuries on. Works of such proto-Romantic suggestiveness and complicity emerged simultaneously with a process of democratisation in the arts, hastened by the Revolution and the growth of a middle class with cultural and political aspirations. The period saw the birth of new 'arts' institutions: academies, galleries, libraries, theatres. There were new commercial opportunities for literary and musical publication, dissemination and performance, for the public exhibition of painting and sculpture, and the sale of prints (see Holt 1979 and Motion 1997: 18–19): all this in turn helped create new markets and audiences. Thanks to lending libraries and reading circles, periodicals, almanacs, voyages, biographies, works of philosophy, pedagogy or theology, and, a little later, the newspaper feuilleton and the serial novel, new ideas of all kinds 'were darting more randomly into the minds of men (and even more of women) . . . Printing was now also for butterfly minds' (Hughes 1979: 6). The growth of this public in turn further encouraged this new kind of textuality: new kinds of art, and new kinds of spectator, reader and listener were being called into existence. In the process, new forms of relationship between spectator and art work were being forged: more personal and intimate, more charged with a sense of context, more active, identificatory, reflective, and engaged, and open to the development of new depths and complexities.

At the same time writers, poets, actors, dancers, musicians, composers, painters and sculptors were themselves claiming a new status and mystique.

The artist was no longer the mere servant of a patron, as, for example, even Mozart had been. In Romanticism emerges the modern idea of the artist, from Byron to Picasso or Pollock, as a unique and driven individual who creates new realities as well as reflecting existing ones: lamp rather than mirror, in M.H. Abrams's phrase (Abrams 1953, cited in Glendinning 1977: 31). This accompanied a shift away from old hierarchies, practices and standards of correctness and taste. Within the new artist–viewer, writer–reader, composer– listener relationships which were evolving there was space for enigma, and for an ever-widening range of moods, feelings and experiences, from the tender and reflective to the erotic and violent.

At one extreme were works such as Byron's *Childe Harold's Pilgrimage*, the first two cantos of which were an instant publishing sensation in 1812. Byron's biographer Fiona MacCarthy has described it as 'the necessary . . . poem of the aftermath of the French Revolution' (MacCarthy 2003: 158). It elicited heightened responses: 'your Pen has called forth the most exquisite feelings I have ever experienced . . . (I am) animated by a new soul, alive to wholly novel sensations and activated by feelings until then unknown', wrote a female fan (MacCarthy 2003: 162). Appealing to the more reflective end of the readerly spectrum, in England, we find Coleridge's 'conversation poems' of the 1790s, and, later, in 1809 and 1810, his journalism, which sought to create and educate a new readership by means of the self-reflection and self-understanding he was attempting to model in his journal, which he entitled *The Friend* (Holmes 1999: 165). His German contemporary Hölderlin wrote: 'a conversation we are, and hear from one another' (Hölderlin 2007: 214).

It is not hard to find in twentieth and twenty-first critical responses to art of the era commentaries endorsing a Romantic/*scriptible* reading. Mozart's music, for example, could produce what his biographer Wolfgang Hildesheimer called

> the awakening and simultaneous stilling of a longing whose nature and origin we become aware of, but not familiar with. Mozart's music reproduces the depth of experience for us without the experience . . . In reality no one understands it, but the little we do understand is enough to suggest the rest, which we are left to interpret . . . More than other composers Mozart elicits receptive misunderstanding . . .
>
> (Hildesheimer 1982: 40–1)

Here is the mid-twentieth-century American critic Morse Peckham on Goethe's *Faust* (the writing of which spanned a period from the 1790s to 1832):

> Goethe offers us . . . not an explanation, rational, logical, philosophically consistent, of the reconciliation [of forces symbolised by God and the devil], but rather the opportunity to experience it. This is the high

nineteenth-century notion of the work of art; like life itself it should offer a rich complexity irreducible to simple statements; it should defy reductivist interpretations. Always, with *Faust*, we feel that the work presents an infinitude of possibilities; just as in interpreting life itself, we feel, or should feel, that we have only done so by an abstraction which leaves heaven only knows how much unaccounted for. So it is with the greatest works of that century. We feel that any interpretation leaves more to be said, that something capable of contradicting our interpretation is still lurking within the work, that there is always a disparity between the orientation we have derived from the work and the complex interactions of the artistic data itself.

(Peckham 1981 [1962]: 120)

A younger Romantic generation in Germany saw even Goethe as too balanced and Olympian. For the critic Glyn Hughes, the work of Ludwig Tieck, for example, is characterised by a persisting 'sense of imbalance between world and self', especially in the late 1790s (Hughes 1979: 30). In Tieck's story *Der blonde Eckbert* of 1797,

the equivocal nature of reality, and the instability of viewpoint, reflected in the narrative technique, causes the whole Märchen[10] to proceed on a knife-edge . . . the symbols, too, are insubstantial and elusive; all is relative, all uncertain, dreamlike, perhaps even dreamt . . . *Der blonde Eckbert* calls normality into question. The senses present us with unreliable data; memory and temporal awareness play tricks . . .; all interpretations are elusive . . .

(Hughes 1979: 33–4)

Richard Holmes summed up Coleridge's *Biographia*, the great culmination of his literary career, in terms of 'its shape-shifting and paradoxes, its intimacy and disguises, its frankness and its fraudulence'. Holmes, like Coleridge's contemporaries, noted its 'extreme shifts in tone, from mournful apologia . . . through sprightly reminiscence and passionate philosophising, to the steady, measured, brilliantly authoritative note of the critical sections'. Anything less complicated and maddening, Holmes continued, 'would not really be Coleridge at all', for the book, largely dictated and thus 'talked into . . . life' in the pattern of an extended conversation, was a kind of Freudian 'talking cure' (Holmes 1999: 378–9).

Morse Peckham found in Beethoven's late quartets, written between 1824 and 1827,

the facing of the unendurably conditional; the acceptance of the unacceptable – In these quartets . . . emerges a new structure, but it is no longer a structure characterised by familiarity and predictability; its character is precisely that it presents the unfamiliar and unpredictable.

(Peckham 1981 [1962]: 165)

Robert Schumann was to challenge the listener to even more destabilising effect: for Charles Rosen no composer had ever before made 'such expressive use of unresolved cadences' as Schumann in *Kreisleriana*, nor had anyone so violated listener expectations as Schumann did when he made use of cheap urban music and vulgar student songs (Rosen 2010: 68).

Romanticism was the product of dis-ease, disquiet and, finally, of mourning: mourning for lost assurances of (socio-political) harmony and quality, teleological certainties, secure landmarks and master-narratives. It also registered the failure of the great invigorating hopes enshrined in Enlightenment, revolutionary idealism and Napoleon, and hope could feel irrecoverable (Brookner 2001). 'I fell when Napoleon did', wrote Stendhal (Stendhal 1973 [1890]: 28). A sense of a future forfeited was shared by Anglo-Saxon literary and political radicals too: Shelley, a leading spokesman for the disillusion of his generation, lamented in 1821: 'we want the creative faculty to imagine that which we know; we want the generous impulse to act that which we imagine; we want the poetry of life' (Wroe 2007b: 21). Byron made a similar declaration shortly before his death at Missolonghi during the Greek war of independence in 1824. '*Cant*', he had noted in 1820, 'is so much stronger than *cunt* in England today' (MacCarthy 2003: 365, 465). Byron exemplified 'the disappointed and disaffected child of the revolution', as his first biographer described him in 1832 (MacCarthy 2003: 542–3); this figure reappeared in guises such as the jaded hero of Musset's *Confession d'un enfant du siècle* (1836), and transmuted into the helpless, delibidinised mid-Victorian aesthete. 'We are all at some funeral', wrote Baudelaire, struggling with his own sense of impotence and commenting on the universal black frock-coat of the bourgeois of the 1840s (Baudelaire 1975–76: II, 494).

Mourning as a human necessity had been registered in art long before Romanticism and psychoanalysis. Perhaps, as Darian Leader has suggested, the place of the arts in any culture is to work as 'a set of instruments to help us mourn': the spectator is involved in 'a process of identifying with the creator, in the sense of some one who could make something out of an inferred experience of loss' (Leader 2008: 86–7). If to confront us with absence and loss is a deeper function of all art, in Romanticism it becomes overt and poignant, and not just in terms of subject matter: mourning was something which the work of Romantic art required the viewer or reader actively to engage in, directly to feel the loss of familiar or ready-made meanings. At the same time, to mourn and thus give up an ideal of what could have been means, potentially, to be open to the shock or pleasure of what is; it is, indeed, a necessary precondition for this. There can come a moment at which there seems to be no choice other than to wonder at it all, to be open to the particular, transient and contingent, and to try to describe things as one experiences them, just as they are. 'Must it be? It must be! It must be!' wrote Beethoven on the manuscript of his last string quartet (no. 16, opus 135; Peckham 1981 [1962]: 165).

From this point of view Romanticism as a journey through loss and disillusion was a stimulant to enquiry of all kinds, a building on Enlightenment. At the same time it was unable to rest from its subversive, critical task of exposing Reason's paradoxes and contradictions, and that Enlightenment which, as Adorno and Horkheimer wrote, 'fixes the transcendence of the unknown in relation to the known' (1989 [1944]: 15). Romanticism was an attempt to reverse the process, to return to experience and the possibility of rediscovering the miraculous in the familiar and everyday. Blake affirmed 'the Holiness of the Minute Particulars': 'Labour well the Minute Particulars', he exhorted (Blake 1988: 205). Novalis wrote of 'romanticising the world'. 'By investing the commonplace with a lofty significance, the ordinary with a mysterious aspect . . . thereby I romanticise it' (Novalis 1989: 56 [no.162], cited in Furst 1980: 3). For the French philosopher Yves Bonnefoy, the crisis in Enlightenment marked the end of what he called *le grand rêve*, the great post-Renaissance dream of a universe that was visibly purposeful and harmonious, as oil painting, above all other art forms, could demonstrate (Bonnefoy 2006); the end of this dream meant a corresponding awakening to disunity, contingency and apparent inconsequence, to the exception that does not prove any rule.

Awareness of this, as for example Diderot had registered it, had also in fact been part of the subtext of Enlightenment, signalling its always incipient crisis. 'Wife? – What is it? –Nothing', goes a snippet of dialogue in *Jacques le fataliste* (Diderot 1970 [1796]: 135). 'July 1789: . . . 14th, Nothing', wrote Louis XVI in his diary on the day of the storming of the Bastille (Pernoud and Flaissier 1965: 45). For many, contrary to Hegel's theses, it was no longer possible to discern unfolding and progressive historical patterns, only to register happenstance. Misrecognition and misunderstanding were unavoidable: Stendhal's Fabrice van Dongen, the hero of *La Chartreuse de Parme*, is in the middle of the battle of Waterloo but doubts that what he is experiencing is a real battle. Mourning might thus also include, if one were brave enough, looking into the heart of one's illusions, blind spots and unfathomable contradictions. Stendhal supplemented his often fragmentary memoirs with enigmatic little maps, attempts to recapture a geography of childhood that end up reading as ciphers of loss and ignorance. He wrote of himself as if he were some unknown other.

> What is this character of mine? I should be hard put to it to say. If ever I meet that intelligent woman again, I shall have to question her closely to find out what I was like in those days. I honestly don't know.
>
> (Stendhal 1973 [1890]: 191, 345–6)

What do others think of me? Why do I forget some things and remember others? How many personalities am I? (Stendhal gave himself over one hundred pseudonyms). Similarly, Percy Bysshe Shelley: 'What is life? What is death? What is consciousness? What is our true history, and what is our destination?' Thus, Ann Wroe, a biographer of Shelley, evoked the urgency of such questioning. If, according to his sister Mary, Shelley's 'persistent enquiries' and 'intense meditations on his own nature . . . thrilled him with pain', it was because he made them 'not as a member of a church or a school of thought but as Shelley unprotected, Shelley alone' (Wroe 2007b: 21). The ever-allusive answers, for Romantics, were to be sought in the personal and specific, with no institutional safety-net.

In 1979 the critics Charles Rosen and Henri Zerner published an important essay on the popularity in the nineteenth century of the ephemeral and relatively impermanent sketch and the caricature, which were of negligible value in the academic hierarchy of artistic genres: the emotional value placed on the contemporary, fleeting and fragmentary added up to a whole new aesthetic (Rosen and Zerner 1984 [1979]). The beginnings of a 'painting of modern life' that was to flourish from the mid-century in Realism and Impressionism lay in an emphasis on the value of the present, mundane historic moment, and on the act of making itself, the traces of a performance, brush-strokes, for example. The annotations, date and time of day, on Constable's studies of clouds underline not only that they are meteorological observations but also that they are records of the unrepeatable moment. Stendhal footnoted his writings with little notes to himself: '18 December 1835, from 2 to 41/2: 24 pages. I am so absorbed by the memories which unfold before my eyes that I can hardly form my letters' (Stendhal 1973 [1890]: 127,139). Traces of Balzac's high-pressure literary performances survive in the form of his heavily annotated proof pages, corrected at the printer's. Turner's later work, with its washes and swirls of paint, is driven by his fascination with the creative and destructive power of the sun and the elements that atomise and disperse the phenomena of the material world. 'How poetic we are in our cravates and patent leather boots' Baudelaire observed in 1845 (Baudelaire 1975–76: II, 407). It was in this attention to an ever-changing present that Romanticism, Rosen and Zerner wrote, was a 'permanent revolution'. The modern artist who was responsive to this ethic was necessarily required to attend to the unprecedented and individual, and to find the specific, telling form of expression to evoke it: from Coleridge's 'plain style' of the 1790s (Holmes 1998: 85–6), to Gautier's insistence on *le mot propre* from the 1830s onwards (Snell 1982: 18 ff.).

Romantic attention to the ephemeral and apparently marginal embraced the overlooked and excluded other: the destitute outsider, *les misérables*. Humanitarian feeling for the underdog, crippled war veterans, widows, foundlings, chimney sweeps, prostitutes, prisoners, had been a strong current in late eighteenth-century literature (Butler 1981: 31). The Romantics turned their attention to victims of slavery and political violence, to beggars, street entertainers, itinerant musicians, the old and impoverished (Goya, Géricault, Baudelaire . . .). In the process they were also developing an acute, pre-Freudian awareness of an internal other. A feeling of being spoken by this other might be terrifying or uplifting. In *A Defense of Poetry* Shelley pictured 'the mind in creation' as 'a fading coal' fanned by 'some invisible influence, an inconstant wind' arising from within (Shelley 1994: 656). This sense found more concrete expression in German, then in French Romanticism in the image of the uninvited, spectral stranger who comes from outside (Béguin 1938). In the tales of Hoffmann, Nodier, Balzac and Gautier, this 'other' might do the writing or painting and create the masterpiece, at the same time threatening the sanity of the host. She might also be an irrestistible erotic *inconnue*, a serpent (Hoffmann 1979) or vampire who threatens to paralyse as well as promise infinite bliss (Gautier 2008 [1837]). Poe's Raven makes explicit the connection between loss of identity, fear of being subsumed by voices without and within, and subjection to death; Coleridge's man from Porlock is the visitor who can bring all imaginative activity to an end.

The stranger (see Kristeva 1991) comes from a 'somewhere else', from an indeterminate zone outside the *polis*, a margin of consciousness that might both threaten and provide fertile ground for the new. Its tourists and inhabitants are themselves exiles, marginal, displaced. An anonymous, almost featureless landscape is the ground for the dramas played out in Goya's etchings, *Los Caprichos*, *Los Desastres de la Guerra* and *Los Disparates*; it is the dead terrain just outside the city on which the executions of the 3 May 1808 take place. In the mid-century another version of this indeterminate landscape appears in Baudelaire's Parisian *zone*, the area just beyond the fortifications of the 1840s, home of the *estaminet*, the cheap wine shop, of prostitutes and rag-pickers. The Romantic generations actively sought out such marginal or twilit conditions.[11] The liminal space, they discovered, was the site both of grief and of creativity.

If it exalted the outsider and the lonely wanderer, Romanticism also celebrated conviviality. The figures contemplating the mountains, forest or sea in the paintings of Caspar David Friedrich are bound to each other in imagination and by friendship, even or especially, one senses, when they are alone. Paintings such as Friedrich's could be commemorations of companion-ship. For it was one of the functions of Romantic art to to form restorative, relationship-affirming bonds; like the Romantic landscape, it offered itself as curative and transformative. In late eighteenth-century Germany a Romantic psychiatry, acknowledged by Freud and represented by such figures as Johann Christian Reil (1759–1813) and Carl Gustav Carus (1789–1869), made therapeutic use of painting, theatre and music (Ellenberger 1970: 199–215, and Bell 2005, Chapters 5 and 6). Etienne Georget, a friend of the painter Géricault, was among French alienists who encouraged his patients (including, perhaps, Géricault himself) to paint or draw (Georget 1972 [1820]). Key to this was faith in the healing power of imagination. Charles Lamb, the friend of Hazlitt, Coleridge, the Wordsworths and Shelley, wrote of the importance of an education in imagination: by arguing for more associations and more fantasy rather than less, he was both developing and opposing the prevailing Enlightened idea, deriving from the philosophy of John Locke, that it is a fixity of false associations that can make us mad. In 1796 Lamb's sister Mary had indeed become mad and killed their mother with a knife. Instead of having her confined in an institution where efforts might possibly have been made to correct her false ideas, Charles cared for her himself for the rest of his life, in a fractious and uneasy relationship that nevertheless produced *Tales from Shakespeare* (Appignanesi 2008: 24–8). Latter-day Lockeans, practitioners of cognitive therapies in various forms, also regard the substitution of 'true' ideas and perceptions from 'false' ones as the mainspring of psychotherapy; departure from a mechanistic, Lockean view in favour of doubt, imagination and relationship is what distinguishes both Romanticism and psychoanalysis.

Imagination, which Baudelaire was to call 'that queen of the faculties' (Baudelaire 1975–76: II, 585), is what can liberate us from fixity and falsehood. Allowing its free play can help restore us to our senses; it is also that which can bring us together. William Hazlitt, in an essay of 1805, argued for the role of imagination and 'disinterest' in creating a mutuality out of our separateness and the 'otherness' which we all share with our unknowable *future* selves. Hazlitt's ideas were taken up by Coleridge and Keats, among others (Hazlitt 1969 [1805]). For Goya and Blake, Coleridge and Keats, Géricault and Baudelaire, the imaginative capacity and the effort to maintain it led, ineluctably, to an awareness that we suffer alongside each other, to compassion. The period left indelible images, visual and mental, of the care of sufferers: Keats in the sickroom of his dying brother Tom, and Keats himself nursed by his friend Severn in Rome in his last weeks. Both Schiller and Coleridge had formative experiences of tending the very ill: Schiller his melancholic colleague Grammont (Dewhurst and Reeves 1978: 177 ff.), Coleridge a dangerously sick comrade in the Pest House at Henley during a brief flight into the military (Holmes 1998: 54). Keats had confronted physical suffering at first hand as a medical student and surgical assistant at Guy's Hospital (Motion 1998: 87ff.). Schiller, who had also been a medical student, was himself watched over by the young Novalis during a critical illness in 1791 (Garland 1976: 642). The elderly Goya left us a self-portrait in which he is cradled by his physician, Dr Arrieta. Romanticism tapped a therapeutic and reparative impulse, a wish to *attend*. That we suffer is one thing we hold in common; compassion, the Romantics hoped, might be built in.[12]

Among the most powerful and moving attempts to represent the sick, voiceless and unrepresented is Géricault's group of five portraits of the insane, made in the early 1820s. They are portraits both of the other (Freud's *der Andere*) and the internal other (*das Andere*). They take Romantic consciousness a step further: not only that our otherness to ourselves and each other is something we fundamentally share, but that it might also be absolute and irredeemable. The portraits illuminate what the philosopher Emmanuel Levinas was to say, in the middle of the next century, about the 'absolutely other':

> The relationship with the other is not an idyllic or harmonious relationship of communion, or a sympathy through which we put ourselves in the other's place; we recognise the other as resembling us, but exterior to us; the relationship to the other is a relationship with a Mystery.
>
> (Levinas 1947: 43; see also Loewenthal and Snell 2003)

*   *   *

Psychoanalysis too was the product of crisis. It was, in Toril Moi's words, 'born in the encounter between the hysterical woman and the positivist man of science', and it too is 'shot through with paradoxes and difficulty' (Moi 1989: 196). In the last decades of the nineteenth century, Freud and Breuer were obliged to listen; they had been hired by some of the wealthiest women in Europe for help with inexplicable, medically impossible symptoms, and they had no other therapeutic or social resource than to listen. They had to learn to listen in a way that was different from the usual way in which physicians listened to their patients (Appignanesi and Forrester 1992). For it was the patient rather than the doctor who, unknown to her, held the key (although the doctors, starting with *Studies on Hysteria*, went on to conceptualise how this could be so). Thus, 'more or less unwittingly', Moi says, Freud opened the way for a whole new understanding of human knowledge.

With roots in Romanticism, this understanding was not, of course, totally new. Psychoanalysis articulates relationships of present and anticipated future to past, as Romanticism did. Like Romanticism it recognises the persistence of the past in the present, in order that the past might be re-evaluated and its ties potentially loosened. This it undertakes through attention to current realities and through a living, present relationship, 'in the transference', just as Romantic artists consciously wished to realise the transformative potential of the present encounter between art work and spectator, reader or hearer. Crucially, the process involves the patient/reader in mourning for the loss of former bearings; psychoanalysis too, like Romanticism, questions the extent to which such bearings are themselves products of fantasy and dream.

The mourning involved in accepting this destabilising and decentering, for psychoanalysis as it was for Romanticism, can also be a new opening out to the contingent and its mystery, to a renewed sense of wonder. For Freud and post-Freudians, in their dealings with the unconscious, there will always be an unassimilable surplus, an extraordinary remainder, as there was for Romantics. Freud wrote of 'the dream's navel', the part of the dream that will always resist interpretation (Freud, S. 1900: 525). Lacan spoke of the 'Real', that which lies beyond language and symbolisation: it is what can emerge in the phenomenologically open-minded encounter with the other and the everyday.

Mourning is involved in holding an analytic attitude as it is in facing the Romantic work of art. Roger Bacon has considered this in terms of accepting castration (Bacon 2006); it can also be thought about and experienced, in Freud's terms in 'Mourning and Melancholia', as a gradual letting-go of cherished meanings and ideas, with an accompanying syphoning off of ego and narcissicism, and all the risk of a sense of personal depletion this can incur. It is, for the therapist in the democratic setting of the consulting room, surrender to a process over which s/he has little control – or indeed no control, no more than either participant has of their own mortality.

Psychoanalysis, like Romanticism, is founded in an acceptance of the 'feminine'. The feminine is immanent in the analytic setting and in analytic attentiveness themselves, in so far as both work to return the patient to the earliest relationship, that is, with the mother. As Christopher Bollas has put it, 'the work of reception derives from the world of mutual communication between infant and mother', and this mutual communication, in turn, 'forms the foundation of the unconscious itself' (Bollas 2009: 15). The feminine, in psychoanalysis as in Romanticism, is generative of 'analytic' attentiveness. Both lean their ear towards the unconscious, and towards its exemplary expression, the dream: dream which 'is the mother', her 'body . . . and . . . oracle' (Bollas 2007: 9). In both Romanticism and psychoanalysis listening differently became a self-imposed requirement.

Yet such listening is always at risk, in crisis; it is undertaken in an emotional and cultural force-field which is always threatening fatally to compromise it. For, as Moi continues,

> if Freud's (and Breuer's) act of listening represents an effort to *include* the irrational discourse of femininity in the realm of science, it also embodies their hope of *extending* their own rational understanding of psychic phenomena. *Grasping* the logic of the unconscious they want to make it accessible to reason . . . When the colonising impulse gains the upper hand, psychoanalysis runs the risk of obliterating the language of the irrational and the unconscious, repressing the threatening presence of the feminine in the process . . .
>
> (Moi 1989: 196–7)

Thus, at the same time, it obliterates itself. As Romanticism required of its audience, psychoanalysis requires the analyst to give up a colonising wish to bring the foreign and the other into an omniscient, Enlightenment gaze. Listening necessarily precedes knowledge and theory; yet it is always at risk of being compromised by theory, since it is also always, to a greater or lesser extent, mediated by theory that threatens to direct and dictate to it. When the crisis is too hot to handle, or the moment of crisis has passed and 'the colonising impulse gains the upper hand', the language of the irrational and the unconscious, the 'feminine', is suppressed, and so too is the very possibility of psychoanalysis.

For Laplanche (1996), Freud was caught in a parallel tension, between a wish to continue the Enlightenment construction of master-theories and a registration of their insufficiency. This manifested itself along various axes, fixed symbolism versus free association, for example. Freud sometimes said he looked forward to a day when physiology or neuro-science would unlock the secrets of the mind; he also felt that contemporary physiologists and psychiatrists were 'trying to take away from dreams their dignity as psychical phenomena', while the contributions of philosophers, amateurs, and popular belief were not to be despised (Freud, S. 1990: 41, 63–4). One can trace across his career an oscillation between Freud the architect of an overarching body of theory, with universalising claims to explanation, and Freud the phenomenologist, open to the contingent and the irredeemably *other*. For Christopher Bollas he was 'in perpetual conflict and in contradiction with himself' (Bollas 2007: 30).

Freud's conflict echoes the great cultural battle of the earlier part of the nineteenth century. Yet distinctions between the opposing forces were never absolute. A search for a new kind of order and new foundations was part of Romanticism. Acknowledgement of chaos and contingency existed in classical Enlightenment, albeit in partly repressed form: this repressed content tended only to be evident on the margins and to re-emerge through play, as, for example, in Diderot's ludic, long unpublished, privately circulated novels. What truly distinguished Romanticism, in contrast, was that it faced the conflict between order and chaos, reason and unreason, openly and head-on, and it was obliged to accept that this was not a conflict it could resolve. Tension, contradiction and permanent crisis were constitutive of Romanticism, and they were, and are, of psychoanalysis.[13]

Is all this really anything new, though? Both radical Romantic openness and the broad attitude required for the practice of psychoanalysis can also be located in far more ancient currents and traditions. Perhaps, after all, Freudian psychoanalysis and its 'unconscious' are merely the expression of the numinous in a 'scientific' form acceptable to a post-Cartesian, post-Newtonian world. Jung arguably returned more directly to source. Christianity has always insisted on the limits of a merely human understanding. Bion recommended that the analyst make use of a searchlight beam of darkness (see Chapter 2); for St Paul there was no choice, we can only ever, in this world, see 'through a glass darkly' (I Corinthians 13: 12). The Old Testament is rich in invitations to listen, to 'incline the ear of our heart' (Proverbs 2: 2); 'be still, and know that I *am* God' (Psalm 46: 10). The most important prayer in Judaism, the Shema, opens with the exhortation 'Hear, O Israel' (Deuteronomy 6: 4). Augustine insisted on listening as an act of love, and on the need to listen in order to distinguish truth from lies (St Augustine 2007: 155 ff.). The sixth-century Rule of St Benedict emphasised that the disciple's part is to be silent and listen (St Benedict 1998: 16). Non-Arabic students of Islam are encouraged to listen to recitations from the Qur'an in Arabic, to open themselves to the divine through giving up the need for discursive sense. Such listening is mandatory in Zen Buddhism; is there a school of meditation that does not privilege it?

The Romantics were not the first to understand that the high road to self-discovery is indirect: 'where I seek myself I cannot find myself', wrote Montaigne in the late sixteenth century. 'I discover myself more by accident than by inquiring into my judgement' (*Essay* II, 10; Montaigne 1991: 40). Montaigne's awareness of creative internal 'otherness' and of a self that is dynamic and conflicted pre-dated and was to resonate with the Romantic generations. 'Provided that he listens to himself there is no one who does not discover in himself a form entirely his own, a master-form which struggles against his education as well as against the storm of emotions which would gainsay it' (*Essay* III: 2; Montaigne 1991: 914).

Montaigne's *Essays* were reflections both on his experience of himself and on his wide reading of Latin literature. Classical antiquity and the Middle Ages, wrote the twentieth-century Catholic philosopher Josef Pieper,

> drew a distinction between the understanding as *ratio* and the under-standing as *intellectus*. *Ratio* is the power of discursive, logical thought, of searching and of examination, of abstraction, of definition and drawing conclusions. *Intellectus*, on the other hand, is the name for the under-standing insofar as it is the capacity of *simplex intuitus*, of that simple vision to which truth offers itself like a landscape to the eye.

Pieper was concerned with an ancient view of the action of mind:

> The faculty of mind, man's knowledge, is both these things in one . . . simultaneously *ratio* and *intellectus*; and the process of knowing is the action of the two together. The mode of discursive thought is accompanied and impregnated by an effortless awareness, the contemplative vision of the *intellectus*, which is not active but passive, or rather receptive, the activity of the soul in which it conceives that which it sees.
>
> (Pieper 1964 [1952]: 26–7)

For much of post-classical and especially post-Cartesian Western history, listening has been undervalued in favour of grasping, expressive, discursive *logos*. Yet, as the psychoanalyst and philosopher Gemma Corradi Fiumara has pointed out (Corradi Fiumara 1990), in thus allowing listening to be eclipsed we account for only half a *logos*: for what is a word, a speaker, without a listener? The ancient current of receptive *intellectus* re-entered the mainstream of Western culture, after a period of Cartesian and Lockean repression, with Romanticism, which reproblematised *intellectus*'s relationship with *ratio*. Perhaps this is what Laplanche was referring to when he said that the 'psychoanalytic cure . . . can have neither sense nor results unless it . . . enters into relation with something pre-existent and fundamental in human existence *and its movement of temporalisation*' (my italics): the re-emergence of *intellectus* and the re-problematising of its relationships was an effect of 'deferred action' or 'afterwardsness', *Nachträglichkeit* (Laplanche 1992: 171; see also Laplanche and Pontalis 1988: 111–14). Through Romanticism, as a Wordsworthian aspiration to 'a simple vision to which truth offers itself like a landscape to the eye', in tension with discursive thought, *intellectus* became available as a vital source of energy in contemporary psychotherapy. In the history of psychoanalysis, *intellectus* held in tension with *ratio* once again became a consciously cultivated therapeutic stance, an attempt to sustain a state of receptivity that could be developed, through training and through apprenticeship both to one's own analyst and to one's own unique, reflected and worked upon experience.

In this sense both Romanticism and psychoanalysis are returns of something repressed. In mid- and late nineteenth-century positivism, Romantic art-and-science was partially re-repressed; it came back to life in another form in psychoanalysis. The 'living intensity' of Freud's Romantic heritage, Vermorel and Vermorel wrote, was 'concealed beneath the pervasive materialism of his [later nineteenth-century] teachers'; once psychoanalysis had established a degree of scientific credibility, however, they note that references to the psychical models of the Romantics vastly increase. The 'stream becomes a torrent' with 'The Uncanny' (1919) and *Beyond the Pleasure Principle* (1920) (Vermorel and Vermorel 1986: 14–15).

Romanticism and psychoanalysis were and are responses to the continuing and endemic crisis in Enlightenment. They are, for the critic Kenneth Scott Calhoon, 'dual expressions of disillusionment with a rationalism that had failed to make good'; they share an 'economy of longing and disappointment of which mourning is a profound index' (Calhoon 1992: 5, 25. Calhoon has argued that both are responses to the loss of a father). For Joel Faflak, Coleridge's coinage of the word 'psycho-analytical' in 1805 points to how Romanticism *invents* psychoanalysis – 'as the struggle for an identity radically divided between its rational . . . theoretical and philosophical . . . and literary or aesthetic impulses'. He proposes that Romanticism's 'psychoanalytic' tropes 'disclose a process of *imagining* psychoanalysis before its codification by theory. Psychoanalysis had to be imagined, that is, before it could be debated in theory, a debate always undone by the psychic process that made it possible' (Faflak 2002: 75; see also Faflak 2008, McDayter 2002). Faflak sets out to remind psychoanalysis of its 'fundamental matrix' in the work of imagination – particularly among the English poets, Wordsworth, Coleridge, De Quincey, Keats – involved in the struggle to reconcile the poles of this divide, a struggle constantly undermined 'by the psychic processes that made it possible' and one that could never be brought to completion.

Like Romanticism, psychoanalysis affronts genre sensibilities; it has been characterised as both a science and *a work of* art (Vermorel and Vermorel

1986: 16, my italics). It is a form of therapy, research and philosophy that is *sui generis*, an 'impossible profession' (Freud, S. 1937: 248). 'Not only impossible, but also very difficult', added the psychoanalyst Adam Limentani (cited in Malcolm 2004 [1981]: inside cover).

*   *   *

A recognisably analytic attitude began to take shape in European culture one hundred years before Freud. It was, like its late nineteenth- and early twentieth-century re-emergence in Freud's consulting room, something born out of historical contingency. It was prompted into being by a kind of art that called a new kind of audience into existence and was simultaneously called into existence by this audience. Art work and spectator entered a new form of, potentially, mutually transformative *dialogue*, complicit and open ended, a dialogue that made space for mystery and the unconscious, and, ultimately, for a new kind of 'psycho-analytical' dialogue between people.

Fear haunts the process. 'Mental illness', as Foucault and others have shown, was invented as a modern category in the late Enlightenment/Romantic period, as something which, if subsumed within a medical discourse, might be thinkable, susceptible to categorization (Foucault 1971 [1961]). The subject of *madness* in the raw is, at first glance surprisingly, rare in the visual arts and literature of the period. Contained within the increasingly hegemonic regime of medical discourse, its terrors were perhaps displaced elsewhere. For the bourgeois Europe of Freud's adulthood, the spectre of the savage horde, a terrifying, nameless, mass, never ceased to make its threat felt. This mass was often cast as feminine, in terms of female sexuality, an echo of the women who marched on Versailles and the *tricoteuses* who sat by the guillotine; it generated some of the earliest sociological theories of the group (see LeBon 1905 [1895]; Thomson 2004: 79–106).[14] It was a terror that had increased across the century as capitalist production took hold (Barham 1993: 31 ff.). It entered into psychoanalysis's picture of dark id forces, and, later on, of unconscious 'internal gangs' (Rosenfeld 1987); into Freud's understanding of dreams as sophisticated attempts to evade censorship, to negotiate between wild desire and social order. But such representations of madness as did occur in the earlier part of the century, in Goya, Géricault, or Nerval, before what Foucault called the great medical confinement, articulate the most feared consequences of the Romantic loosening up; this did, for a Hölderlin, Nerval or Schumann, end in madness. Such works, along with other products of Romanticism, allow the viewer/reader a sense of that edginess, that un-at-homeness and readiness to dwell in an unnerving, marginal zone, which needs to be one of the dimensions of analytic attentiveness.

Chapter 2

The analytic attitude

An overview

Freud's classic statement of the analytic attitude is contained in his 'Recommendations to Physicians Practising Psycho-analysis', one of the series of papers on technique of 1912–15. He formulates it in terms of the requirement on the analyst's part to maintain 'evenly distributed', or 'suspended', 'hovering', 'circling' or 'free-floating attention' (*gleichschwebende Aufmerksamkeit*):[1]

> The technique ... consists simply in not directing one's notice to anything in particular and in maintaining the same 'evenly-suspended attention' (as I have called it) in the face of all that one hears ... as soon as anyone deliberately concentrates his attention to a certain degree, he begins to select from the material before him; one point will be fixed in his mind with particular clearness and some other will be correspondingly disregarded, and in making this selection he will be following his expectations or inclinations. This, however, is precisely what must not be done. In making the selection, if he follows his expectations he is in danger of never finding anything but what he already knows; and if he follows his inclinations he will certainly falsify what he may perceive. It must not be forgotten that the things one hears are for the most part things whose meaning is only recognized later on.
>
> It will be seen that the rule of giving equal notice to everything is the necessary counterpart to the demand made on the patient that he should communicate everything that occurs to him without criticism or selection. If the doctor behaves otherwise, he is throwing away most of the advantage which results from the patient's obeying the 'fundamental rule of psychoanalysis'. The rule for the doctor may be expressed: 'He should withhold all conscious influences from his capacity to attend, and give himself over completely to his "unconscious memory".' Or, to put it purely in terms of technique: 'He should simply listen, and not bother about whether he is keeping anything in mind.' What is achieved in this manner will be sufficient for all requirements during the treatment ...

This job description is a salutory reminder of the radical nature of the Freudian project. 'The post-holder will be expected to concentrate on nothing in particular, to refrain from conscious exertion of any kind, and listen.' Freud is unequivocal: 'What is achieved in this manner will be *sufficient for all requirements during the treatment*' (my italics).

Over time, connections and nodal points begin to form themselves in the analyst's mind, emerging from material that at first seems chaotic and unconnected; the analyst must allow himself 'to be taken by surprise'. He must also model himself on the surgeon who

> puts aside all his feelings, even his human sympathy, and concentrates his mental forces on the single aim of performing the operation as skilfully as possible . . . A surgeon of earlier times took as his motto the words: *Je le pansai, Dieu le guérit.*[2] The analyst should be content with something similar.

The analyst is the servant of a process; through his refusal to substitute 'a censorship of his own for the selection that the patient has forgone', he positions himself to hear from the patient's unconscious. Freud then elaborates on this with another analogy:

> To put it in a formula: he must turn his own unconscious like a recep-tive organ towards the transmitting unconscious of the patient. He must adjust himself to the patient as a telephone receiver is adjusted to the transmitting microphone. Just as the receiver converts back into sound waves the electric oscillations in the telephone line which were set up by sound waves, so the doctor's unconscious is able, from the derivatives of the unconscious which are communicated to him, to reconstruct that unconscious, which has determined the patient's free associations.

At the same time he was at pains to insist that this is not a merely technical or mechanical matter, for

> if the doctor is to be in a position to use his unconscious in this way as an instrument in the analysis, he must himself fulfil one psychological condition to a high degree. He may not tolerate any resistances in himself which hold back from his consciousness what has been perceived by his unconscious; otherwise he would introduce into the analysis a new species of selection and distortion which would be far more detrimental than that resulting from concentration of conscious attention . . .
>
> (Freud, S. 1912: 110–15)

The analyst is emotionally on the line. He must be able to face and resist what he may come up against in himself. In 1923 Freud revisited the topic in two encyclopaedia articles, and now he suggested a widening of the focus of evenly suspended attention to include more of the analyst's own unconscious: the analyst might 'surrender himself to his own unconscious mental activity' in order 'to catch the drift of the patient's unconscious with his own unconscious'.

He went on to make this further, important comment: 'It is true that this work of interpretation was not to be brought under strict rules and left a great deal of play to the physician's tact and skill . . .' (Freud, S. 1923: 238). This might sound (in the Strachey translation at least) apologetic or ambivalent, as if Freud felt that the work of unconscious-to-unconscious listening and subsequent interpretation ought to have been better codified or standardised. Yet he was, later, unambiguously rueful about how some of his followers seemed to read him. In 1928 he wrote to Ferenczi:

> For my recommendations on technique which I gave back then were essentially negative. I considered the most important thing to emphasise what one should not do, to demonstrate the temptations that work against analysis. Almost everything that is positive that one should do I left to 'tact', which has been introduced by you. But what I achieved in so doing was that the obedient ones didn't take notice of the elasticity of these dissuasions and subjected themselves to them as if they were taboos. That had to be revised at some time, without of course revoking the obligations.
> (Falzeder and Brabant 2000: 332, cited in
> Jiménez 2008: 582–3)

Freud censures 'the obedient ones' for turning obligations into taboos – or, to put it another way, for making rigid rules out of the requirement to avoid anything that might close down on the possibility of the new and unknown, of the unconscious, emerging in analysis. He underlines the 'elasticity of these dissuasions' and the role of personal 'tact', which he had noted himself and praised Ferenczi for stressing (Ferenczi always emphasised the tremendous complexity of the mental and emotional work demanded of the analyst: see Jiménez 2008: 582. He was also to pay dearly at Freud's hands for his therapeutic freedom of mind).

The apparently relaxed attitude Freud displayed in his letter to Ferenczi is in contrast to the rigorous examination the analytic attitude has received from subsequent theorists, particularly in France. For Serge Leclaire, writing in the 1960s, the analytic attitude was simply an impossibility. Listening was never unproblematic; Freud's 'rules of analytic attention are impossible to uphold'. Leclaire compared the situation Freud outlined in his 'Recommendations' to 'some mad undertaking in which a blind navigator without a compass invites his passenger to take the wind whichever way it blows'. Leclaire continued,

> Quite obviously, this is an untenable position, and Freud was the first to say so. Indeed, who could ever seriously claim to succeed in erasing all his prejudices, giving up all the secret preferences that constitute the order of his world, his very way of seeing, feeling, loving, listening? With such a claim, the severe psychoanalyst evokes, in the worst case,

the schizophrenic's world from which all possible order vanishes and, in the best case, of the obsessive endlessly employed in contesting the established order so as to give himself the illusion of overcoming his attachment to it . . . one could imagine that there are psychoanalysts who, applying the letter of the law of floating attention, make it their duty never to hear anything.

(Leclaire 1998 [1968]: 12–13)

The neutrality of the analyst, Leclaire continued, 'aims only to describe a certain affective or libidinal position'; it must always be supplemented by, be in tension with, theory. For the analyst does orient himself, have an order of reference by which to make connections between elements gathered in the sessions. He does not solely rely on his reverie, or counter-transference, or mere intuition (Leclaire 1998 [1968]: 13).

Thus, as Leclaire put it, a 'double requirement' is imposed on the analyst: he must have a system of reference, a theory; he must set aside any system of reference and theory. Leclaire reminds us that the Freudian order of reference is, in the final analysis, sexual and libidinal. Is reference to, for example, the central fact of sex sufficient guarantee of respect for this double requirement? How? There is, for Leclaire, the unavoidable, underlying question touched on in Chapter 1, above: 'how can one conceive a theory of psychoanalysis that does not annul, in the very fact of its articulation, the very possibility of its practice?' On one hand, the requirement to keep an absolutely open ear; for 'floating attention designates precisely the sort of lateral listening that is better able to grasp fringe phenomena, obstacles, or shadows than the exaggeration of a sign in its place or the well-balanced harmony of an elegant argument' (Leclaire 1998 [1968]: 66). On the other hand, the need to hold on 'to the very principle of an open logic that . . . takes account of the facts of sex and *jouissance*':

. . . the always recurring difficulty of psychoanalysis, which no institution will ever be able to resolve, derives from the fact that it is vulnerable, on the one hand, to the degradation of a closed systematization and, on the other, to the anarchy of intuitive processes . . . The rigourousness of unconscious desire, its logic, is revealed only to whoever respects simultaneously these two apparently contradictory requirements that are order and singularity.

(Leclaire 1998 [1968]: 15)

Laplanche and Pontalis, in their dictionary entry on 'Attention, (Evenly) Suspended or Poised', also point to theoretical and practical difficulties which, they note, are already suggested by the self-contradictory nature of the term. In one way, since unconscious structures come to light only in multiply-distorted forms, evenly suspended attention makes sense, since it is 'the only truly objective attitude' adequate to 'an essentially distorted object'. From the analyst's viewpoint, however, there is a problem: if the goal is direct communication between one unconscious and another, with the analyst's unconscious relating to that of the analysand like a telephone receiver to a transmitting microphone, how can his attention not be oriented by his own unconscious motives? How, furthermore, can the analyst, in interpreting or making historical constructions, not give special attention to particular material, comparing and schematising it? – 'the rule of suspended attention must be understood as an *ideal*' (Laplanche and Pontalis 1988: 43–5).

For André Green, 'benevolent neutrality', at least, is not a contradiction in terms; coldness and indifference are certainly not required. As for the analyst's unconscious motives, Green accepts that analytic listening 'is just as much a matter of receptivity and availability to the productions arising from the analyst's own unconscious which he will not only have to tolerate but to understand as well'. In fact, evidence of the spontaneity of the manifestations of the analyst's unconscious can contribute to the analytic communication and may be preferable to the artificiality of attitude that Ferenczi denounced (Green 2005: 36). Green also addressed the problem of the analyst's departure from 'pure' suspended attention when the moment comes, as it inevitably does, for the selection of particular material. There are, he writes, two phases. First, the analyst attempts to listen, in as free-floating a way as possible, to what the patient says. He already has two listening perspectives simultaneously in mind, however: conflictuality within the patient, and the possible (transference) messages that the patient's speech may contain for the analyst. He attends to the movement of the patient's discourse 'towards and away from a meaningful nucleus or . . . nuclei which are trying to enter consciousness'. Thanks to free-floating attention, the analyst may then be able to 'notice these variations intuitively even if one does not know the exact nature of the focal point around which they gravitate'. When this does appear, suddenly, sometimes clearly or as if accidentally, 'floating attention undergoes a change of state and becomes investigative acuity' (Green 2005: 43).

These points of reference, conflictuality and transference, Green regards as mandatory for the practice of psychoanalysis. There are, of course, within Freud and certainly post-Freud, nuances to such 'systems of reference' and the ways in which they are held in mind by practitioners. In his book *The Analytic Attitude* (Schafer 1983), Roy Schafer concluded that no single concise formulation for this attitude in its hypothetical totality exists, however beautifully exemplified across the field of analytic writing it may be. Schafer cited Anna Freud, Ferenczi, Abraham, Klein, Reich, Fenichel, Glover, Strachey, Freeman, Reik, Kris, Lowenstein, Annie Reich, Jacobson, Eissler, Greenson, Kohut, Erikson, Winnicott, Hartmann and Loewald among others who had written more or less explicitly on the topic, some of whom, at least, should not be counted among 'the obedient ones'. The analytic attitude eludes monolithic definition. Theoretical emphases within these various contributions are different, Schafer pointed out. Anna Freudians, for example, might think in structural terms, with the emphasis on the inner world of the patient – about maintaining, as Anna Freud recommended, a position 'equidistant' from id, ego and superego (Freud, A. 1993 [1936]: 28). Others stressed the inter- as well as the intra-psychic. Theodor Reik, who borrowed the term 'the third ear' from Nietzsche, particularly emphasised how much the analyst's own inner world required his attention if he was to be able to catch the dialogue between one mind and another (Reik 1948: 246).

The relevance of discussions on technique to an understanding of the analytic attitude will, wrote Schafer, be differently construed by different readers; some contributions are more controversial than others. There is variation as to what should be the major features of the analytic attitude; and there is always the specific context, that made up by the particular analyst and analysand, the nature of what the analysis is struggling with at any particular time, and the phase of the analysis. Consequently, Schafer continued, 'the project of presenting a definitive set of generalisations about the analytic attitude cannot be undertaken very hopefully, for these generalisations will serve only as the roughest of guidelines for sorting out . . . the full, the compromised, and the failed analytic attitude'. What is more, such generalisations could end up sounding like a proscriptive admonition to 'be a good analyst' (Schafer 1983: 3–5). A comparative study of views of the analytic attitude might ultimately reveal very different assumptions about what it means to be human.

Schafer nevertheless did not give up trying to 'set forth standards of excellence'. His book recommends an attitude of neutrality and an avoidance of either/or thinking; an insistence on holding at all times to the effort to interpret psychic reality; the aim to help the patient understand his or her past and present life; promotion of an atmosphere of safety, an empathic stance, a sense of appreciation or wonder, an openness to multiple histories and different narrative structures, and an affirmative insistence on finding value in even the most apparently destructive of the patient's behaviours and attitudes.

There have been plenty of other useful attempts to provide blanket or dictionary definitions. Roudinesco and Plon, for example, noting that the phrases 'rule of abstinence' and 'analytic attitude' are sometimes used interchangeably, offer this:

> The rule of abstinence is a corollary of the fundamental rule and designates the totality of methods and attitudes brought to bear by the analyst to make it impossible for the patient to have recourse to substitute forms of satisfaction in order to save himself from the suffering which constitutes the motor force of analytic work.
>
> (Roudinesco and Plon 1997:19)

In practice, according to the particular personality and style of the practitioner, there may be overlap between different systems of reference, and none would be the wholly exclusive frame of reference for any particular 'school'.[3] For Kleinians, it might be the state of the transference and counter-transference; for analysts from the British Middle Group current and past configurations of object relations; for Kohutians, the ego-state; for Lacanians the operative structure (hysteric, perverse, psychotic); for Jungians, the operative archetype, or state of integration–deintegration; for those influenced by Bion, location on the grid; for Meltzerians, the patient's place in the mother's body, from head to claustrum, and so on.

Parallelling and, arguably, underlying all ways of conceiving of a listening, analytic orientation is phenomenology. Phenomenology was fundamental to the development of Lacan's thought and this is widely acknowledged (see, for example, Roudinesco 1993: 129 ff.). However, the influence of phenomenology on psychoanalysis in general often seems to be under-explored, by Anglo-Saxon commentators at least, even though Freud attended the psychologist and phenomenologist Franz Brentano's lectures, with their 'refreshing and seductive' ambiance, as a student (Gay 1988: 29).[4] The phenomenologist, wrote Edmund Husserl, modern phenomenology's founding father, must begin 'in absolute poverty, with an absolute lack of knowledge' (Husserl, cited in Moran 2000: 126).

> Initially this meant refraining from preconceived ideas drawn from philosophy and the sciences, but gradually it came to mean the most radical form of *self-questioning*, involving a kind of Cartesian overthrow of all previous assumptions to knowledge, and a questioning of many of our 'natural' intuitions about the nature of our mental processes or the make-up of the objective world. Nothing must be taken for granted or assumed external to the lived experiences themselves as they are lived.
>
> (Moran 2000: 127)

It was surely a phenomenologist's attempt to bracket off preconceptions and resist the wish to privilege one thing over another, to maintain calm attentiveness, which Freud was recommending in 1912.

In Britain the best-known spokesperson for an existential-phenomenological stance has been R.D. Laing. Laing was trained as a psychoanalyst as well as a psychiatrist, and was highly critical of both psychoanalysis and psychiatry in their institutional forms; experience and scientific 'objectivity', he reminds us, belong to two different registers, and to conflate them in therapeutic practice is to risk doing violence to the person who comes in search of meanings (see also Cotton and Loewenthal 2011).[5] There are UK trainings in which, alongside psychoanalysis, the phenomenological tradition takes centre stage, from Husserl and Heidegger through to Foucault and Derrida and the post-modern 'turn to language': that at the Philadelphia Association, for example, founded by Laing and colleagues in 1965, or at Roehampton University. Phenomenology foregrounds the experience and practice of listening themselves: 'words, vowels, phonemes are so many ways of singing the world', wrote Maurice Merleau-Ponty in *Phenomenology of Perception*. The 'phonetic gesture' breaks a primordial silence; for both speaker and listener it makes manifest 'a structuring of experience, a modality of existence' (Merleau-Ponty 1979 [1945]: 218, 224, 214). Such listening is, furthermore, the foundation of an ethics:

> if by means of reflection I find a pre-personal subject in myself, alongside the subject who perceives . . . if the world perceived remains in a state of neutrality, neither verifiable object nor dream . . . this world can remain undivided between my perception and his, the I who perceives has no particular privilege which rules out an I who is perceived, both are beings . . . exceeded by their world who can, consequently, be exceeded by one another.
>
> (Merleau-Ponty 1979 [1945]: 405)

An analytic stance in all its forms involves, like phenomenology, a humbling acceptance that the listener just like the speaker belongs within and is subject to a world. It is also a radical refusal of the claim to know for, and better than, the other, to be 'the subject supposed to know', the position which, for Lacan, the new patient will typically give the analyst (Evans 1996: 196–7). It is an insistence on speaking from somewhere else, if only because we are all in any case always already somewhere else: 'I am thinking where I am not, therefore I am where I am not thinking', said Lacan in his famous reversal of Descartes's *Cogito ergo sum* (Lacan 2007: 430). 'Hands off the theorisation of the patient! Hands off!' admonished Lacan's erstwhile student Jean Laplanche (Laplanche 1992: 70). Neither join in with the patient's stories about himself nor try to replace them with new and better stories: that, Laplanche wrote, is the patient's job, just as for Lacan it was the analysand who was to do the analysis. Like the phenomenological stance, an analytic attitude can perhaps be gauged by whether or not, through its commitment to 'mere' observation and description, it allows both patient and analyst a breathing space, free from the accumulated clutter of knowingness, demand, authoritativeness or ready explanation, so that both might become more available for the mysterious meeting with a common but ultimately unknowable otherness.

For the position required of the analyst vis-à-vis the patient is, in a sense, akin to that of the neonate in Laplanche's account of development (Laplanche 1989 [1987]). The newborn is inevitably open to the enigmatic unconscious sexual messages of the adult carer, but these will always exceed the baby's capacity to translate them, impelled to translate as he or she is, for it is the enigmatic message itself that produces the need for translation. The analytic setting is analogous to an originary and traumatic situation of seduction, which, from the unconscious or not so unconscious point of view of the patient, it recreates (what does the analyst want?); the analyst's position too might be conceived of as a willed recreation of the child's original situation vis-à-vis the adult's (patient's) unconscious sexual messages which he must, however, resist translating. The enigmatic message demands respect *qua* enigma: it is also axiomatic for Laplanche that the adult patient's speech should be approached by the analyst as if it were a foreign language. Rather than taking 'the contingent status of his own language as solid and fixed' the analytic listener needs to let himself 'be violently moved by the foreign language ... he must enlarge and deepen his own language by means of the foreign language'. Otherwise, the analyst ceases to be an analyst; he becomes less a translator than a transferrer, less an 'Übersetzer' than an 'Übertrager', blindly caught up in his own emotional perspectives, his transferences, without acknowledgement of their contingency (Laplanche 1992: 201).

For the newborn, furthermore, the unconscious sexual message of the adult is transmitted through the body, the breast and the skin-to-skin contact of ordinary infant care. What Laplanche also crucially does – something occluded or ignored in much psychoanalytic writing, in spite of Freud's reminder that 'the ego is primarily a bodily ego' – is to bring an awareness that in the consulting room are two sentient bodies, sexual and visceral. Laplanche is rare among contemporary psychoanalysts in his bypassing of a post-Cartesian mind–body split, and in his refusal of a notion of pure 'psychic reality': all communication passes through the body (see Roustang 2006 [2001]: 18–19).

Within this tradition in psychoanalytic thought, the overt content of what the patient says is likely to be seen as relatively unimportant, and the encounter with the foreignness of the unconscious correspondingly valued. Both the patient's psyche and the analytic setting, the interpersonal space of the session, tend to be seen as theatres for the staging of unconscious conflicts. Christopher Bollas, for example, at a time when perhaps matters of transference and counter-transference occupied a more central place for him, wrote:

> The classical model's theories of evenly suspended attentiveness and neutrality were never intended to imitate interpersonal reality, but rather, to portray the intrapsychic through the projective possibilities of the interpersonal where the object's reply is of the self's own making. The structure of two allowed the internal figures and dynamics of one to speak.
> (Bollas 1999: 49)

Similar views can be heard from across the Channel:

> The analyst learns to be disinterested in the narrative content of what is said. He thus adjusts himself to the [unconscious] position of the analysand, whose speech has the sole function of turning unconscious representations into verbal metaphors. That is what free-floating attention

('l'égal suspens') is about. Instead the analyst allows his attention to float on the disturbances constituted by certain plays of association and analogy, because here, like silhouettes in a Chinese shadow play, figures returning from the depths of unconscious memory can emerge. Analytic listening, in the presence of the manifest, seductive familiarity of narrative speech, is thus a disobliging kind of listening . . . This ascetic, frustrating listening partakes, paradoxically, of a real benevolence . . . by virtue of being, in the same way as a sensory organ in relation to the external world, a *perceptual tool for unconscious reality*. Too much empathy on the analyst's part for the subject's suffering, too much curiosity about history and life events, too much concern with the prospect of cure, or too much interest in an approach based on forms of psychopathology, tend to destroy this listening's power to initiate a process.

(Rolland 2006: 29–31)

The French philosopher Paul Ricoeur elaborated the theatrical metaphor in his account of psychoanalysis as a hermeneutics:

the development of Freudian theory may be looked upon as the gradual reduction of the idea of a psychical apparatus . . . to a topography in which space is no longer a place within the world but a scene where roles and masks enter into debate; this space will become a place of ciphering and deciphering.

(Ricoeur 1970, cited in Calhoon 1992: 18)

The most single-minded post-Freudian initiatives in thinking about the value and difficulty of 'a disobliging kind of listening', 'not troubling to keep anything in mind in particular', have come from the Kleinian tradition, above all the work of W.R. Bion. The 'only point of importance in any session is the unknown', Bion famously insisted in a short and explosive paper of 1967, 'Notes on Memory and Desire'. The analyst must 'cultivate a watchful avoidance of memory' and avoid any desire, for results, cure, or even understanding. Psychoanalytic observation, he wrote, 'is concerned neither with what has happened nor with what is going to happen but with what *is* happening'. The only measure of 'progress' will be 'the increased number and variety of moods, ideas and attitudes seen in any given session' (Bion 1967: 17–18).

Bion's cultural background, like that of other British analysts of his generation, included the English Romantic poets (see Williams and Waddell 1991; White 2006). He made his debt to Romanticism explicit, enlisting Keats's idea of negative capability, to which he alluded in different contexts (Bion 1984b [1970]: 125; 1990: 45, 47) as a potent evocation of the analytic attitude. Bion used the idea of reverie to encourage openness to the unconscious communication from the patient. At the same time, the analyst's reverie is in itself a communication *to* the patient: the analyst who is able to maintain a state of reverie imparts something to the channels of unconscious communication themselves, just as a mother's reverie in the presence of her child is a 'psychical quality . . . imparted to the channels of communication, the links with the child' (Bion 1962: 36). Bion alludes to the change that takes place – a jointly experienced increase in 'the number and variety of moods, ideas and attitudes' – merely by virtue of the analyst being able to maintain reverie.

Throughout his work his advice to analysts was to listen to what the patient says as if listening to a dream. In the early 1960s he characterised the analyst's capacity to sustain such listening as 'alpha function', 'a working tool in the analysis of disturbances of thought', which can 'provide [both the analyst's and the patient's] . . . psyche with the material for dream thoughts, and hence the capacity to wake up or go to sleep, to be conscious or unconscious' (Bion 1962: 308). Bion drew attention to the affinity between dream and psychoanalysis itself:

> Anyone who has made careful notes of what he considers to be the facts of a session must be familiar with the experience in which such notes will, on occasion, seem to be drained of all reality: they might be notes of dreams made to ensure that he will not forget them on waking. To me it suggests that the experience of the session relates to material akin to the dream, not in the sense that dreams might be part of the preoccupation of the session but that the dream and the psycho-analyst's working material both share a dream-like quality.
>
> (Bion 1984b [1970]: 70–1)

For Kleinians and therapists informed by the Kleinian tradition notions of projection and introjection are crucial: the psychic mechanisms underlying intersubjecivity, whereby, to use Kleinian metaphors, we 'put emotional states into each other' and unconsciously take them in from each other. Klein developed this thinking further with the concept of projective identification (Klein 1946), which can be summarised as that which leads the recipient of the projection of the other's affective state to identify with it as if it were all his own (see Laplanche and Pontalis 1988: 356–7). These ideas have been further developed by Betty Joseph (Joseph 1985, 1987), as well as by Bion and others, all within the context of the great importance Klein ascribed to the transference.

Even in his pioneering, pre-analytic work with groups, Bion stressed the importance of the group therapist's ability to shift points of view, to 'see the reverse as well as the obverse of every situation', as required in the well-known optical illusion of the open-sided cube (Bion 1989 [1961]: 86 ff.). He also framed this ability to shift vertices in terms of 'binocular vision': analytic work throws up phenomena 'that require stereoscopy to make them manifest' (Bion 1984b [1970]: 43).

Ignacio Matte-Blanco's 'bi-logic' made similar demands on the analyst. Bi-logic, which Matte-Blanco developed out of mathematical 'set' theory, identifies two principles at work in all thinking: the principle of Generalisation and the principle of Symmetry. Eric Rayner and David Tuckett have commented that for Matte-Blanco 'human experience can be conceived as structured by the existence of up to an infinite series of strata in which our capacity to recognize differences declines as the amount of symmetrization increases' (Rayner and Tuckett 1998: 26–7). Thus, Matte-Blanco could write:

> If the attention of the observer remains focused on the first level, that of consciousness, then he will only be aware of the concrete individual; and if he lets himself be permeated by the underlying levels, this infinity will unfold itself before him, though in an unconscious manner . . .
>
> (Matte-Blanco 1975: 170)

In his attempts to conceptualise the kind of work required for listening to the unconscious, Bion developed his mathematised 'grid', which he introduced in *Learning from Experience* in 1962. The grid systematised and made graphic the complexity of shifting vertices in which the analyst is involved. K ('knowledge') and minus-K, L ('love') and minus-L, and α and β function were elements in an exploration of problems 'fundamental to learning', and an attempt to convey emotional experience, both the patient's and the analyst's (Bion 1962: v).

Bion also made use of the visual metaphor of projection in an image that seems to draw partly on theatre, with its spotlights, and partly on his experiences of war.

> Instead of trying to bring a brilliant, intelligent, knowledgeable light to bear on obscure problems, I suggest we bring to bear a diminution of the 'light' – a penetrating beam of darkness: a reciprocal of the searchlight. The peculiarity of this penetrating ray is that it could be directed towards the object of our curiosity, and this object would absorb whatever light already existed, leaving the area of examination exhausted of any light that it possessed. The darkness would be so absolute that it would achieve a luminous, absolute vacuum. So that, if any object existed, however faint, it would show up very clearly. Thus, a very faint light would become visible in maximum conditions of darkness.
>
> (Bion 1990: 20–1)

In his wilful blinding of himself (Bion 1984b [1970]: 43),[6] his putting himself in the dark, his deliberate ignorance and refusal to know about and for his patient, his 'capacity for tolerating [the] analysand's statements without rushing to the conclusion that [he knows] the interpretations' (Bion 1990: 45), the analyst becomes in his own person a means of absorbing, taking into himself as if through his light- and dark-sensitive skin, the unconsciously projected communication of the patient; he identifies this in himself, thanks to projective identification, in his own feeling state. The later Bion, in the later 1960s and the 1970s, increasingly came to value faith and intuition, and described an analytic attitude that involved an openness to what he designated as 'O', which is both a kind of Platonic ground of being, an unknowable reality, and the unknown as the new, the not yet foreseen or evolved (White 2006: 194–5). He summed this up in 1970:

> What matters is the unknown and on this the psycho-analyst must focus his attention. Therefore 'memory' is a dwelling on the unimportant to the exclusion of the important. Similarly, 'desire' is an intrusion into the analyst's state of mind which covers up, disguises, and blinds him to, the point at issue: that aspect of O that is currently presenting the unknown and unknowable though it is manifested to the two people present in its evolved character. This is the 'dark spot' that must be illuminated by 'blindness'. Memory and desire are 'illuminations' that destroy the value of the analyst's capacity for observation as a leakage of light into a camera might destroy the value of the film being exposed.
>
> (Bion 1984b [1970]: 69)

This means, in the words of Bion's commentator Michael Eigen,

> an appreciative sensibility for what remains out of reach. The very taste of experience gains new meaning. The subject learns the gesture of repeatedly starting from scratch, of living in a wall-less moment and sensing his walls in a way that makes a difference.
>
> (Eigen 1985: 326, cited in White 2006: 194)

Bion's writing aimed in a way similar to Lacan's to engender this necessity in the reader, the need to start from scratch.[7]

'O' has also received this commentary, from Neville Symington:

> Bion says that one cannot strive for this state but that one can only 'become' it. It is possible to be receptive to pure giving. It is this and only this that moves the heart, that melts stubbornness, that dilutes the madness in whose grip we find ourselves. All the theories, all the schools of psycho-analysis or psychotherapy are dust and ashes if this purity of giving is absent. This is why psychotherapy if it is anything brings healing through this giving; it only works if this generous spirit is present. The spiritual is woven then into the very fabric of what we do as psycho-analysts, as psychotherapists.
>
> (Symington 2008: 498–9)

The analytic attitude, thus conceived, is imbued with a profound, spiritual generosity. It can be sufficient in itself:

> I believe that if I listen to this patient, if I am prepared to hear what he has to say, if I am prepared to see what I can see if the patient comes to me, then, although the patient cannot understand what I say to him if I am using ordinary language, he may be able to understand the fact that I have not run away, I have not shut him up in a mental hospital and I am ready to arrange to see him tomorrow . . . If the analyst is prepared to listen, have his eyes open, his ears open, his senses open, his intuition open, it has an effect upon the analysand who seems to grow; the session provides the mind of the patient with what, if it were a matter of physical experience, one could say was 'good food'.
>
> (Bion 1990: 131, see also Khair Badawi 2011)

For D.W. Winnicott, the search for a sense of one's creative self could only come from 'desultory formless functioning', a 'rudimentary playing, as if in a neutral zone', in the company of a responsive other who, crucially, is able to reflect back emergent signs of creativity. To proceed therapeutically is thus 'to afford opportunity for formless experience' in which we experience ourselves as no longer 'either introvert nor extrovert' but

> in the area of transitional phenomena, in the exciting interweave of subjectivity and objective observation . . . in an area that is intermediate between the inner reality of the individual and the shared reality of the world that is external to individuals . . .
>
> (Winnicott 1985 [1971]: 75)

The analytic attitude might also be thought of as a means of staying open to the human context – not only to the in-between but also to the all-around, which would, of course, include the analyst too. Winnicott's concern with very early, pre-Oedipal states of undifferentiation, in which 'there is no such thing as a baby', before the baby begins to achieve a sense of his own boundaries and separateness from the mother or primary carer, led him to conceive of the analytic attitude as something like what he called 'primary maternal preoccupation' (see White 2006: 21). This implies not only that the analyst become absorbed in his patient like a mother with a baby, attuned to the non-verbal expressions of the baby's states; it also suggests a kind of environment-mind, a form of dreamy protecting attentiveness within which the patient/ baby can pursue their own organic development with little impediment or impingement (the latter a key Winnicottian term). The analytic attitude, in this idiom, is the sustaining of a state of mind in the therapist in which mind is an open space available for the patient to move into, to come and inhabit and, crucially, shape as his own. This is a vision of profound responsiveness,

Freud's not troubling 'to keep anything in mind in particular' modulated into a kind of active passivity in which the analyst is not just another subjectivity but a kind of interactive ecology.

The French analyst André Green has developed aspects of Winnicott's thinking. He has put forward the notion of the *active matrix*, composed of the patient's free association, floating attention and listening, stamped with the analyst's benevolent neutrality, forming a *dialogical* couple in which the analysis is rooted' (Green 2005: 33). In his paper 'The Dead Mother' Green stressed the importance of the analyst maintaining an attitude of lively alertness to the patient who is beset by an internal deadness, in an invitation for the patient to come and occupy the mental space offered (Green 1996 [1980]: 163). In a similar vein, another French-speaking analyst, Danielle Quinidoz, has insisted on the necessity of using 'words that can touch': the analyst's words need to be 'capable of simultaneously evoking fantasies, thoughts, feelings and sensations if [patients] are to be able to unfold their psychic freedom and creativity to the full' (Quinidoz 2003, back cover).

Recently, Ken Israelstam has drawn on Winnicott to elaborate a concept of the 'dialectical edge', a pivotal point within the 'rich, ambiguous and unsettling tapestry of the core dialectical tensions . . . generated in the patient-analyst relating'. It is a 'fluid, emotionally evocative threshold, where there is maximum potential for change, as well as for homeostatic stagnation'. The outcome is critically dependent on the therapist's capacity to contain and hold the 'arousing and intense affects – such as anxiety, dread, excitement and passion – that are inevitably generated at these pivotal relational moments' (Israelstam 2007).

Analysts and therapists will, by definition, bring their own unique cultural and personal styles to analytic practice. This has led to moving personal evocations and accounts of the lived analytic relationship: Enid Balint (Balint 1993: 10–17), Nina Coltart (Coltart 1986: 185–99) and Neville Symington have provided particularly lively examples. The last two also drew special attention to what Symington called 'the analyst's act of freedom': the role of the analyst's personal spontaneity in precipitating change (Symington 1986b: 253–70).

A British post-Romantic sensitivity to the aliveness of nature and landscape, to pastoral and agricultural metaphor, to art and a certain spirituality or mysticism, has led to a style of practice that is characteristic of the Independent school. Masud Khan valued 'the sovereignty of intensity, immediacy and imagination' in the analytic space (Khan 1983: 24), a 'dream space' for the patient – and by implication the analyst – for '*lying fallow* . . . a mode of being that is alerted quietude and receptive wakeful lambent consciousness', that without which no real growth can take place (Khan 1983: 183, cited in White 2006: 29). Such a sensitivity gives, in the words of Jean White, 'space to the patient – space to be in an unorganised state without demands for analytic compliance, space to be private and silent, space to become and articulate themselves in their own unique idiom' (White 2006: 37). Within this English-speaking tradition, which stretches from Marion Milner to Thomas Ogden and Christopher Bollas, the aesthetic experience is privileged; this involves a respect for what therapy can share with art: its 'mysterious ability to evoke from within our own unknown depths surprises to us about ourselves and what (and whom) we have been unwittingly harbouring' (Grotstein 2002: 78, cited in White 2006: 27).

In her pre-analytic writings, under the pen name Joanna Field, Milner discovered for herself 'that there were two kinds of attention, both necessary, a wide unfocussed stare, and a narrow penetrating kind, and that the wide kind brought remarkable changes in perception and enrichment of feeling' (an echo of Pieper's *intellectus* versus *ratio*). She wrote of the analytic hour as a blank space, a 'framed gap', an emptiness: her experiences and meditations lead her close to Buddhism and Eastern mysticism, and to reflections on the nature of the divine. Fascinated by the effort to draw and paint, and the difficulty of 'losing oneself in an activity', she recalled quoting Cézanne to a patient, on the capacity to achieve unmindfulness (Milner 1987b: 81). The parallel between the analytic setting and the work of visual art, in its frame, was possibly first drawn by Milner (Milner 1987b: 80 ff.): both the analytic and the picture frame inherently invite us, as patients and spectators, to adopt a state of receptivity.

Adam Phillips, coiner of the phrase 'free listening' (Phillips 2002: 31), has suggested 'the comedian and the lover and the mystic' as models for an analytic state of mind, which might make space for humour, surprise and the erotic as well as the unknowable (Philips in Molino (ed.) 1997: 133, cited in White 2006: 37). It is a current that has touched post-Kleinians too, notably Bion's influential interpreter Donald Meltzer, author (with Meg Harris Williams) of *The Apprehension of Beauty* (1988). Meg Harris Williams and Margot Waddell's *The Chamber of Maiden Thought* (1991) is a monument to this British tradition, an exploration of the literary and Romantic roots of the psychoanalytic model of mind (in Shakespeare, Milton, Blake, Wordsworth, Coleridge, Keats and others; see also Glover 2000).

The idea that the analyst needs carefully to monitor his own shifting feelings and moods, as an intrinsic and vital part of the work, is current and widespread; far from being the impediment to a proper analysis, as Freud originally thought, these 'counter-transference' phenomena are, in this view, an invaluable contribution. Exploration of the 'counter-transference' was rigorously undertaken, from the 1950s onwards, by members of the British Kleinian school, latterly with particular reference to projective identification, from Paula Heimann's classic paper 'On Counter-Transference' of 1950 (Heimann 1950) through to the more recent contributions of Betty Joseph (Joseph 1985, 1987) and others (see Hinshelwood 1991: 255–62). The American Harold Searles was an early and courageous explorer of his own feeling states, writing, for example, in 1959: 'I have found, time after time, that in the course of work with every one of my patients . . . I have experienced romantic and erotic desires to marry . . . the patient' (Searles 1986: 284).

The Polish-born Argentinian analyst Heinrich Racker published an important exploration of the theme in his book *Transference and Counter-Transference* (Racker 1982 [1968]). He enlisted a Chinese story to illustrate the unconscious dimension of the 'free-floating attention' that is required. An old sage lost his pearls. He sent his eyes to search for them, but his eyes did not find them. Next he sent his ears, but they did not find them either. Then he sent his hands, but with no success. So he sent all his senses out to search for the pearls but they did not find them either. 'Finally he sent his *not-search* to look for his pearls. *And his not-search found them*' (Racker 1982 [1968]: 17). Racker explains that the analyst, 'upon identifying himself with the patient's thoughts, desires, and feelings, [surrenders] simultaneously to free association; [he] creates an internal situation in which he is disposed to admit all possible thoughts and feelings in his consciousness'. If he is well identified with the patient and has fewer repressions, 'the thoughts and feelings which emerge in him will be, precisely, those which did not emerge in the patient, i.e. the repressed and the unconscious'. However, 'there are times, as Freud warned, when the analyst's work is impeded by impulses and feelings that emerge in him towards the patient which are alien to his function of understanding and interpreting the patient's resistances and infantile complexes', and it is overcoming this kind of 'counter-transference', the analyst's own resistance, that 'is . . . decisive for the transference and its working-through, and . . . decisive for the whole treatment' (Racker 1982 [1968]: 17–18).[8]

Since the mid-1980s several generations of psychotherapy and psycho-dynamic counselling students in Britain have been informed by Patrick Casement's *On Learning from the Patient* and his subsequent publications. For Casement, the analyst's resistance and 'mistakes' may be not just things that need to be overcome but important contributions in themselves to an under-standing of the patient's unconscious communication within the dynamics of the therapist–patient relationship. Casement also usefully extrapolates from the Freud of *The Interpretation of Dreams* the idea that the unconscious has no respect for conventional, sequential grammar, subject–verb–object. One must listen for alternative or simultaneous grammatical possibilities, especially, but not only, when listening to dreams: all the hearer can be sure of is that some subject, not necessarily that of the manifest material, is acting (or has or will act) on some object, in some adverbial way. In the footsteps of Reik he points to the need for practitioners to cultivate an 'internal supervisor' as a guide. This requires both a conscious, imaginative effort to make trial identifications, to try to put oneself in the patient's shoes, and a readiness to learn from one's own spontaneous feelings in the session (Casement 1990 [1985]).

Such ideas have in turn fed into a growing recognition of the inter-subjective dimension of the analytic meeting. The idea of analysis as 'a dynamic play of subjectivities' is currently a widely shared one – by among others the American analyst Jessica Benjamin and the Frenchman André Green (White 2006: 26). Indeed, it has given birth to a new 'Relational' school. This relational perspective is a 'democratic co-created view of the therapeutic relationship in which the therapist's subjectivity is always present' (Orbach 2007: 9), in which the patient can enter into 'a study of his own subjectivity' (Orbach 2007: 15). Phillips, not a signed-up Relationist, has said something similar: 'We could think of psychoanalysis as an enquiry into the equality of listening; into the senses in which we can be equal to what we hear' (Phillips 2002: 31). This does not mean, for Relationalists or for Phillips, that patient and analyst quite become equals, for mutuality is not the same as symmetry; what counts is the sensibility informing the analyst's participation (Mitchell 1997). Relationalism's roots are partly in existentialism and phenomenology; one of its central concerns is for the listening, relating analyst, in the inter-subjective field, to avoid objectifying the other: 'There is a difference between listening as representing the other and listening as a wordless, pre-reflective, non-representational attunement out of which words emerge' (Frederickson 2009: 64). Thinking about inter-subjectivity has led to further theorisation, in terms, for example, of complexity theory, requiring of the analyst a 'complexity sensibility' (Coburn 2009: 190), or of a 'post-Cartesian', Heidegger-informed, psychoanalytic intersubjective-systems theory, a 'phenomenological contextualism' (Stolorow 2011).

These theoretical developments aside, in some senses the idea of inter-subjectivity seems nothing new. For Jungians, current 'Relational' ideas might seem to offer little more than a watered-down version of what Jung himself was passionately advocating from the 1920s onwards. 'I confront the patient as one human being to another. Analysis is a dialogue involving two partners', he wrote in *Memories, Dreams, Reflections* (Jung 1963: 131). Jung left little doubt as to where he stood. No one, he wrote, has the right to practise psychotherapy who has not 'himself undergone a thorough analysis, or can bring such a passion for truth to the work that he can analyse himself through his patient'. He will merely have 'the petty conceit of his authority' to cling to, and 'his whole work will be intellectual bluff'. For

> How can the patient learn to abandon his neurotic subterfuges when he sees the doctor playing hide-and-seek with his own personality, as though unable, for fear of being thought inferior, to drop the professional mask of authority, competence, superior knowledge, etc? The touchstone of every analysis that has not stopped short at partial success, or come to a standstill with no success at all, is always this person-to-person relationship, a psychological situation in which the patient confronts the doctor on equal terms, and with the same ruthless criticism that he must inevitably learn from the doctor in the course of his treatment ... the patient must have the right to the freest criticism, and a true sense of human

equality . . . in my view, analysis makes far higher demands on the mental and moral stature of the doctor than the mere application of a routine technique, and also that his therapeutic influence lies primarily in this more personal direction.

(Jung 1993 [1928]: 137–8)[9]

Within psychoanalysis, probably the most influential late twentieth-century spokesmen for the inter-subjective dimension of the analytic meeting and the importance of the analyst's sensibility is the American Thomas Ogden. Since the 1990s, Ogden, from within a broadly Reikian tradition, has brought considerable refinement to an understanding of analytic inter-subjectivity. He has written of 'the complexity of the dialectic of individuality and inter-subjectivity', and claims that

a principal task faced by the analyst is to recognize and make use of the largely unconscious feeling states generated intersubjectively in the analytic relationship. The importance of the analyst's close attentive-ness to the nuances and details of the events in the analytic hour is a well established facet of contemporary analytic thought . . . In addition . . . an indispensable avenue in the effort to get a sense of my uncon-scious experience in and of the analytic third [that which is generated unconsciously and intersubjectively] is the use of *reverie* (Bion 1962) . . . I include in the notion of reverie the most mundane, quotidian, unobtrusive thoughts, feelings, fantasies, daydreams bodily sensations, and so on that usually feel utterly disconnected from what the patient is doing or saying at the moment . . . Reverie, like the manifest content of dreams, is an aspect of conscious experience that is intimately connected with unconscious experience . . . Thus the analyst's use of his reverie experi-ence is in my view a central component of analytic technique.

(Ogden 2001a: 20–1)

At the same time, like an exercise in art appreciation practised upon the analyst's own internal world, a stance such as the one adopted by Ogden, when he recommends listening to the patient's dreams as to a poem (Ogden 2001a), might seem to involve the analyst in the risk of becoming so absorbed in his own sensibilities as to make the patient disappear. Robert Caper, a Kleinian from the American West Coast, notes that what is important is that the analyst has been able to think about the patient's projections, 'not how much (or little) trouble he has had to go to in doing so' (Caper 1999: 114).[10] He similarly criticises the intersubjective or Relational school for locating the experience of the analysis 'somewhere *between* the patient and analyst, in such a form that the respective contributions of each cannot be resolved . . . analysis, after all, means resolution into components' (Caper 1999: 67). Yet it would be a mistake to dismiss Ogden, in this most cursory of readings, as a mere willowy aesthete among analysts; he must also, as he wrote in a commentary on Winnicott, be able to face both the patient's and his own destructiveness, to live for example 'with the inevitable destructiveness of love' (Ogden 2001b: 305).

A Lacanian understanding would take a different form, in so far as Lacanians would see both analyst and patient as subject to a third term – language – which structures the unconscious. They too would object to an Ogdenian reliance on counter-transference, seeing it as a naive insistence on staying caught in the Imaginary, in a delusive specular relationship. Lacan's expression 'the analyst's desire'

> refers not to the analyst's counter-transferential feelings but rather to a kind of 'purified desire' that is specific to the analyst – to the analyst not as a human being with feelings but as a function, a role . . . it is a desire that focusses on analysis and only on analysis . . . [it] is not for the patient to get better, to succeed in life, to be happy, to understand him- or herself, to go back to school, to achieve what he or she says he or she wants, or to say something in particular . . . it is an enigmatic desire that does not tell the patient what the analyst wants him or her to say or do . . . it is an unflagging desire for the patient to come to therapy, to put his or her experience, thoughts, fantasies and dreams into words, and to associate to them . . . it is not the kind of desire that anyone who wants to can maintain without first going through a long period of analysis him- or herself. It is . . . what Lacan considers the motor force of analysis.
>
> (Fink 1997: 6–7)

For Lacan, the analytic attitude equates with the analyst's desire to carry on being an analyst, and the desire for the patient to attend sessions. Free-floating attention for Lacan meant, as it did for Bion, 'having ears *in order not to hear*, in other words to pick up what is to be heard'. Lacan described this as 'a second subjectivity' (Lacan 2001 [1953]: 50, cited in White 2006: 169). Lacan, wrote Bruce Fink, an American Lacanian,

> reminds his students over and over to stop trying to understand everything, because understanding is ultimately a form of defence, of bringing everything back to what is already known. The more you try to understand, the less you hear – the less you can hear something new and different.
>
> (Fink 1996: 149)

For in the end the analyst's desire 'is a desire to obtain absolute difference' (Lacan 1998: 276); the patient's desire can only be reached by the most meticulous attention on the analyst's part to language itself:

> the term 'free-floating' does not imply fluctuation, but rather evenness of level . . . what need can an analyst have for an extra [Reikian 'third'] ear,

when it sometimes seems that two are already too many, since he runs headlong into the fundamental misunderstanding brought on by the relationship of understanding? I repeatedly tell my students: 'Don't try to understand!' and leave this nauseating category to Karl Jaspers and his consorts. May one of your ears become as deaf as the other one must be acute. And that is the one you should lend to listen for sounds and phonemes, words, locutions, and sentences, not forgetting pauses, scansions, cuts, periods, and parallelisms, for it is in these that the word-for-word transcription can be prepared, without which analytic intuition has no basis or object.

(Lacan 2007: 394)

For

You must start from the text, start by treating it, as Freud does . . . as Holy Writ. The author, the scribe, is only a pen-pusher, and he comes second . . . Similarly, when it comes to our patients, please give more attention to the text than to the psychology of the author – the entire orientation of my teaching is that.

(Lacan 1988a: 153, cited in Evans 1996: 13–14)

He summed up in 1973, punning on his famously punning formulation *le nom(n) du père* (the name/no of the father), *les non-dupes errent* (non-dupes err): if you insist that you can't be fooled, that you always get it, you are in the wrong place (Lacan 1973). Reading Lacan's transcribed seminars, like reading Bion, can itself be a generative and often humorous encounter with the unconscious (White 2006: 44), a way of fostering an analytic attitude in oneself. Similarly, the writings of Julia Kristeva, who was profoundly influenced by Lacan, can evoke the kinds of experience she describes. Her concept of the *chora* is of particular relevance to this discussion. Borrowed from Plato, the *chora* designates the 'pre-imaginary, undifferentiated space of the mother-baby dyad' (White 2006: 60), and implies a need for the analyst to be alert to the non- and pre-verbal, the manifestations of what Kristeva termed the semiotic, a sort of pre-Oedipal compost of 'sound and melody, rhythm, colours, odours' out of which speech and the Symbolic will emerge (Kristeva 1995 [1993]: 104). Kristeva's thinking invites a sensitivity to tones and nuances of voice, movements of the body, to which Winnicottians might be especially receptive.

Ways of thinking about the role and importance of analytic listening continue to be developed in depth. The British Middle Group analyst Michael Parsons has argued for a 'genuinely free-floating' inward listening that would be distinct from the 'self-monitoring inward listening for something' as conceived in theories of counter-transference, in which the analyst monitors her responses to determine whether they are a hindrance – analyst resistance

– or the results of a communication from the patient. Such listening according to Parsons could hardly said to be free; analysts 'in this case would be treating themselves in just the way that they try not to treat the patient'. Instead, the analyst might listen 'to whatever there is to be heard' (Parsons 2007: 1442). There should be no limits to what might be heard from the inside, from what William Blake called the 'unfathomed caverns' of the ear (Blake 1988: 145).

The analyst needs to become an 'analytic listener to herself' (Parsons 2007: 1442) in the sense that s/he needs to develop a certain kind of mental space, an 'internal analytic setting' complementary to, and in some respects more important than, the external setting (room, chair, couch, timing, payment, etc.). This is a space within which the analyst can allow sessions to be there 'for patients to discover how to use them'; it allows the fullest possibility for apparent boundary breaches in the external setting to become contributions to a shared analytic understanding. The analyst's 'freedom of self-experience' is more than his ability to free associate; it is also 'freedom from considerations that operate elsewhere in the analyst's mind' (Parsons 2007: 1444–5). This, Parsons implies, is more than a matter of 'identification' or empathy, but something perhaps closer to what the Romantics called 'imagination': the heterosexual analyst's availability, for example, for experiencing homoerotic feelings. Parsons supports his argument by quoting from Seamus Heaney: Heaney, the reader of Eliot's *The Waste Land*, who found he had to give up the erudite search for meaning and instead to *listen* to the poem, to allow it to reverberate inside him so that he might experience its sounds and its life echoing in his own body (Heaney 2002: 34–5, cited in Parsons 2007: 1446). Such listening distinguishes between abstracting meaning and hearing it. This is a vital distinction for the analyst. Parsons cites Heaney's poem *The Rain Stick*: 'a poem about listening which embodies, and makes happen, its own multiplicity of listenings'. What is required, in poet and analyst, is a mastery of technique, something which, for Heaney, is not only about craft and skill; it is also a plumbing of the depths of oneself.[11] The poet's (analyst's) technique thus involves

> a definition of his stance towards life, a definition of his own reality. It involves a discovery of ways to go out of his normal cognitive bounds and raid the inarticulate: a dynamic alertness that mediates between the origins of feeling in memory and experience and the formal ploys that express these in a work of art.
>
> (Heaney 2002: 19, cited in Parsons 2007: 1447–8)

This rephrasing or reframing of the analyst's impossible position, as Leclaire defined it, does nothing to gloss over the difficulties; what it does offer is purchase on the distinction between deciphering and hearing, between a mere 'series of intersecting monologues' and a genuine 'analytic conversation'. Such a conversation can 'evoke capacities, and functions, in an analyst's psyche, of which he was not previously aware', as long as he is open to the potential for this to happen. Such personal work takes place in an area 'beyond counter-transference'. In making the point that this does not mean the analyst is parasitising the analysis for his own self-analytic purposes, Parsons finds himself emphasising, almost as an aside, something that writers on the analytic attitude, concerned with general principles, often overlook: that analytic listening, the analyst's internal setting, is the setting 'for a particular analysis' undertaken by two particular people (Parsons 2007: 1452–4). It is personal, unique and unrepeatable, for both participants.

A related perspective has been offered by the British psychoanalyst Christopher Bollas in his views on analytic attentiveness. Bollas's argument, developed over the last dozen or so years in a sequence of books (Bollas 1999, 2002, 2007, 2009), can be broadly outlined.

There is a 'Freudian pair' (Bollas 2009: 19 ff.). The analysand's role is to free associate. This, Freud's 'fundamental rule', is not, as many analysands fear, a requirement to disclose deep dark secrets. It is, rather, to report in as much detail and with as much texture as possible whatever happens to be on his or her mind. Freud asked for a 'narrative of the ordinary . . . to hear from the *everyday*' (Bollas 2007: 11). The analyst's part is to maintain evenly hovering attention, in order, in Freud's words, to 'catch the drift' of the patient's unconscious (e.g. Bollas 2007: 36–7, 72). Every analyst, Bollas has said, should have this phrase pinned to his wall and should read it every day (Bollas 2007: 13). In Bollas's view, this aspect of psychoanalysis has been tragically overlooked, partly because Freud himself developed it very little, giving far greater theoretical attention to repression, as enshrined in his topographical model of mind. Yet Freud himself stated, albeit almost in passing, at the beginning of his 1915 essay 'The Unconscious', that 'Everything that is repressed must remain unconscious; but let us state at the very outset that the repressed does not cover everything that is unconscious' (Freud 1915: 166).

Indeed, the existence of a non-repressed, non-dynamic unconscious is implicit in much of the *Interpretation of Dreams*: this is the receptive or descriptive unconscious. Freud's theory of dream work implicitly recognises, Bollas argues, that the dynamic, censorship-determined unconscious must operate through 'categories of reception and representation' which have not been brought into being by censorship and repression. This too must be the receptive unconscious through which unconscious-to-unconscious communication is possible, that allowed by the analyst's 'stoical' (Bollas 2009: 9), evenly hovering stance (Bollas 2007: 36–7).

If Bollas sees this neglect as tragic, it is because generations of analysands have been let down by psychoanalysis, their unconscious communications unheard or closed down, as a result of selective listening on the parts of their analysts: 'the analyst *intervenes* and incarcerates the analysand's unconscious thinking' (Bollas 2007: 19, 54), because he is on the look-out for a certain kind of material. The analyst would be waiting for a rare evasion of censorship, a slip of the tongue or a dream, which might disclose the presence of the castration complex, the drive derivative, or the ego position. In particular, Bollas has deplored the overuse, the tyranny even, of the 'here and now transference interpretation', which, he argues, can work intrusively to collapse the analysand's (unconscious) 'wish to be unconsciously communicative'. It might also be the analyst's 'resistance to free association' (Bollas 2007: 6–7, 85–100).

Such analysis has 'lost sight of how the *analysand* works within psychoanalysis' (my italics; Bollas 2007: 54–5). It has lost sight of what the analysand already brings, and what, as can be seen in other spheres such as poetry, drama and music, we do as human beings anyway – that is, derive pleasure from creating and discerning sequences and patterns. The over-riding aim of psychoanalysis is to 'introduce the patient to his own unconscious mind' (Bollas 2007: 21); by immersing herself in the patient's world the analyst 'catches the drift' of his unconscious as it emerges sequentially, probably over a lengthy period, from the patient's narrative. Such indeed was what Freud called the 'classical method': to 'follow the chronological order in which [the patient's utterances] appeared' (Freud, S. 1923: 11; Bollas 2007: 8). Crucial to this process is a recognition, following Freud, of the patient's fundamental, if unconscious, and often unconsciously resisted, wish to communicate, co-operate, and grow. For, as Freud wrote in 1915, 'the *Ucs.* [the Unconscious] is alive and capable of development, and maintains a number of other relations with the *Pcs.* [the Preconscious], amongst them that of co-operation' (Freud, S. 1915: 190; Bollas 2007: 7). It is indeed a receptive unconscious. Under the force of the epistemophilic drive, the drive to know and understand (that which the analyst must put into temporary suspension), the analysand unconsciously works on multiple issues, on old and new questions; the analyst's role is to co-operate in the process, 'to become a working partner in the way we all think'. What maintains the impetus, the investment in working on psychic issue, is *pleasure*: we are driven to resolve the unpleasure of mental pain through understanding and thought, and 'thinking is ultimately in the service of the pleasure principle'. The analyst's role is thus 'dependent on what the patient creates. . . . By reflecting on their lines of thought we indicate to the analysand how rich a source of thinking he or she really is' (Bollas 2007: 556).

Perhaps Bollas, along with Bion when he wrote of the increased range of the patient's moods, had Coleridge in the back of his mind: 'Are not vivid Ideas themselves a sort of pleasure, as Music whether sad or lively, is always Music?' (Coleridge, 1804, in Holmes 1998: 1).

Bollas (2007) has proposed a symphonic model as a metaphor for grasping the sheer complexity of ways within which, in an analytic session, unconscious communication can take place. This enables him to picture, to a high degree of sensitivity and detail, both the sequential nature of the communication(s), and the great range of its possible vertical components: the multiple means, from pitch, volume, timbre, colouration and so on of voice, to bodily sounds ('biomusic' – Bollas 2007: 45), gestures and postures, to silences, and including transference–counter-transference manifestations, through all of which and more the patient pursues her wish for unconscious-to-unconscious understanding. The symphonic metaphor also enables Bollas to illustrate the way in which the strands of the analysand's unconscious thinking periodically come together in 'nodal points' and in so doing open up new lines of unconscious questioning (Bollas 2007: 44). Bollas, for all his powerful insistence on returning psychoanalysis to its proper roots in the Freudian pair, in free association and free listening, sees himself as a pluralist; the choice, he has said, is not to be or not be a pluralist, but 'whether one is a pluralist or a totalitarian' (Bollas 2007: 7). On the grounds that all theory is a form of perception and on the basis of an appreciation of 'the value of psychoanalytic theories as forms of perception' (Bollas 2007: 77), he would advocate that analysts familiarise themselves with as much psychoanalytic theory as possible, to suit their individual, unconscious predelictions – provided they are then able to forget all about it in the session.

In the process of pursuing this fertile line of thinking Bollas has inevitably evoked the analytic situation in his own personal idiom, as indeed every theorist must, however great their commitment to impartiality or objectivity. For

> Psychoanalysts have not adequately written about the profound but deeply generative aloneness of the psychoanalyst, his patient . . . and the psychoanalysis. I know that I cannot describe the place where I work, even though the terms 'evenly suspended attentiveness' or 'reverie' or 'the analytic attitude' are fortunately there as signifiers I can use, but do they really designate life in this place? . . . Psychoanalysis takes place between two people yet it feels as if it lives within the deepest recesses of my private life.
>
> (Bollas 1999: 11)

Coleridge would have had no difficulty understanding this.

Analytic attention is at the service of unconscious process, a process essential for creativity and growth. Romanticism, as a constant state of crisis, intuited psychoanalysis. If in important respects Romantic openness adumbrates analytic listening, and neither can be reduced nor confined to simple definition, it was an openness to a powerful sense of there being enigmas, 'fringe phenomena, obstacles, shadows', the whole phenomenology of the unconscious, to which psychoanalysis was later to give a degree of substance and definition. The tension between the analyst as phenomenologist, and the analyst as theorist, will be revisited from different perspectives in the chapters that follow: what permanently restless movement between openness and supposed knowledge does the work of art instigate in the viewer/reader/listener? How much, following Bollas, might we be helped to hold to our theories as mere 'forms of perception'? How much does the work of art, like the enigmatic message of the Laplanchian primary carer, expand the viewer's unconscious and activate a drive to translate and participate – like the analyst who becomes, in the patient's unconscious, 'the *cause* of the movement animating his speech' (Green 2005: 44)?[12] How much might echoes in the psyche/soma of the viewer/reader/listener/analyst/patient persist long after the encounter?

Chapter 3

Goya and the dream of Enlightenment

'This is the season of evil thoughts and words and actions', wrote the Spanish painter Francisco Goya y Lucientes in a letter to his greatest friend, around Hallowe'en 1787.

> I must confess that I was frightened and confused at first, but now? Well now, now I have no fear of Witches, goblins, ghosts, thugs, Giants, ghouls, scallywags etc., nor any sort of body except human . . .
>
> (Symmons 2004: 194)

Since the later nineteenth century Goya (1746–1828) has been regarded as one of the great masters of Western art, on a par with his seventeenth-century precursors Velázquez and Rembrandt with whom (and only whom) he wished to be compared. He is the first truly 'modern' painter, the first great artist of a post-religious age. His example was decisive for Manet and thus for the whole modern movement in art; his influence on Picasso, the Surrealists and many others in the twentieth century is huge. In this century the Chapman brothers, Jake and Dino, pay him a homage which is no less apt for being larded with irony and violence.

Goya can help the analyst stay alert to forms of aliveness, even unwelcome ones, in the deadest material – as to Bion's pinprick of light in a searchlight beam of darkness. In his work there is always a tension, never resolvable, between the two poles of light and dark, life and death, and he never allows the spectator to settle with one or the other, in a facile celebration of life nor a horrified turning away from death. He can help us be on our guard against doing either in the presence of our patients; he keeps us in touch with the tragic. Anyone coming to him for the first time is likely to be struck both by the astringency of his visual commentaries, and the sheer breadth and depth of his sympathies. He requires us to endure our anxiety, as he finds ever more inventive ways of confronting us with what lurks in the shadows: the repressed and denied, rage, perversity, malignant narcissism, the power of the collective and social unconscious. At the same time death drive, in Goya's work, is always linked to eros, and eros is inalienably present in the sheer animal physicality of his bodies, the raw drive inherent to life even in the direst circumstances. Reason and unreason in Goya are always mutually implicated. Their collision seems to generate the work. There is no madness, wrote Michel Foucault in an extraordinary passage at the end of his *Histoire de la folie*,

> except as the final instant of the work – the work endlessly drives madness to its limits; *where there is a work of art, there is no madness*; and yet madness is contemporary with the work of art, since it inaugurates the time of its truth.
>
> (Foucault 1971 [1961]: 288–9)

Goya's life story is worth rehearsing in a little detail. It embraces both robust sociality and deep solitude; it spans the period of Europe's greatest historical upheavals and it was significantly shaped by them. Goya came from an artisanal background in Aragon; his father had been a master-gilder. Over his very long career he was in contact with just about every facet of contemporary Spanish culture and society: Goya the painter of royalty was also a man of the people, steeped in popular custom and tradition. In the 1760s he found ecclesiastical and aristocratic patrons in Zaragoza and then Madrid; he was employed for five years in the 1770s making designs for the Royal Tapestry Factory, married shrewdly, was elected to the Royal Academy of Fine Art, and over the next decade worked at the court of the Bourbon king Charles IV, where he came into contact with the leading intellectuals of Spanish Enlightenment, *ilustrados*. For contemporaries he was both a 'philosopher painter' and an ambitious 'painting monkey' (Symmons 2004: back cover); in 1789, at the start of the French revolutionary decade, he was appointed Court Painter, and by the end of it he was First Court Painter. In 1792 he was struck down by illness, possibly meningitis, or lead poisoning, which was intermittent for three years, and left him, at the age of 47, permanently deaf. His illness and convalescence coincided with the September massacres in Paris, the execution of Louis XVI and the Terror.

On his recovery, he resumed his official career and at the same time produced a series of small uncommissioned paintings, including a madhouse scene. In 1799 he published *Los Caprichos*, the first of his series of satirical etchings, which teem with monsters, animals, strange hybrids and witches alongside priests, monks, prostitutes and smartly attired young men and women. He painted the entire royal family with, to modern eyes, startling frankness, and received important commissions from the queen's lover Manuel de Godoy, for whom he made the famous naked and clothed *majas*. He himself was probably the lover of the young Duchess of Alba. The major political events of his lifetime, the Napoleonic occupation of Spain in 1808 and the War of Liberation (the 'Peninsular War') which followed, once more brought to the fore his identification with ordinary people and their sufferings, as can be felt in the two paintings of 1814 commemorating popular uprising and French recrimination ('The Second of May 1808' and 'The Third of May 1808'), and in the posthumously published etchings *The Disasters of War*. The Spanish patriot Goya would undoubtedly have shared the sense of fiercely split loyalties of some of his enlightened, French-leaning (*afrancesado*) friends.[1] For the rest of his life Goya occupied an in-between position. Public and private Goya co-existed 'in a species of schizophrenia' (Williams 1976: 102), and this reflected explosive tensions within Spanish society itself. The Goya who had a living to make painted Napoleonic officials during the occupation, then, in 1812, a joyful allegory of the brand-new Spanish constitution (at the time the most liberal in the world), and, in 1814, the victorious Duke of Wellington (they did not hit it off).

The restoration of the Catholic, Bourbon king Fernando VII heralded a period of political reaction and repression: Fernando was driven by a wish to eradicate all traces of the liberal – the word was first used in a political sense in Spain, during the War of Independence – politics of the *ilustrados*. He revoked the 1812 Constitution (Williams 1976: 110; Carr 1982: 118–19), in the words of his decree, 'as if it had never been'; it was 'to be erased from the annals of time'. Goya, vulnerable on more than one count, underwent a process of 'purification', and was also called before the newly re-empowered Inquisition to account for the 'Naked Maja'. His continuing livelihood depended on his relations with the regime. Increasingly solitary and in straitened circumstances, his isolation exacerbated by age and deafness, he worked on *The Disasters of War*, the *Tauromaquia*, etchings of bull-fighting scenes, and another series, *Los Disparates* (mad or absurd ideas). He produced further small, probably uncommissioned, imaginative 'cabinet' paintings, including a second scene in a madhouse. In 1819 he bought a house on the outskirts of Madrid, known as the Quinta del Sordo ('the house of the deaf man'), the walls of which he decorated with the frescoes which were later christened 'The Black Paintings': depictions of cannibalism, witchcraft and blindly driven crowds. They have an enigmatic, haunting, terrifying quality unmatched in Western art.

He survived another major illness, and commemorated this in a tender, moving self-portrait of 1820 with his physician. In 1824, following renewed political repression (supported this time by a French monarchist invasion, 'The Hundred Thousand Sons of St Louis'), the 78-year-old painter was given medical leave to take the waters in France. He settled in Bordeaux, where liberal friends had already found refuge, and visited Paris; he left just too soon to see Constable's *Haywain* and Delacroix's *Massacre at Chios* at the Salon. He experimented with the new medium of lithography, made startling miniatures on ivory, and produced drawings, dream images and street scenes of the urban poor, beggars and entertainers, which register with undimmed vividness a response to human suffering and resourcefulness (see Brown and Galassi 2006). He died in Bordeaux, aged 82, in 1828.

This chapter focuses in some depth on three images: one very familiar, the etching of 1797–99 entitled *El sueño de la razón produce monstruos* (*The Sleep of Reason Produces Monsters*), showing a seated, male figure, his head and arms resting on a table, surrounded by nocturnal creatures; another etching, no. 79 from the same series, *Los Caprichos;* and the second small oil painting of a madhouse, probably made in 1816. Two of these images have had an extraordinary afterlife, as key elements in a modern repertoire of ways in which Western culture has pictured to itself questions of the relationship between reason and imagination, sanity and madness. The 1816 *Madhouse* features on the cover of Roy Porter's *Madness: A Brief History* (2003). The repining figure with his attendant monsters has appeared on countless book jackets; it is *the* image of the crisis of Enlightenment. Other pictures too claim attention in this context: Goya's late self-portrait as a sick man with his doctor; and, although they are not in central focus here, the Black Paintings, the *Pinturas Negras*. Yet, once glimpsed, these terrible images can hardly be kept out of mind. Their unspoken presence, like the Lacanian 'Real', haunts the following pages. In a sense, what is there to be said about them? They address a Nietzschian, Dionysian substratum or core (Fafalk 2002, 2008); they show a madness of 'glances shot from nowhere and staring at nothing' which for Foucault 'eats away faces, corrodes features'. Madness in the Black Paintings 'has become man's possibility of abolishing both man and the world' (Foucault 1971 [1961]: 281).

Goya can get under the skin like no other.[2] Here is how the French poet and philosopher Yves Bonnefoy has characterised his capacity for registering disturbance and the uncanny. He is writing about the Tapestry Cartoon known as *The Mannikin*, which shows four young women, in an idyllic landscape, holding an outstretched blanket from which they are tossing a fashionably dressed life-sized dummy into the air (see Figure 3.1).

   Bonnefoy finds

> an absolute absence of meaning, except to bring to mind everything the human project instinctively rejects if it perceives it . . . that rigid piece of wood [the mannikin], shown in the full light of day, is a darkness lurking right inside the light which spills over colours and forms . . . What is this game into which the girls are throwing themselves? What is that desire which rises in them . . .? . . . One might wonder, as a first thought, if this apparent game is not a simulacrum of torture, if it does not seek out the pleasure of imagining inflicting torture. But even torture is still an aspect of the order of the world, it can be spoken about, desired or condemned. What Goya succeeds in making visible resides lower down in what exists, beyond the grasp of words . . . Yet that grasp is the only entity to which men and women can appeal, following rumours of the death of God which are abroad as the young painter works . . . he freezes one with fear.
>
> (Bonnefoy 2006: 29–31)[3]

Figure 3.1 Francisco José de Goya y Lucientes, *The Mannikin*, oil on canvas, 1791–92.

In the 1790s Goya established friendships with influential *ilustrados*, such as the poet and dramatist Leandro Fernández de Moratín, and the philosopher, writer and statesman Gaspar Melchor de Jovellanos, reformers who looked towards France and Britain as sources of hope for a backward, economically and educationally benighted Spain. While as sons of a profoundly Catholic country the *ilustrados* did not always share the atheism of the French philosophes, Goya's enlightened friends in Madrid were nevertheless informed by the sceptism and the radical materialism of the eighteenth century, with its implication, as Bonnefoy puts it, that there is nothing to be understood beyond the immutable laws of matter. The idea that the universe could be accounted for in terms of Christian faith was no longer one in which educated Europeans could feel confident; perhaps there was no guaranteed existence outside or greater than the finite, beyond the material body into which one happened to be born, with all its appetites and drives (Bonnefoy 2006: 18).

The Western, Renaissance tradition of painting, Bonnefoy argues, had been founded in this confidence; painting visibly manifested what he calls *le grand rêve*, the great dream, in which a colourful, sensory world, bathed in unifying light, was of a continuous piece with the will of the divine. Its breakdown in the eighteenth century, manifest in painting (consider the airy lack of solemnity of Tiepelo's depictions of God and angels, for example) as much as in philosophy, might also be considered an awakening. One might argue that Goya, attracted to the ideas and representatives of Enlightenment, had already awakened from this dream; Bonnefoy elaborates on this idea in a discussion of one aspect of the painter's craft, and a crucial one for Goya, drawing.

He contrasts two kinds of drawing. There is drawing that engages with the purely sensory aspects of reality and the impressions the artist receives from them, delighting in their life and the pleasures they promise. Such was the drawing that has underpinned 'the great dream' since it emerged in fifteenth-century Flanders and Italy. But there is another kind of drawing, less concerned with the sensory substance of what is than with 'the purely mental, the fugitive, the unspeakable, even'. This proceeds with rapid strokes, 'brief inflexions, the slightest tremble in the tracing of a contour'; it has eyes only for

> emotions and thoughts which belong, essentially, to the invisible but which none the less make themselves known in gestures and on faces, skilled of course as the observer's subsconscious is in discerning, even in a stranger, poorly disguised impatience, fleeting pleasure or fear, or a rush of pique or anger.
>
> (Bonnefoy 2006: 27)

This other kind of drawing, says Bonnefoy, has been viewed with suspicion or fear since the dawn of Western civilization and certainly since the triumph of Christianity, for 'it brings the hidden into view and thus at every instant threatens to reveal that there is more in human beings than that which religious or political norms allow' (Bonnefoy 2006: 27–8). Such was the drawing at play in *The Mannikin* and other Tapestry Cartoons; it is also, and this is of particular relevance for Goya in the 1790s, the suggestive, subversive drawing of the caricaturist.

Goya's illness of the early 1790s caused him to have frightening hallucinations. On his recovery, he started to make a kind of painting virtually without precedent in the history of art (Glendinning 1977: 25). Recent and contemporary political traumata in France could not have worked better to undermine and demolish 'the great dream'; Goya meanwhile was discovering that a capacity for unsettling the foundations of that dream was inherent in painting itself, in so far as painting in oils was the best suited of all the arts to constructing a persuasive idea of a substantial and coherent universe (Bonnefoy 2006: 48–9). Goya now produced small, uncommissioned works on subjects he had seen or invented, one of which was the first of his two paintings of madhouses, the *Corral de locos* (see Figure 3.2).

Figure 3.2 Francisco José de Goya y Lucientes, *Yard with Madmen* (*Corral de locos*), 1794. Oil on tin-plated iron. Algur H. Meadows Collection. Meadows Museum, Southern Methodist University, Dallas, Texas. MM.67.01.

Goya claimed in a letter that he had witnessed at first-hand this scene of fighting, naked figures, and their guardian with his whip, in the madhouse at Zaragoza (Symmons 2004: 238). His 'I saw this' might be read as a statement of how much, faced with events that were turning the last years of the century upside-down, Goya was committed to seeing things as they were, as faithfully as possible (Bonnefoy 2006: 51): that is, not only as he might have seen or recorded them optically, but as he experienced, imaginatively apprehended or 'dreamed' them. The etchings of *Los Caprichos* were a continuation of this project; Goya's work of the 1790s began radically to blur distinctions between what might be seen with the eye, and what with the mind's eye; it simultaneously cast the substantiality of the ordinary, visible world into doubt.[4]

El sueño de la razón

In a beautiful portrait of 1798 (see Figure 3.3) Goya depicted his friend Jovellanos, *ilustrado*, *afrancesado*, reader of Rousseau, as an embodiment of late eighteenth-century sensibility. Jovellanos was also a poet; Goya painted his portrait while Jovellanos was Minister of Justice. In the painting, the Minister's pens and papers are on the desk on which he leans. The goddess Athene presides, in the shadows: Jovellanos is the epitome of wisdom and balance. He is *un homme bien pensant*; he and his French contemporary the reforming doctor of the insane Philippe Pinel would have recognised each other as kindred spirits. His elegantly folded legs are part of an eighteenth-century body language, a physical etiquette quietly expressive of sublimated appetites. He is the man of Reason, and the new man of feeling.[5] Yet he also seems open to profound and uneasy questioning, and in this respect too his portrait catches the mood of the times. Spain had experienced no anti-monarchical revolution in the 1790s; in many ways it continued to be 'a traditional society, where everything was apparently regulated from above by laws, decrees and custom'. In such a society, however, 'nothing was a greater destabilising factor than *political* uncertainty. To be "unsure of the future", "not to know what to expect", [itself] represented a rupture with the Old Order's "monolithic mental and operative system"' (Fraser 2008: 84, citing Juana and Castro 1991: 75–89).

Goya's series of etchings *Los Caprichos* (Madrid, 1799) was no doubt in part a product of his friendships with *ilustrados*, and of an ideological commitment to *las luces*. If confirmation of this is needed, one need only consider what the etchings are not: Goya makes no appeal to religious faith. Goya may have had help from an enlightened literary friend, the playwright Moratín, for example, in composing the text of the advertisement for the series. This appeared in the *Diario de Madrid* of 6 February 1799 and promised 'a series of prints of imaginative subjects [*asuntos caprichosos*], invented and etched by Don Francisco Goya'. On one level this text, albeit in unspecific terms, seems to establish an enlightened, satiric intent, and to suggest that the etchings will stigmatise superstitious, priest-ridden 'black' Spain. The artist,

Figure 3.3 Francisco José de Goya y Lucientes, *Portrait of Jovellanos*, oil on canvas, 1798.

it says, 'is convinced that the criticism of human error and vice (although usually thought to be the domain of rhetoric and poetry) can also be the aim of painting'. He has

> selected from among the multitude of follies and errors that are common in all civilized societies, and from the popular prejudices and deceitful practices authorised by custom, ignorance, and utility, those he believes to be most appropriate for submitting to ridicule, and which stimulate at the same time the imagination of the artist [*fantasía del artifice*].
>
> (cited in Schulz 2005: 99–102)

A closer reading, however, reveals this text to be 'a deeply anxious and conflicted document, one that constructs an ambiguous and problematic position for the viewer to occupy' (Schulz 2005: 99). It creates a disorienting oscillation in the reader, an uncertainty as to what to expect. On one hand it reads as a statement of rational, academic, neoclassical orthodoxy, and on the other as a justification for the creation of wild and fantastic hybrids. Its 'shifting topography', notes the art historian Andrew Schulz, 'would have puzzled even the most astute contemporary reader' (Schulz 2005: 101–5).

Complexity and indeterminacy surround *Capricho* 43, the famous *Sleep of Reason* (see Figure 3.4). In an earlier conception this was to have been the frontispiece to the series, which was itself to have been called *Sueños*, dreams. Different contemporary manuscript commentaries exist on different sets of the *Caprichos*, none of which is likely to have been composed by Goya himself (Schulz 2005: 118). The caption to a preparatory drawing, this time in Goya's own hand, reads: 'The artist dreaming [*El Autor sonando*]. His only purpose is to banish harmful, vulgar beliefs, and to perpetuate in this work of caprices the solid testimony of truth.' This would support a reading of the print as an enlightened document, at least if we can ignore a lingering sense of irony, a feeling that the artist may be protesting too much ('his only purpose . . .' – what other purpose could he have had?) For the print, like most in the series, is neither self-explanatory nor self-contained. In the *Diario de Madrid* announcement Goya had explicitly drawn attention to the visual nature of his undertaking; the prints exist in a visual context. It is hard to ignore, once it is registered, the echo of Jovellanos's pose, the similarly folded legs, in the closely contemporary portrait. The concordance of enlightened mind and body is broken, parodied; sensibility has become breakdown.

The frontispiece for the series as published is an apparently conventional self-portrait, in which Goya shows himself in not-quite full profile; he is wearing French-style clothes and a top hat, which again seem to set him up as an enlightened liberal (see Figure 3.5). Yet this is also an image of unsettling self-objectification. The art historians Victor Stoichita and Anna Maria Coderch, who wrote a remarkable study of Goya, note that no one can see their own profile and draw it without some intermediate system of

Figure 3.4 Francisco José de Goya y Lucientes, *El Sueño de la razón produce monstruos*, plate 43, *Los Caprichos*, etching and aquatint, 1799. Image © Biblioteca Nacional, Madrid (Spain).

Figure 3.5 Francisco José de Goya y Lucientes, *Self-Portrait*, plate 1, *Los Caprichos*, etching and aquatint, 1799. Image © Biblioteca Nacional, Madrid (Spain).

objectification. Goya presents himself in the third person, as a 'he', where a full-face portrait invites an 'I–thou' relationship; to contemplate a profile is always to contemplate an 'other'. At the same time he, and we, are implicated. By twisting his head slightly towards the spectator, he shows his awareness of this, our common condition: he is both object and subject, allowing himself to be observed, and observing (Stoichita and Coderch 1999: 175–8). It might be thought about, in Merleau-Ponty's terms (Chapter 2), as a portrait in which an 'I who perceives has no particular privilege which rules out an I who is perceived' (Merleau-Ponty 1979 [1945]: 404). Numbered 1 in the series, it can be taken as the first caprice; for Goya's 'left eye, half covered by the heavy eye-lid, and the oblique gaze with which he looks at the world are probably the key to the whole series' (Stoichita and Coderch 1999: 178).

The *Caprichos* were undoubtedly as mysterious and enigmatic for contemporaries as the text announcing them; it does not seem to be the case, as has sometimes been claimed, that they were once transparent, and that the keys to their elucidation have simply been lost. One author, writing in 1811, suggested they were like riddles for the viewer to puzzle out, 'fitting for exercising the skill of the young and . . . testing the power of penetration and liveliness of understanding of every kind of person'. They contain 'subtle notions' which everyone approaches 'in his own way and according to his own field of knowledge' (cited in Schulz 2005: 114). The anonymous manuscript commentaries attest to the divergent readings the images elicited; they also point to the inherent difficulty of translating the images into textual form (Schulz 2005: 118).

The visual nature of what we are experiencing is further underlined by the strong possibility that in *El sueño de la razón* it is the sleeping artist himself we see; his table is his work table. Yet what is subject and what is object; what 'grammatical' sense do we make of what we see? That in his sleep the figure actively creates in his mind and dreams the creatures which crowd in on him? Or that it is the creatures who are the moving agents, the subjects, who smother the mannikin-like artist-object and send him to sleep, or move him to create? In the published print, an owl seems to be proffering him his etching tool. In another preparatory drawing, in which the work table is explicitly an etching press, Goya showed his own head floating above the dreaming artist. He floats outside himself. He can stand outside himself and reflect upon what he is experiencing, as the analyst must – at the risk, however, as Goya seems to remind us, of disassociation or disembodiment. With which of them, the disembodied head in the preparatory drawing, or the sleeping figure, is the viewer to identify, in order to 'see' the image?

The figure is certainly in the vortex of a crisis. There is also a sense, of course, to which post-Romantic and post-Freudian viewers might be particularly receptive, that Goya was dealing both with a contemporary Spanish social and political malaise, and with the great eruptions of his own interior of a few years previously: 'the visions of his fever removed the barrier which the dark tribes of the blood are usually forbidden to cross' (Bonnefoy 2006: 43). We need to be able to imagine (art historians have seemed reluctant to do this) his utter isolation during the long months of his illness, suddenly deaf, dizzy, sick, disoriented, unable to stand without falling, hearing terrible noises in his head and hallucinating, in his dreams and in waking trances, all kinds of human and animal figments and hybrids, together with fragments of speech, snippets of remembered or overheard conversations, proverbs and popular sayings, bits of stories.[6] It was as if the cracks in *le grand rêve*, which had allowed the uncanny to enter the Tapestry Cartoons, had opened up into great fissures, and the visible and the instinctual combined to reveal the larger extent of their domain. Merely to look, writes Bonnefoy, 'when you are deaf, is to risk being unable to say no to the epiphany of non-sense'; to be hallucinating too is to expose oneself to 'radical doubt about the foundations of the world's usages and customs' (Bonnefoy 2006: 40).

Goya's hallucinations had also been the hallucinations of a painter. Convalescing from his illness, still half-way between waking and dreaming, half in and half out of his body, he had stayed in the house of his friend Sebastien Martinez in Cadiz, in whose collection he would have seen English satirical prints, caricatures by Hogarth and Gillray, alongside works by Blake, Fuseli and Piranesi (Bonnefoy 2006: 42). Goya was a man already acutely attuned to the visible, and at the heart of things, professionally alert to all the visible signs of 'the world's usages and customs'. He was able to transmute them into two-dimensional images, into another form of waking, conscious dreaming, the metal point in his hand moving freely across a giving wax surface, while words echoed in his mind.[7]

The work/the figure might lend itself too to being thought about as a life-saving, Lacanian *sinthome*. The *sinthome* is 'the particular modality of the subject's *jouissance* . . . [it] is what "allows one to live" by providing a unique organization of *jouissance*'. The *sinthome* intervenes to bind together the three Lacanian registers of Real, Symbolic and Imaginary; it works to knot together that which cannot be knotted (Evans 1996: 188–90). Goya in the late 1790s was caught between multiple contradictions, producing lines of extreme tension and potential fracture, personal as well as societal: his own class background and enthusiasms and relation to 'black' Spain; his position as courtier within a regime which was itself uncertain as to its status, absolute or enlightened; his attraction to *las luces* and French ideas; his likely love affair with an aristocrat (see Williams 1976). Lacan used the example of James Joyce to develop the idea of the *sinthome*: Joyce managed 'to avoid psychosis by deploying his art as *suppléance*, as a supplementary cord in the subjective knot . . . a new way of using language to organize enjoyment'. The *Caprichos* may be Goya's Joycean epiphanies, 'experiences of an almost hallucinatory intensity which were then recorded in enigmatic, fragmentary texts'. For the *sinthome*/*capricho* is ultimately 'immune to the efficacy of the symbolic . . . unanalysable . . . inevitably beyond meaning' (Evans 1996: 188–90). This account catches something of the mystery of *Los Caprichos* and their enduring hold, their surplus, unanalysable residue – all that they have in common with the later Black Paintings and the Freudian dream.

Perhaps, from a more existential perspective, as Bonnefoy has suggested, the satirist was indeed made ill by the conditions he addressed, rather as Jung wrote of the therapist becoming ill, indeed *needing* to become ill, with the patient (Jung 1993: 171–2). The art historian Janis Tomlinson has made use of Mikhail Bakhtin, particularly Bakhtin's account of Dostoyevsky's 'polyphonic' novels, to supplement such a reading. For Tomlinson, the image shows

> the dozing artist . . . who relinquishes control of the world he creates. The author's voice – in *Los Caprichos* as in Goya's oeuvre as a whole – is subsumed by a multitude of other voices: the traditions of art addressed, the personalities of the subjects portrayed, the projected desires of the patrons or intended public.
>
> (Tomlinson 1992: 7–8)

In this reading, the image is emblematic of Goya's work as a whole. It gathered contemporary voices; it needs to be considered as the product of a rich and complex matrix, which included the artist himself and a polyphony of desires, anxieties, intentions. It is an invitation to dialogue or multilogue.

Materially, the finished etching is a negative in itself, a reversal: in the etching process the plate is a negative of the print, dark for light, light for dark. The paper receives the impression of the plate: etching itself might be said to picture a radically receptive state of mind. *El sueño de la razón* engages the spectator in a conjunction of powerful visual experience and text(s); finally, the two are irreconcilable. Visually, it is this light–dark opposition that first impacts. The opposition of light to dark was, as Jean Starobinski has underlined, *the* visual metaphor of Enlightenment; it is explicitly drawn upon in a study for the etching (see Figure 3.6). In this metaphor the light of reason and good sense is meant to banish darkness, vice and superstition, as, perhaps, in the triumphant finale of Mozart's *Magic Flute*, of 1791: 'the rays of the sun drive out the night' (Starobinski 1979: 29). Goya's light, however, does not seem to want to behave like this (Mozart's and his librettist Schikaneder's light is not so unequivocal either). In the light–dark metaphor, in Goya and late Enlightenment, the one needs the other. Light and dark are in a dialectical relationship. A similar dialectic is evident in the accompanying, anonymous text in the so-called 'Prado' manuscript: 'Fantasy abandoned by reason [when it sleeps] produces impossible monsters: united with her she is the mother of the arts and source of all their marvels.' Reason alone is impoverished; she needs supplementing with fantasy. But reason and fantasy are *not* united in the image. The collapsed figure is situated in a gulf between them. There are further textual ambiguities: *sueño* is sleep, or sleepiness, drowsiness; or dream.

Figure 3.6 Francisco José de Goya y Lucientes, *Sueño 1*, preparatory drawing, pen and sepia ink over chalk, 1797–98.

Is it that this is what happens when Reason falls asleep? Or is it that Reason itself is a sort of dream? A dream that produces monsters, like the revolution of the intellectuals, which devours both its progenitors and its children? Approached in this way the apparently enlightened message, like the plate that generated the etching, reads as its opposite, its negative.

Monsters result whichever reading is in play. The light of Reason, far from driving out the dark and archaic, reveals not 'marvels' but lively 'monsters', which are only half-tamed; they may be creatures of the night, bats, owls, cats, but they are also relatively familiar and close to home. The vivid elements of fantasy, the figments that live in the darkness but can nevertheless be *shown* (the word monster or *monstruo* derives from the Latin *monstrare*, to show) are not, after all, so very foreign.

The word *razón* itself means different things in different constructions and contexts: 'rightness' (as in the phrase *tener razón*, to be right) or 'common sense'. As one ponders, subtle differences and shifts of meaning unfold and fold back over each other, as in a dream. The print invokes dreaming. It deconstructs itself in the spectator's mind, exposing the limitations of linear and monologic thinking. It catches the spectator up in its dialectic of light and dark, and in a tangled web of textual meaning and imaged counter-meaning, in undecidability, indeterminacy and surplus. It invites us into a full-on engagement not merely with 'the dark' but with the nature of this engagement itself.

In whatever mode we find ourselves engaging with the image, there certainly does seem to be a connection between *disembodiment* and the production of monsters, a detachment from the animal drives. There is the disembodied head of the preparatory drawing, and the sense, in the published print, of the artist fatally lost inside his own skull, his body no longer the poised organism of the Jovellanos portrait but a mannikin-like absence, a sort of Enlightenment doll. In his graphic body language Goya was the satirist of disembodiment. Schulz's recent work lends some support to such a view (Schulz 2005): Goya's work implicates the viewer in the problematics of his/her own physicality. For perhaps our shared embodiment is the only ground on which it is possible for humans to have 'common sense'.

Late eighteenth-century contemporaries were involved in another kind of aspiration towards commonality. In the plinth in one of the preparatory drawings (Figure 3.6) are the words: 'Universal Language. Drawn and Etched by F.co de Goya. Year 1797'. The reference is to a very old idea: the myth of the 'universal language', which eighteenth-century grammarians and philosophers had revived as part of the larger Enlightenment dream of universality. In the previous century, this hoped-for universal language had been that of dream itself; Stoichita and Coderch reproduce the cover of a volume published in Bologna in 1683 by one Guiseppe Maria Mitelli, *L'Alfabeto in sogno*, which shows a sleeping artist resting his folded arms and head on a plinth (Stoichita and Coderch 1999: 173). In the 1790s and early

1800s cultured Spaniards became aware of the universal language idea 'by way of experiences such as hypnosis, mesmeric telepathy, teaching and entertainment. These were probably the same people who attended demonstrations of magic lanterns and fantascopes ... members of the most progressive intelligentsia in Madrid ...'. An article in the *Diario de Madrid* in September 1799 reveals that participants included the Duke and Duchess of Osuna, major patrons of Goya and the purchasers of one of the first sets of the *Caprichos* (Stoichita and Coderch 1999: 174); it is not hard to imagine that the magic lantern and phantasmagoria, perhaps too the camera obscura and the peepshow, played a part in the generation of the etchings (Bird 2004).

The September 1799 *Diario* article went on to say that these demonstrations aimed to show 'the pre-eminence of images in inter-human communication ... "This mute and purely ocular language can easily be converted into a spoken language destined to the hearing since it presents the true prototype of a universal language"' (Stoichita and Coderch, 1999: 171–4). One can begin to imagine what this dream of a universal language might have meant personally to the profoundly deaf Goya; his deafness is a subject to which we shall shortly return.

Marat versus Capricho 79

The 1790s produced another celebrated image of a repining male figure next to a box or table, a writing implement in one hand and, like Jovellanos, a letter in the other: Jacques-Louis David's *Marat assassiné* of 1794 (see Figure 3.7). Its impact too partly depends on a relationship between image and text. The dedicatory words *À Marat. David*, inscribed on the wooden bath, underline the painting's status and function, as a homage to a fallen hero. It is as unambiguous as possible in its message, and clear in its intent on the viewer: to inspire admiration and mourning. The viewer is invited to join the painter in his grief, now made resoundingly public; the invitation implies the necessary universality of such grief. The painting is an exemplary neoclassical statement. It is readily legible and coherent, a thoroughly rational construction in three-dimensional space: it would be easy to draw a geometrical ground-plan. It contains too a recognisable appeal to tradition: it is like a *pietà*, but this works merely to underline its secular allegiance ('This is not a *pietà*'). David's Marat is a secular Christ. Contemporaries would have grasped this; it was all part of David's conscious skill as a constructor and manipulator of meanings. The empty space above is itself resonant: it contains no angels, saints or *putti*. Neither is it populated by monsters. The painting is, in Barthesian terms, *lisible*, and in Bakhtinian terms, monologic. It tells us what to think.

Goya's *Capricho* 79 (see Figure 3.8) is the last but one in the series as published in 1799, and the caption reads *Nadie nos ha visto* ('nobody has seen us'). It seems to show a claustral cellar. There is, on the face of it, a moral

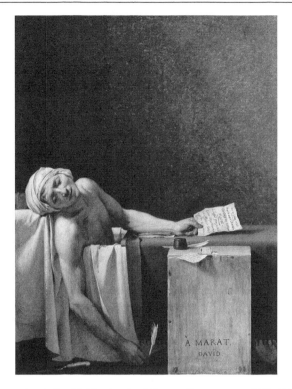

Figure 3.7 Jacques-Louis David, *The Death of Marat*, oil on canvas, 1793. © Musées royaux des Beaux-Arts de Belgique, Bruxelles (dig. photo: J. Geleyns/ www.roscan.be).

message: the vice of drunkenness is being mocked, and it is clear enough from the image itself that the additional target is the priesthood. The anti-clerical revolutionary Marat would have approved. The accompanying text, however, from the 'Prado' manuscript, is tangential: 'And what does it matter if the goblins go down to the cellar and have four swigs, if they have been working all night and have left the scullery like gleaming gold?' (Goya 1969 [1799]). Is this displacement onto a popular superstition, about goblins who clean by night, a ploy to evade the Inquisition's censors while still allowing encoded references to ecclesiastical cupidity and moral grubbiness?

This conjunction of verbal and visual text is also anti-classical in its ambiguities and the audience skills required to read it. They are skills of free association and of the street. The barrel is probably the first thing we see: without thinking an eighteenth-century Spaniard might have identified it as a *bota*, an oak barrel in which sherry is matured. The cool, high warehouses of sherry-producing South West Andalucia in which very large such barrels are housed are known as 'cathedrals' (Goya had, of course, been in this part of Andalucia in 1793–94, during his illness). The word *bota* is also used, more

Figure 3.8 Francisco José de Goya y Lucientes, *Nadie nos ha visto*, plate 79, *Los Caprichos*, etching and aquatint, 1799. Image © Biblioteca Nacional, Madrid (Spain).

commonly, for the famous Spanish boot-shaped leather drinking vessel with a spout, perfect for communal, carnival drinking.

In their analysis of the *Caprichos* and of this one in particular, Stoichita and Coderch point out that the viewer is required to attend both to the visible form of the image and to the ambiguous content. Goya, they suggest, is employing a 'conceit'. 'Conceptism' was a literary style from the previous century, which survived as a popular way of constructing meaning, unconstrained by the enlightened requirement for transparency, lack of ambiguity, and manifestly improving purpose. The Spanish baroque writer Baltasar Gracián, *conceptismo*'s leading exponent, wrote in 1647 that a conceit (a *concepto*) is 'an act of understanding that expresses the correspondence between objects', a visual para-language. It is more than just punning; in the sixteenth century, Stoichita and Coderch recall, Rabelais had made the wordplay *divin/du vin* (priest/wine) (Stoichita and Coderch 1999: 197–9). To work, Goya's conceit also needs the spectator to mouth words and thus actively and democratically participate in the generation of meaning, which similarly works on the principle of condensation, two images in one, although in the case of the *capricho* one image is verbal and one is visual. Having noticed the obvious barrel the ingenious Castillian spectator, who would sound his Vs like Bs, would come to see that the wretches are *devotos de la bota*. For the viewer, pleasure and satisfaction; for the artist, conscious of what he was doing, pleasure in exercising a playful skill. (For the therapist, a reminder of a ludic resource at her disposal when approaching, say, a dream; for the patient, perhaps unconscious of what he is doing, pleasure too.)

This skill was also close to that which was known, in the language of the Academy, as *invención*, that is, conscious attention to the elaboration of meaning through playful, encoded and possibly subliminal messages, decipherable by those educated as to their (probably classical) referents. *Invención*, however, which Goya had already amply deployed in the Tapestry Cartoons (Tomlinson 1989), was usually reserved for history painting, the highest category in the academic hierarchy of genres. Here, in a humble etching, was a surfeit of *invención*, a mere caprice or, to use the initial title of the series, dream. Goya's democratic dream-work, combining high and low, implied an inversion of cultural values, something liberating and insurrectionary. It registered the impact of the French Revolution. These 'devotees of the bottle' are engaged in an 'upside-down worship' (Stoichita and Coderch 1999: 199); in *Los Caprichos* and increasingly in his work Goya presents a carnival 'world turned upside-down'; the number of headlong-falling figures in his work is worth noting.

The playful readings of *Capricho* 79 above by no means exhaust the image, and it is one of the more straightforwardly satirical of the series. It withholds; it retains its awesome ambiguities and polyphonies; *Los Caprichos* was originally advertised for sale on the Calle del Desengaño, the Street of Disappointment. What is the standing figure? A shadow? Another monk? The bogey-man? What of the (apparently) masked figure on the left, who is raising his glass to the standing shade, which seems to be inviting him to drink, like the *Commendatore* at the end of Don Giovanni? Something about the back of his head might suggest the artist himself. Goya 'relinquishes control of the world he creates' and we must join him. Let us turn to the madhouse.

The Madhouse

Goya's second madhouse (see Figure 3.9) was almost certainly painted around 1816; this crowded, multi-figure painting is smaller than reproductions might suggest, measuring 45 × 72 centimeters, or about 18 × 28 inches, and it hangs in the Real Academia de San Fernando in Madrid.

Before the eighteenth century, madness was generally portrayed visually as divinely inspired frenzy, a 'life-giving' aspect of religion (Rosen 1998: 121), or else perhaps a wage of sin. Pieter Bruegel the Elder's *Dulle Griet* (*c*.1564) is a sort of holy fool. The fifteenth- and sixteenth-century image of the Ship of Fools, which probably emerged from the medieval practice of banishing the mad to boats and ships to sail from place to place, was also a humanist satire of the Catholic Church (see the book by Sebastian Brand of 1494, and the more or less contemporary painting by Hieronymous Bosch in the Louvre). In sixteenth- and seventeenth-century literature madmen are depicted as either serious or comic, 'congenitally foolish' like Shakespeare's Don Adriano de Armado in *Love's Labour's Lost* or Molière's Harpagon in *L'Avare*, or driven mad, like Lear or like Orestes in Racine's *Andromaque* (Rosen 1998: 116).

Figure 3.9 Francisco José de Goya y Lucientes, *The Madhouse*, oil on board, 1816. Museo de la Real Academia de Bellas Artes de San Fernando, Madrid (Spain).

Goya's 1816 madhouse is one of a handful of very potent images, in eighteenth- and early nineteenth-century art, of mad people in an asylum. It is situated between Hogarth's *Bedlam* scene from *The Rake's Progress* (1735) and Goya's own earlier *Courtyard of a Madhouse* (c.1793–94), and Théodore Géricault's portraits of the insane of 1822.[8] It is part of the new, 'strange but momentous dialogue with Madness' which the eighteenth century had opened. Kant's *Critique of Pure Reason* (1781) had operated 'on the frontiers of human reason' (Stoichita and Coderch 1999: 146–7): 'It was as though classical reason were once more admitting to a proximity, a relationship, a quasi-resemblance between itself and the figures of madness' (Foucault (1971 [1961]: 204, cited in Stoichita and Coderch 1999: 147). Since Foucault published his *Histoire de la folie* in 1961, the strangeness of this dialogue has not ceased to fascinate and tax scholars.

The iconography of madness was defining a 'new thematic register' in the years around 1800 (Stoichita and Coderch 1999: 147). In *The Anatomy of Melancholy* (1621) Robert Burton had affirmed that we are all capable of being 'brain-sick' because we are all subject to falsehood and error; divine revelation was the only certain means of separating truth from illusion (Rosen 1998: 117). By the end of the eighteenth century, with the decline of religious faith, the idea that we could all go mad was securely linked to the intolerable conflicts and traumata of everyday, social existence. This could be seen, for example, in the life of the mad English poet William Cowper, or the German poet Jakob Lenz (the subject of Georg Büchner's *Lenz* of 1839), or in Wordsworth's portrayals of madness rooted in 'the ordinary lives of the poor and the middle class' (*The Thorn*, *The Ruined Castle*, *The Idiot Boy*) (Rosen 1998: 117–18).

In contemporary literature, madness could be enlisted to highlight injustice, particularly towards women, as in Wollstonecraft's *Maria: or, The Wrongs of Woman*, of 1798: the heroine confined to an asylum by an unscrupulous relative. Madness was gathering a multitude of other meanings too; it was becoming attractive, for example as a 'refuge from unbelief – from Bacon, Newton and Locke', as William Blake claimed the spirit of Cowper had told him. In 1796 Charles Lamb, echoing a character in Goethe's *Werther* and anticipating the sentiments of Gérard de Nerval, recalled to Coleridge the 'pure happiness' he had experienced while himself locked up in an insane asylum: 'Dream not Coleridge, of having tasted all the grandeur & wildness of Fancy, till you have gone mad.' Madness was gaining 'a new ideological charge', as a source of creative energy (Rosen 1998: 113–14).

In another register, the Marquis de Sade's novel *Juliette* of 1797 contains a remarkable madhouse scene. In the work of de Sade, himself imprisoned as insane throughout the Napoleonic period, scholars have seen a sort of upside-down or mad reverse of Enlightenment: Adorno and Horkheimer (1989 [1944]: 81–119) took the view that de Sade's scenarios of unbridled sexual gratification showed up the ruthlessness, the dispensing with the tutelage of the other, inherent in enlightened reasoning. For Lacan, de Sade's *The Philosophy of the Boudoir* was the fulfilment and vindication of Kant (Lacan 2007: 645 ff.; see also Stoichita and Coderch 1999: 145).

In a social sense, as Foucault also showed, madness was becoming both domesticated and invisible. The mid-eighteenth century had been the heyday of madness as spectacle and entertainment (Hogarth showed the fashionable audience which would descend on hospitals such as Bethlem); Goya's madhouses hark back to this period, which may in any case have lasted longer in the Iberian peninsula than it did in the north. At the same time the paintings coincide, chronologically, with enlightened, revolutionary reforms under the physician Philippe Pinel, which freed the insane from incarceration with common criminals and led to the great nineteenth-century European asylum-building project. The beginnings of the talking cure can be seen in Pinel's 'moral treatment', a regime of persuasion, example and initiation into the world of orderly work. Yet this was a narrow window, historically: the ascendancy of Pinel and his followers, in Foucault's and others' analysis (e.g. Goldstein 2001 [1987]), marks the annexation of madness to medicine, the beginnings of psychiatry and the notion of 'mental illness': Foucault's 'great confinement'.[9]

Goya was working on the cusp of these broad developments. At the end of the *Histoire de la folie* Foucault offered tantalisingly suggestive descriptions of the two madhouse paintings. One depicts confinement and control, the old way, in which the mad are locked up together with criminals, or in private asylums, while the second, perhaps hinting ironically at the Pinelian system and its classifying impetus, reveals 'bodies in their dark freedom'–something beyond and outside the enlightened Pinelian universe. Foucault points both to a more dire abjection, and to a bodily surplus, a *jouissance*. The images are very far from the objectifying glance of medical illustration, like that which was to characterise the engravings in, for example, Jean-Etienne Esquirol's *Des maladies mentales* (1838), and very far indeed from later nineteenth-century depictions of the heroes of psychiatry (Robert Fleury's painting *Pinel Releasing Lunatics from their Chains* of 1887, or Brouillet's *Charcot Lecturing*, 1897). Goya's images, especially the second, implicate *us*, as ourselves creatures or prisoners of the imagination, wayward and suggestible.

The 1816 *The Madhouse* also coincides with the restoration of Fernando VII, politically repressive and administratively chaotic; Goya was in a sort of internal exile. The painting might be viewed as a depiction of people driven mad by years of war now followed by crushing oppression. It might also be read as an encoded satire on the state of the nation, like the *Caprichos*. With its king, priest, savage and military figure, it invites, and frustrates, a detailed allegorical and satirical reading: the pillars of state power, court, Catholic Church and army in crazy disconnection from each other, with a possible reference as well, in the figure of the savage, to the Latin American empire which was currently wresting itself from Spain's grip.

The Madhouse is also a polyphony, with echoes as multiple as those reverberating from the late eighteenth-/early nineteenth-century category of 'madness' itself. It has three similarly proportioned companion pictures, which, if they were made to be seen as a set (as they can be seen today, hanging together in the Real Academia), provide the viewer, now as we may safely assume then, with contextual nudges as to how the painting might be approached. There is a scene from the Inquisition, a village bullfight and a procession of flagellants: all are what Erik Erikson would have called 'deathly rituals' (Erikson 1977). They work to underline the hellishness of the scene with the mad. Each, as a potential satire of 'black', Catholic and reactionary Spain, undertaken from a liberal viewpoint, covers its tracks: the scene from the Inquisition and the flagellants seem to be located as past rather than present features of the national landscape, which they once more were; the bullfight, for all its tawdriness, could pass for a celebration of a distinctly Spanish popular custom (Goya was in any case well known as an *aficionado;* in 1815 he had been working on the *Tauromaquia* etchings). All are public spectacles of cruelty and punishment. Furthermore, there are echoes and cross-references across the four paintings, 'quasi-resemblances', in Foucault's phrase (cited in Stoichita and Coderch 1999: 147) – for example, horns and hats, in the bullfight and madhouse. Such echoes and resemblances can be found in Goya's wider *oeuvre* too. The figure in 'The Madhouse' with the (also slightly archaic) three-cornered hat and outstretched arm, who paradoxically works 'to centralize and decentralise the composition in equal measure' (Stoichita and Coderch 1999: 149), resonates with the so-called *Colossus* of 1812; the half-hidden figure who seems to be labouring at something just behind him echoes *The Forge* of 1811, both paintings made during the War of Independence and referring to it. In 1816 Goya would also have been working on the plates for the *Disasters of War*, with its multitudes of suffering, often naked figures. In Bakhtinian terms, the painting is a 'mosaic of citations', a 'palimpsest of traces' (Bakhtin 1981). Perhaps, too, in their shared darkness, all four paintings bear another trace: in 1815–16 the world was darkened by the ash from the volcanic eruption of Tambora, in Indonesia, the largest in recorded history. The first year of the pan-European Restoration, 1816, was known as the 'year without a summer', during which Mary Shelley wrote *Frankenstein.*

The painting is also in conversation with images by other artists, none too distant in time: with Hogarth's Bedlam scene, with the prisons, the *Carceri,* etched by Piranesi, which Goya would have seen in Moratín's collection, and with the work of the neoclassical school of Goya's contemporary David. The painting's irony emerges all the more clearly when it is seen in relation to David, his *Oath of the Horatii* (1787), for example, and the echo would not have been lost on educated, French-leaning contemporaries. *The Madhouse* is constructed according to recognisably neoclassical principles: a frieze-like arrangement of naked and semi-naked, mostly male, figures, with musculature like that of Greek or Roman statues, their gesturing bodies in poses that visually echo each other and seem expressive of a range of feelings and reactions, is deployed against an indeterminate, stage-like architectural background, under a raking light, and, to complete the illusion, within geometrically coherent space, emphasised by flagstones seen in perspective.

Yet in most other respects, not least in its overt subject matter, it transgresses neoclassical norms. It subverts the visual language of Enlightenment, and the seamless relationship between neoclassical form and content. It offers the viewer no noble sentiment, no exemplary behaviour, in the way that David's *Oath* did, with its unmistakable message about manly patriotic duty. *The Madhouse* emerges even more starkly as an ironic commentary if compared to the naked male figures in David's great sketch for his *Oath in the Tennis Court* of 1789, in which classically naked figures are the templates for modern heroes of the beginning of the Revolution. In Goya's painting the spectator is not at the Davidian theatre, being elucidated and uplifted, but a participant at the abject spectacle of the asylum. Might the inmates, in fact, be putting on a play, like that in Peter Weiss's *Marat-Sade*, with the foreground-seated figure with the horns the director or the prompter? The question of the external spectator's, our, presence remains open: are we there for the purpose of having our own rationality and its importance confirmed, or for lurid, erotic sensation? In David, reason and determinacy of meaning prevail; in Goya, profound, unsettling indeterminacy. The palace has become a basement; light itself does not uniformly reveal, but casts deep shadows that harbour mysteries. In another respect too *The Madhouse* departs from Davidian procedure. It looks as if it was made by a spontaneous, free-associative process rather than through careful pre-planning; there are no known preparatory sketches and nothing to suggest preliminary drawing on the canvas. It is possible that it evolved and unfolded itself across the surface, like a sentence with spontaneous, semantic depths.

The painting, in Janis Tomlinson's Bakhtinian analysis, constructs an audience. Its probable original owner was a liberal merchant, Manuel García de la Prada, a supporter of French rule in the War of Independence, and a suspect, like Goya, under the new regime (Goya's portrait of de la Prada, of 1805–8, is in the Des Moines Art Center, Illinois). Another possibility is that it may have belonged to the *ilustrado* Moratín himself (Tomlinson, 1992: 162 ff.). In this reading Goya exercised his *invención* in order to transmit encoded messages to receptive, like-minded friends. The painting invited their engagement; it positioned them 'dialogically', as 'listeners' for visual echoes, and thus as participants in the co-construction of meaning, within a context of shared, underground (basement) meanings. As with the *Caprichos*, the key to catching and building these meanings, catching their drift, was a readiness to indulge, in private, in the pleasure of play, in a form of free-floating attention. As has been seen in the discussion of *Capricho* 79, the participant listener might also be called upon to speak.

Yet we are not de la Prada, or Moratín, we cannot be complicit in the way either of them might have been. Time has passed; we can try to reconstruct, as art historians do, but we also have, cannot avoid having, our own associations, in a present relationship with the image. If there were multiple encoded messages to de la Prada or Moratín, which do not disclose themselves too readily but with which they were equipped to engage, how and what can we hope to hear?

We come up against multiple uncertainties straightaway: ambiguities, erotic suggestions. Can we trust our peripheral vision, should we pay attention to it? *Is* that oral sex taking place in the shadow on the far right? What is happening in the middle, on the right? Stoichita and Coderch see 'a heaving mass of naked bodies' orgiastic display . . . strategically enveloped in dense shadow' (Stoichita and Coderch 1999: 149). These authors have persuasively analysed 'the general eroticisation of the viewer' in eighteenth-century art; they also point to how, in the voyeuristic madhouse scene in de Sade's *Juliette*, in which the director of the institution gets his naked charges to 'indulge in a thousand extravagences', everything similarly 'takes place on the fringes of the visible' (Stoichita and Coderch 1999: 142, 147).

Words or phrases might come to us; where might they lead if we also try to imagine our way into a contemporary Spanish frame of mind? What a mess all this seems! *–¡Esto es un cachondeo! Cachondear de uno* means to mock at or satirise someone. The adjective *cachondo* can mean 'on heat'; *ser cachondo* is 'to be sexy', while *estar cachondo* means 'to be horny'. We are in the realm of the drives. Free association to 'horns', for example, might lead us to link 'horn', the bull's horn, as an emblem of Spain, to 'hearing aid'. The seated figure unmissable in the foreground, an internal spectator of the picture, seems to be using one of the horns he holds as exactly that, just as perhaps Goya himself may have used some such aid in order to try to catch something of the inchoate rumbling around (or was it inside?) him. What do *we* hear? This figure has a back like that of a Hercules: a naked and beautiful Hercules opens the mad floor show in de Sade's *Juliette* (Stoichita and Coderch 1999: 147–8); recall too the naked, muscled, sadistically impaled male figures in the *Disasters*. The figure has a second horn in his other hand, pointing outwards and upwards towards the anus or the groin of the standing figure with the three-horned, tricorn, hat (a *tricornio* in Spanish). Now we have three horns, an over-determination of them. What do *we* project, in our claims to 'objective' reading? *Cornudo*, as well as 'horned', means 'cuckolded'. The painting certainly seems to deal with the themes of betrayal, emasculation and humiliation: Spain/liberal ideals betrayed. With its embodiments of authority (political, ecclesiastic, military, tribal), with their identifying insignia, it is a play about malign power relations; it is also a commentary on the instability and flux of sign itself. The one gestural sign that offers legibility, transparency, is that of the seated pope or priest-like figure in the right foreground, who seems to be blessing the spectator(s); but his sign makes at best only ironic, at worst no sense.

But still the thought returns: *is* there something more articulate going on, if only we could decode better, read the clues? Goya was after all a deaf-signer.

He wrote to his friend Martin Zapater in 1798 that Jovellanos, who was sitting for his portrait, was communicating to him in sign language (Symmons 2004: 253). A school for deaf signing, on the model of a school set up in Paris in 1754 by a French *abbé*, Charles Michel de l'Epée, opened in Madrid in 1805 (see Plann 2007). Was this the universal language hoped for by the grammarians of Enlightenment, a world language of sign based on the ur-language of sign that deaf people seemed spontaneously to adopt?

Here is another deaf person, David Wright, entering a crowded room. The speaker is remembering his first day, as a child, at a school for the deaf in 1927. This school required its pupils to speak, and forbade signing; they had, however, evolved a secret, vernacular gestural language of their own.

> Confusion stuns the eye, arms whirl like windmills in a hurricane . . . the emphatic, silent vocabulary of the body – look, expression, bearing, glance of the eye; hands perform their pantomime. Absolutely engrossing pandemonium . . . I begin to sort out what's going on. The seemingly corybantic brandishing of hands and arms reduces itself to a convention, a code which as yet conveys nothing. It is in fact a kind of vernacular . . . though not a verbal one . . . All communications were supposed to be oral . . . we relaxed inhibitions, wore no masks.
>
> (cited in Sacks 2000 [1989]: 11)

The pandemonium described here is tantalisingly close to that depicted by Goya. He alerts and sensitises us to the nuanced, wordless language of body and gesture. The codes or conventions at play in the painting, however, do not go on to disclose precise meaning; the painting just does not function like that, however skilled a reader one is. It is instead a commentary on the world of sign in general, the constant pull to find meaning, and the fact that all communication is contextual. There is no *ydioma universal*, universal language. What, then, about the claim that the *Caprichos* were feeling their way towards a universal language of dream? Even if Goya had subscribed to this idea in the late 1790s, it seems highly unlikely that he would have held it by 1816. The idea that dream, or signing, might be the key to a universal language is itself an illusion of *le grand rêve*.

Goya can seem to challenge us across the centuries: can we let in those meanings which might begin to emerge when we allow ourselves to float in this sea of signs? The work of Goya's old age challenges us further. The *Disparates* and the Black Paintings confront us with a *jouissance*-imbued night of the soul. Like the navel of the dream they 'reach down into the unknown' (Freud 1900: 525). Yves Bonnefoy offers a fascinating understanding of the place of the Black Paintings in Goya's work and in the history of the Western world: they were a form of cleansing. Like *Los Caprichos*, they followed hard upon the heels of a major illness, that in which Goya portrayed himself with his doctor, Doctor Arrieta, in 1820 (see Figure 3.10). It is a key painting. It

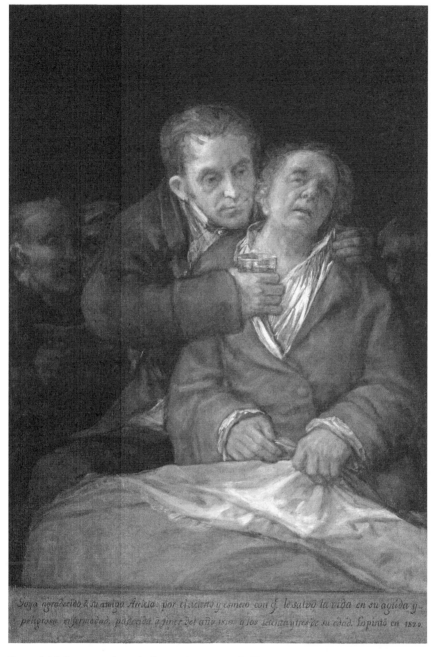

Goya agradecido à su amigo Arrieta: por el acierto y esmero con q' le salvo la vida en su aguda y
peligrosa enfermedad, padecida à fines del año 1819. à los setenta y tres de su edad. Lo pintó en 1820.

Figure 3.10 Francisco José de Goya y Lucientes, *Self-Portrait with Dr Arrieta*, oil on canvas,
1820. Minneapolis Institute of Arts, The Ethel Morrison Van Derlip Fund.

draws on the popular, Catholic, Mediterranean tradition of the *ex voto*, a painting hung in a church in which a survived accident or illness is recorded, usually by an amateur artist, in thanks for the intercession of the Virgin or of a saint. In Goya's painting there is no saint, only a dedication 'to my friend Dr Arrieta', together with the dates and details of the illness. The doctor supports the patient from behind. The patient turns his head away and his hands clutch at the sheets. He is in a fever, a trance, close to death. He is being gently and stubbornly brought back into life, into ordinary human contact, in a disinterested gesture which, Bonnefoy writes, gives proof 'that here is something else . . . that has reality other than the slaverings of dark voracity'. For dimly discernible in the background of the painting, abysmal figures menace, reminiscent of the demons of *Los Caprichos* and elsewhere: they are for Bonnefoy 'the beyond of the human condition, in its absolute non-sense'. They are, however, countered by 'the none the less real fact of the . . . devotion of one being for another being' (Bonnefoy 2006: 70, 73). Goya's late discovery in this painting, one that had been latent throughout his work, and showed itself in the tenderness of some of his depictions of young women, was the possibility of an equally absolute compassion, 'the only thing that is real in a universe where all is illusion except suffering'. There was a work of negation (*un travail du négatif* – Bonnefoy 2006: 75) to be done, so as to make a space for what, if it existed at all, might be of enduring human value. Goya undertook this work with unparalleled urgency and persistence.

'I am still learning'

Walter Benjamin wrote about an 'optical unconscious' (Benjamin 1969 [1936], 1979 [1931]), that world of unforeseeable, inassimilable visible contingencies that photography makes manifest. There also undoubtedly exists another, parallel kind of cultural, visual unconscious. A photograph of 1937 shows a more recent philosopher with a Foucauldian 'quasi-resemblance' both to Jovellanos and the dreaming etcher: Freud sits at his writing desk, surrounded by Egyptian idols, with a monster chow at his feet and a bust of his own head above him (Freud, E. *et al.*, 1985: 271). To suggest this visual lineage may help us focus anew on the question of what Freudians are open to hearing, and on how Freud positioned himself to hear, including from himself. In another portrait, a cartoon by Ralph Steadman, Freud's legs are twisted around each other in a most un-Jovellanos-like manner: an unmistakably phallic cigar in hand, he writhes in his chair with erotic, possibly homo-erotic, frustration, clutching at his groin and overlooked not by the goddess of wisdom but by Michelangelo's half-naked dying slave (Steadman 1982: 74–5).[10]

The kind of analytical attention to which Goya invites us is analogous to that self-blinding suspension of intellect recommended by Bion, his famous 'penetrating beam of darkness . . . so absolute that it would achieve a luminous, absolute vacuum' (Bion 1990: 20–1). It is just this kind of light–dark reversal that the *Caprichos*, the *Sueño* in particular, invites us to reflect upon.

Who is in analysis with whom? Goya's work can seem to speak directly to the viewer's unconscious, and the unconscious, as Freud wrote, 'speaks more than one dialect' (Freud, S. 1913: 177). If Goya's work constructed an audience, it was perhaps in the way the patient constructs, stage-directs, an analyst (Caper 1998), who must in turn be open to thinking about how she is being constructed and positioned. The analyst thus constructed refuses, however, to comply, and insists on remaining enigmatic. The work of art, 'in the place of the analyst' (Brousse 2007), occupies this position too. It frustrates our attempts to bring it to a closure. It can show us ourselves, just as the patient can, our own voracity, terror and chaos, emerging on the margins or in the dark centre of our emotional vision. A *capricho* is a good interpretation. The viewer/analysand asks: 'What does he mean? What does he want?' *Che vuoi?*, as Lacan framed it. Forces from within and without, social masks, roles and narratives, move us like puppets, unless a good *capricho* can shift us out of it. We find ourselves, in Foucault's terms, called to account, 'arraigned by that work of art and responsible before it' (Foucault 1971 [1961]: 289).

Aún aprendo – 'I am still learning' – is the title of one of Goya's last drawings, made during his final exile in Bordeaux. It shows an ancient, stooped, bearded man in a shroud-like smock leaning on sticks and moving, painfully slowly, towards us. As ever, the caption is double-edged: 'I am still interested in life'/'I am now having to learn this new thing, to get about on these sticks' (Lubbock 2001: 27–8).

Chapter 4

Hölderlin, Novalis, word without end

Johann Christian Friedrich Hölderlin (1770–1843) is a giant of European literature; for Georg Lukács he was 'one of the purest and most profound elegaic poets of all time' (Lukács 1968 [1934]: 151). He is not, like Goethe or Schiller, a household name in the English-speaking world, yet he is often regarded as the German poet *par excellence* (Fehervary 1977: 91), on a par with Rainer Maria Rilke, one hundred years his junior. Martin Heidegger indeed bracketed the two poets together in a famous essay, *What are Poets For?*, the title being one of Hölderlin's own questions (Heidegger 1975a). He never founded a 'school'; as Heidegger and Lukács agreed, he could have no successor.

Hölderlin's work is a striving for classical clarity, and he is 'Romantic' in so far as his poetry is a recognition that such clarity was no longer compatible with truthfulness of utterance. In a sense the struggle to find this compatibility and to articulate his failure to do so are the whole subject of his poetry; perhaps the madness of the second half of his life was the only resolution possible. He, and Novalis, might help attune therapists to the importance of the particular word spoken – this word, not that – and to the fact that the word is always contingent and inadequate: it always only approximates to the state of psyche or the experience to which it merely points. As readers, we must read between and around the lines, in uncertainty as to whether or not we are on the right track. We might also, in the process of reading Hölderlin, come to a renewed respect for the patient whose impenetrable speech may have earned him a psychiatric diagnosis but which is for him a way of trying to reach exactitude and truth.

Hölderlin struggles with the limitations of language, or, to put it another way, with the unconscious as obstacle. Novalis, in this respect a Jung to Hölderlin's Freud, finds language's explosive, liberating resources: the unconscious as a creative source. He brings home the inherent vitality of words. Novalis, pseudonym of Friedrich, Freiherr von Hardenberg (1772–1801), was the youthful genius of German Romanticism. He died young, and leaves us a picture of himself as a polymathic enthusiast for life who is nevertheless constantly aware of an unreachable 'beyond'. Steeped in *Naturphilosophie* and flourishing in the post-Kantian climate of German Idealism, he is driven to find the immanence of a beyond in the phenomena of this world. It is also an internal beyond. 'The world is a universal trope of the spirit, a symbolic image therefrom' (Novalis 1989: 74 [no. 262]).

The German Romantics, from the Schlegel brothers onwards, were intensely aware that the word was never to be taken for granted. Halting readers of German, like the present author, may be particularly well placed to resonate to this, by virtue of their linguistic disability and inevitable struggles with the foreign language. It is an experience to be taken to heart in the consulting room, when the therapist who appears to speak the same language as the patient may feel tempted to assume familiarity and relax his or her doubt as to the meaning of what is being spoken. For both Hölderlin and Novalis, the word is not for easy domestication – like the Lacanian, linguistically structured unconscious.

German Romanticism: some background

In Goethe's poem *Erlkönig*, 'Erlking', of 1782 (Goethe 1964: 80–2), a father, galloping through the night, attempts to calm the dying child he holds in his arms, for the child sees and hears, in wisps of mist, shimmering willows and sighing wind, the Erlking calling him to his domain. The poem was written towards the end of the *Sturm und Drang* (storm and stress, or storm and urge) period, within which Romanticism, in German-speaking Europe, found some of its roots. It asserts the power of the irrational against tired Enlightenment certainties. It also lends itself to analysis in terms of precisely the positioning the therapist must refuse but towards which he is always tempted. 'The father's efforts to demystify nature are intended less to achieve understanding than to obliterate mystery' (Calhoon 1992: 33). The analyst is constantly doing battle with his own anxiety, with the temptation to try to manage it by a reversion to Enlightenment method, that which Adorno and Horkheimer characterised as itself a radical form of mythological anxiety, born out of primitive dread of unpredictability and death (Adorno and Horkheimer 1989 [1944]: 16).

The atmosphere which hangs over the forests, mountains and seashores in Caspar David Friedrich's paintings can also be unnerving. Alongside evening calm, companionship and reflection, there is also a strange and insistent disquiet, a sense of loss and lostness. The early German Romantics were engaged in a search for the fulfilment of an intuition that there is an essential unity of things. It was a search they generally undertook in full knowledge that the possibility of such fulfilment had passed, if it had ever really existed. The search must nevertheless ceaselessly be renewed and reformulated; the Romantics were led to eschew facile accommodation, to espouse unfinishable-ness or non-closure to the point of breakdown. This could bring with it a sense of supreme wonder, and fearful vertigo. 'On this height I often stand, my Bellarmin', wrote Hölderlin in the late 1790s, in his epistolary novel *Hyperion*,

But an instant of reflection hurls me down. I reflect, and find myself as I was before – alone, with all the griefs of mortality; and my heart's refuge, the world in its eternal oneness, is gone; Nature closes her arms, and I stand like an alien before her and understand her not . . .
(Hölderlin 1965 [1797, 1799]: 23)

'Every day,' Hölderlin wrote, 'I have to invoke the absent god again' (letter of June 1795, in Hölderlin 2009: 143). Hölderlin's question 'where have the gods gone?' (his poetry is full of questions) was far from academic or idly speculative. If the gods have gone, where does that leave us? In Freud's Cartesian reversal, we are who we are because we are barely intelligible to ourselves; it is this unintelligibility that defines and distinguishes us as human. The Romantic discovery, especially in Germany, was of the need to seek a language for this predicament: for the unknowability, unpredictability and 'otherness' of the individual and collective 'us', and the problematic relation of the human to the natural world and the divine. It was a predicament that underlined the individual's isolation; at the same time the 'us', in German Romanticism, the family of like-minded friends, was correspondingly valued. The search for meaning must be undertaken both in solitude and in the group, in letters, journals, symposia, lectures, love, a constant to and fro of communication.

For this generation the post-Revolutionary present 'symbolised sheer difference'.

The signs of the times were disheartening, confusing, and radically unprecedented. Hölderlin wrote *Ein Zeichen sind wir, deutungslos* ['A sign we are, meaningless']. Faced with a new, unpredictable future, the present appeared incomplete and lacking in interpretation . . . The notion of discontinuity disrupted the once-cherished belief in the teleological progress of human time

wrote the critic Alice Kuzniar. In philosophy Kant's 'continuous development in the pure religion of reasoning' became Johann Gottlieb Fichte's will towards unrelenting striving (Kuzniar 1987: 19–21). There was a shared sense among the young and educated, those who were reaching adolescence and maturity in the 1790s and the Napoleonic era, that real life was elsewhere (Roy 1969: 8). It is this sense that links the two major currents of response, the literary – the Schlegel brothers, Novalis – and the philosophical, the line that stretches from Hölderlin's friend and fellow student Hegel to Feuerbach to Marx. For if 'German Romanticism is the literary offspring of the French Revolution . . . the Marxist revolution is the messiah-like child of German Romanticism' (Roy 1969: 8). These currents intermingle. But while there was an inexorable logic to the Hegelian dialectic and the Marxian unfolding of history, for the literary Romantics the 'elsewhere' was only approachable along what Hölderlin called 'an eccentric course' (Kuzniar 1987: 4). 'The writer's narrative will chart out the points at which it must swerve aside . . .' (Kuzniar 1987: 19–21); it is to just such swervings that the psychoanalyst must learn to be attentive.

Hölderlin

Hölderlin was born near Stuttgart to a wealthy family, in the same year as Hegel, Wordsworth and Beethoven (Constantine 1996: 7). His father died when he was two, his step-father when he was nine. He was brought up by his mother and grandmother, with a sister and younger half-brother; he started writing poetry when he was 14, and even in his teens viewed childhood as a lost idyll; like Coleridge with the River Otter in Devon, the Neckar was a source of childhood delight and poetic awakening. At 18, in 1788, he went to the theological seminary at Tübingen where he met Hegel and Schelling and was inspired by the Declaration of the Rights of Man and the French Revolution (Constantine 1988: 21–4). He met Schiller in 1793, who published some of his poems; he started work on *Hyperion*, a novel with a Greek setting, and in 1794–95 spent a few months in Jena, the hub of Romantic poetic ferment. He moved to Frankfurt, which he called a mercantile 'hell of people living badly' (Constantine 1988: 59), as tutor to the family of a banker, with whose wife, Susette Gontard, he fell in love. 'Diotima' in *Hyperion*, she embodied Hölderlin's Hellenic ideal. In 1798 he left the household and after 1799 he and Susette did not meet again. His mature poetic style developed in the second half of the 1790s; his adult career as a poet spanned a period of only ten years. From 1798 to 1800, the time of his most intense creativity, he was in Homberg, living with a friend; in 1800 he returned home, became a tutor again, and then, in 1802, during a brief peace in the Napoleonic wars, joined a household near Bordeaux as a tutor. In June, he walked the thousand-odd kilometres back to the family home in Nürtingen in a disturbed state; Susette Gontard died in the same month. For the next two and a half years he worked, often agonisingly slowly and in deep unhappiness, on important poems such as *Patmos, Der Ister*, and *Mnemosyne*, making far-reaching redrafts of others, such as *Brod [sic] und Wein* and *Heimkunft*, and revising translations of Sophocles's *Oedipus* and *Antigone* (Constantine 1988: 265–6). For a short time he was the ducal librarian in Homberg, and in 1806 was committed, insane, to a clinic attached to the University of Tübingen. He spent the last thirty-six years of his life, from 1807, in the house of a Tübingen carpenter, living in a tower with a view over the Neckar.

Impenetrability: a thicket of words; short regular building blocks of four-line stanzas, a few brief fragments, many more slabs of verse, more like breeze blocks, compared to the four-line bricks, or covering whole pages with grey type. This is just the selected verse, in a dual-language edition. A thicket, containing buildings. On entering, in repeated short forays, for the thicket can repel and discourage, some other sense or order begins to make itself felt. An orientation. There seems to be some critique of Enlightenment rationality, which has a familiar ring: 'Cold hypocrites, of gods you dare not speak! / You're rational!' (*Ihr habt Verstand!*) (Hölderlin 2007: 17) and a plea for something more authentic; an admiration of Napoleon: 'But this young man's spirit, / The quick – would it not burst / Any vessel that tried to contain it?' (Hölderlin 2007: 5). There are repeated references to rivers: Ganges, Rhine, Neckar, Ister (Danube), a 'fettered river'; and to Greece, Greek literature and philosophy – Sophocles, Socrates – and gods and heroes – Titans, Vulcan, Ganymede, Diotima, Chiron – next to titles relating to modern Germany – the River Main, Stuttgart, Heidelberg, Germania. There are epigrams, odes, elegies, and hymns; *Hyperion*, and fragments of a verse tragedy, *Der Tod des Empedokles* (*The Death of Empedocles*).

Where does he fit? First impressions catch some of the tensions and paradoxes of his work. He is both a passionate modern, dealing with the specifically contemporary, and a classicist with a debt to Schiller and Goethe's 'Weimar' classicism. During his ten years of poetic activity he was in contact with both older poets. There is voluminous correspondence. He seems to be attempting great modern mythologies, which finally fall into fragments, to marry ancient Greece with a nascent Germany. These mythologies seem, like the necessary breakdown of an analytic patient's narratives, to comment on their own impossibility, a mythology of absent gods. At the same time, alongside the mysterious and transcendent, Hölderlin deals with the everyday and familiar; for there are earthly, tantalising compensations, tantalising because of their promise of something more. Often Hölderlin displays a Keats-like sensuality in his response to nature, whether that of the Rhineland in high summer, with its ripening peaches and the blossom of rose bushes as tall as trees (Hölderlin 2007: 140–1), or an imagined Greek and Mediterranean nature:

> . . . their pomegranate ripens, the orange glints
> In a green night and richly the resin drips
> From mastic trees . . .

> . . . *sein Granatbaum reift, wenn aus grüner Nacht*
> *Die Pomeranze blinkt, und der Mastyxbaum*
> *Von Harze träuft* . . .
>
> (Hölderlin 2007: 54–5)

He alerts the reader (as the analyst with her patient must be alert) to manifestations of spontaneous, unbidden life. There is a return, however, time and time again, to heart-rending absence; Hölderlin is also ever the poet of 'absence and longing' (Constantine 1988: 17).

> Spring comes. And everything, in its way and kind,
> Blossoms. But he's far off; is no longer there.

Has gone astray; for all too good are
Genii; heavenly talk is his now.

Der Frühling kömmt. Und jedes, in seiner Art,
Blüht. Der ist aber ferne; nicht mehr dabei.
Irr gieng er nun; denn allzugut sind
Genien; himmlisch Gespräch ist sein nun.
                    (Hölderlin 2007: 106–7)

The distinctly modern, post-Revolutionary ring in Hölderlin's voice can be
heard through this comparison, between one of Goethe's and one of his own
most famous short poems. First, Goethe's *Wandrers Nachtlied II, Wayfarer's
Night Song II*, written in 1780 and revised in 1813.

Über allen Gipfeln
Ist Ruh,
In allen Wipfeln
Spürest du
Kaum einen Hauch;
Die Vögelein schweigen im Walde.
Warte nur, balde
Ruhest du auch.

[Over all the hilltops is calm. In all the treetops you feel hardly a breath
of air. The little birds fall silent in the woods. Just wait, soon you'll be
at rest too.]
                    (Goethe 1964: 50)

Goethe's lullaby-like verse with its soft consonants and simple rhyming
scheme, complete with satisfying internal rhymes, seems to breathe calm over
the reader. It speaks of death, but death as peaceful, blissful, closure.
Hölderlin's *Hälfte des Lebens, Half of Life*, is in a different register.

With yellow pears hangs down
And full of wild roses
The land into the lake,
You loving swans,
And drunk with kisses
You dip your heads into water, the holy-and-sober.

But oh, where shall I find
When winter comes, the flowers, and where
The sunshine
And shade of the earth?
The walls loom

Speechless and cold, in the wind
Weathercocks clatter.

Mit gelben Birnen hänget
Und voll mit wilden Rosen
Das Land in den See,
Ihr holden Schwäne,
Und trunken von Küssen
Tunkt ihr das Haupt
Ins heilignüchterne Wasser.

Weh mir, wo nehm' ich, wenn
Es Winter ist, die Blumen, und wo
Den Sonnenschein,
Und Schatten der Erde?
Die Mauern stehn
Sprachlos und kalt, im Winde
Klirren die Fahnen.

(Hölderlin 2007: 170–1)

Like Goethe, Hölderlin has taken a scene from picturesque nature as his starting point, but where Goethe is limpid and lucid, Hölderlin offers us strained syntax, odd word order and a baffling neologism; the reader has to work to make meaning cohere. Goethe's evening calm is Hölderlin's mild excess and delirium – over-hanging pears, kissing, dipping swans, holy-and-sober water – and the poem meets the prospect of winter and death with an impotent protest. Goethe's evening stillness is now a chill wind. There is no consolatory speech, only walls, no warm breath of words, only a metallic clatter.

Where Goethe offered a sense of seamless connection, in Hölderlin there is a tension between sensuality, embodied experience, and the signs, the words for these experiences. The always tenuous, elusive and problematic correspondence between the two keeps us alert and makes us listen hard. They are self-consciously German words too: Hölderlin was striving to articulate the conditions for a specifically German spiritual revolution. The words used the way Hölderlin used them must have sounded strange to contemporary native speakers (let alone a poor reader of German two centuries later). There is an effect of estrangement, *Entfremdung*. This is frequently explicit, as for example in *Hyperions Schiksaalslied*, *Hyperion's Song of Fate*, of 1798, with its tumbling typography (it was set to music by Brahms in 1868):

You walk above in the light,
  Weightless tread a soft floor, blessed genii!
    Radiant the gods' mild breezes
      Gently play on you
        As the girl artist's fingers
          On holy strings.

Fateless the Heavenly breathe
 Like an unweaned infant asleep;
  Chastely preserved
   In modest bud
    For ever their minds
     Are in flower
      And their blissful eyes
       Eternally tranquil gaze,
        Eternally clear.

But we are fated
 To find no foothold, no rest,
  And suffering mortals
   Dwindle and fall
    Headlong from one
     Hour to the next,
      Hurled like water
       From ledge to ledge
        Downward for years to the vague abyss.

Ihr wandelt droben im Licht
 Auf weichem Boden, seelige Genien!
  Glänzende Götterlüfte
   Rühren euch leicht,
    Wie die Finger der Künstlerin
     Heilige Saiten.

  Schiksaallos, wie der schlafende
   Säugling, athmen die Himmlischen;
    Keusch bewahrt
     In bescheidener Knospe,
      Blühet ewig
       Ihnen der Geist,
        Und die seeligen Augen
         Bliken in stiller
          Ewiger Klarheit.

 Doch uns ist gegeben,
  Auf keiner Stätte zu ruhn,
   Es schwinden, es fallen
    Die leidenden Menschen
     Blindlings von einer
      Stunde zur andern,
       Wie Wasser von Klippe
        Zu Klippe geworfen,
         Jahr lang ins Ungewisse hinab.

(Hölderlin 2007: 24–7)

There was 'no foothold, no rest'; Hölderlin revised and rewrote frequently. Important late poems such as *Patmos* and *Brod und Wein* were worked and reworked: 'the written text', wrote Alice Kuzniar, 'must forfeit its authoritative, completed status to future revision . . . What matters . . . is correct utterance and vigilance against error.' As Hyperion said of his beloved, 'I can speak of her only fragmentarily – a word here, a word there. I have to forget what she is in her completeness if I am to speak of her at all . . . if I am not to die of delight in her and die of grief for her' (Hölderlin 1965 [1797, 1799]: 72). Every time his writing 'comes close to a possibly false depiction of divine return, he swerves aside to correct his former statement . . . Hölderlin's manuscript is a palimpsest of variants' (Kuzniar 1987: 170).

Thus one can – must? – read late Hölderlin intertextually or hermeneutically, 'applying insights gained from one work to another'. In this way the reader might come to a closer appreciation of something else which marks his texts, his principle of *Wechsel der Töne*, 'alternation of tones': 'reversals and interruptions, by different poetic voices pitted against one another'. Kuzniar is still left, however, with a question, one that also faces the analyst trying to catch the unconscious drift of the patient's speech: is Hölderlin merely 'exploring alternatives, or does he establish a hierarchy to their succession?' He was, she seems to suggest, perfectly conscious of this question himself; he 'deftly plots these various conflicting moments', in *Patmos* (Kuzniar 1987: 137–8) and elsewhere.

We are a sign, without meaning, wrote Holderlin in a version of *Mnemosyne* (Kuzniar 1987: 138). What, then, is the status of the sign? What comes across from the versions of this and other poems is a sense of the coming and then the going, the ebb and flow of the elusive theme. The gods come and go in human capacity to conceive of them. 'Marvellous is her favour, Night's, the exalted, and no one / Knows what it is or whence comes all she does and bestows', begins the second stanza of *Brod und Wein* (Hölderlin 2007: 151): the lines cast us, kindly, into a state of wonder and perplexity.

Then there is the issue of translation. The problems of the translator echo those of the analyst. Hölderlin's German is sparse, precise, both formal and colloquial, founded in his native Swabian dialect. One must look between the gaps/lines at the same time as trying to *hear*. The reader might like to make his or her own comparison of Hölderlin's major English and American translators, David Constantine (Hölderlin 1996), for example, or James Mitchell (Hölderlin 2004b).[1] Mitchell may be the most immediately appealing; it is easy to contrast him favourably with more demanding precursors in the field. Michael Hamburger is the translator I use here. He is praised by Hölderlin's biographer David Constantine as a 'mimetic translator': he stays as close as he can to the word order and the meter of the original. In this sense he is a 'Lacanian', 'word-for-word' translator (see Lacan 2007: 394, and Chapter 2 in this volume). Here, for example, is his rendering of the opening lines of *Brod und Wein*: 'Round us the town is at rest; the street, in pale lamplight, falls quiet / And, their torches ablaze, coaches rush through and away' (Hölderlin 2007: 151). The original reads:

> *Rings um ruhet die Stadt; still wird die erleuchtete Gasse,/ Und, mit Fakeln geschmükt, rauschen die Wagen hinweg.*
>
> (Hölderlin 2007: 150)

For all its slight stiffness – or perhaps precisely because of it – Hamburger succeeds best in conveying the sudden sense of movement at the end of the couplet: his 'coaches rush through and away' catches the little flourish of the 'hinweg', as carriages and wagons disappear from the imagined, town-bound spectator through the suburbs and out into the darkness (where the Erlking may be waiting). Hamburger also does his utmost not to steer the reader towards one preferred reading or another. As the writer of the cover notes for the Anvil edition of his translations observes, he confronts us with the darkness of Hölderlin's own words (Hölderlin 2004a). He respects the enigma.

Another of Hölderlin's translators, Gode von Aesch, has underlined how much the translator's mission 'is not to bring the foreign text to the reader but the reader to the foreign text'; he cites Ortega y Gasset, who insisted on translation's potential to enrich the translator's language (Gode von Aesch 1965: 17). The translator must pay careful attention both to meaning and to atmosphere, refined by his textual, intertextual, contextual and biographical knowledge. Hölderlin's deliberately naive tone in, for example, *Die Wanderung* (*The Journey*), required for Michael Hamburger the translation 'free as' rather than 'free like' swallows, in the line *Frei sei'n, wie die Schwalben, die Dichter*: 'free as swallows the poets are'. A simile, because it is a rhetorical, poetic artifice, would have been 'out of tone', out of tune with Hölderlin's colloquial Schwäbisch. When similes occur it is precisely because 'one thing is *not* like another'; we are merely asked to suspend disbelief and accept. The translator must be alert and sensitive enough to avoid this, and to understand how far the 'as', which is closer to a folk-form of speech in which one thing is simply allowed to *be* another, invites and opens the reader's capacity for mental and emotional activity. Swallows are driven to migrate, they are not free at all; their mobility is compulsive, like the poet's, perhaps. Like the poet, too, they have more than one home and are at greatest risk between homes. Thus there emerges a 'whole complex of implications – even the danger incurred by Hölderlin in his strenuous imaginative flights and the price [madness] he had to pay for them . . .' (Hamburger 2003: xiv).

This single image of the swallow, with its problem of translation, retains its echo when we come to other parts of the work. In *Lebenslauf* (*The Course of Life*), an ode written between 1798 and 1803, the poet almost seems, through an analysis of the limitations of freedom, to have found resolution. Not for nothing, the poet writes, does our arc, which is never a straight line, bring us back to our starting place; he learns

to grasp his own freedom
To be gone where he's moved to go

. . . verstehe die Freiheit,
Aufzubrechen, wohin er will
(Hölderlin 2007: 60–1)

Hamburger writes of the 'reticence and impersonality' of Hölderlin's poems, which was based on the poet's own sense of the limitations of his scope and vision; he subjected himself to a severe discipline of the imagination. He moved from generic to vivid, sensuous terms; from figures to images. He combined the directness of common speech with daring elipse, inversion, ambiguity and obscurity (Hamburger 2007: xxiii–iv). Here, for example, are some lines from *Der Ister* which, in Hamburger's translation, have a quality that is both naive and deeply mysterious:

> Yet almost this river seems
> To travel backwards and
> I think it must come from
> The East.
> Much could
> Be said about this. And why does
> It cling to the mountains, straight? The other,
> The Rhine, has gone away
> Sideways. Not for nothing rivers flow
> Through dry land. But how? A sign is needed . . .

> *Der scheinet aber fast*
> *Rükwärts zu gehen und*
> *Ich mein, er müsse kommen*
> *Von Osten.*
> *Viels wäre*
> *Zu sagen davon. Und warum hängt er*
> *An den Bergen gerad? Der andre*
> *Der Rhein ist seitwärts*
> *Hinweggegangen. Umsonst nicht gehn*
> *Im Trok5nen die Ströme. Aber wie? Ein Zeichen braucht es . . .*
> (Hölderlin 2007: 256–7)

Elsewhere, but not, interestingly, in the verses of his madness, the language can fragment. A psychoanalytic reader might be struck by how, as in this example from *Wie wenn am Feiertage . . . As on a holiday . . .* , things start to fall to pieces when an absent father is invoked, who has a 'ray' which recalls

Freud's Schreber. The poet's hold on the Symbolic seems to be threatened, like Schreber's, as he approaches the void lurking behind a failure of Oedipal organisation. In this view, to extrapolate from the case made by Laplanche (Laplanche 1961), Hölderlin's life's work was devoted to warding off this threat.[2]

> For if only we are pure in heart,
> Like children, and our hands are guiltless,
>
> The Father's ray, the pure, will not sear our hearts
> And, deeply convulsed, and sharing his sufferings
> Who is stronger than we are, yet in the far-flung down-rushing storms
>
> The God, when he draws near, will the heart stand fast.
> But, oh, my shame! when of
>
> My shame!
>
> . . .
>
> *Denn sind nur reinen Herzens,*
> *Wie Kinder, wir, sind schuldlos unsere Hände,*
>
> *Des Vaters Stral, der reine versengt es nicht*
> *Und tieferschüttert, die Leiden des Stärkeren*
> *Mitleidend, bleibt in den hochherstürzenden Stürmen*
>
> *Des Gottes, wenn er nahet, das Herz doch fest.*
> *Doch weh mir! Wenn von*
>
> *Weh mir!*
>
> . . .
>
> (Hölderlin 2007: 176–7)

Like all poets, he raided the inarticulate, but few before or since have dared make the struggle so overt, so much their poetic (non-)ground.

It may come as no surprise to learn that since Hölderlin's work began, in the mid-nineteenth century, to attract wider attention, there have been multiple and highly contrasting critical understandings, different ways of responding to or appropriating his œuvre. Nietzsche wrote an important essay on him in 1861: Hölderlin exemplified the revolt of the Genius. For Wilhelm Dilthey and Stefan Georg, following Nietzsche, he was the poet of inwardness and pure aesthetics. For the great Marxist critic Georg Lukács and other, particularly German-speaking critics of the left, Hölderlin was the quintessential intellectual 'caught between the utopian and tragic dimensions of history' (Fehervary 1977: 11). In the 1920s, 1930s and during the Second World War (Fehervary 1977: 11), Hölderlin was the dark, Nordic poetic and militaristic inspiration for the German Youth Movement (Fehervary 1977: 24). He lent himself to Nazi vulgarisation: his despair stemmed from the fact that he never got to meet Hitler and enjoy living in the Third Reich, the coming of which he had dreamed (Lukács 1968 [1934]: 147–8). Martin Heidegger, the Nazi-appointed rector of the University of Freiburg, delivered an important lecture course on him in 1942, and in a certain sense regarded his whole philosophical life's work as 'a dialogue with Hölderlin' (Heidegger in 1966, cited in Wolin 1993: 113).[3] Hölderlin was, for Heidegger, 'the pre-cursor of poets in a destitute time' who does not, however, 'go off into a future; rather, he arrives out of that future, in such a way that the future is present only in the arrival of his words' (Heidegger 1975a: 142).

For other pre- and post-war existentialists Hölderlin was the foundational poet of the existential curse; he could be seen, for example, as belonging to a lineage Hölderlin–Kierkegaard–Heidegger/Sartre (Gode von Aesch 1965: 14). For Laplanche, who published his doctoral thesis on Hölderlin in 1961, *Hyperion* was less a novel about aloneness in the universe than about inter-subjectivity. The poet's later insanity might be understood as *l'absence d'un défaut* (Laplanche 1961: 132), the absence of a lack, and the consequence of a failure of Oedipal mourning; poetry and myth helped hold Hölderlin together before he tipped into psychosis. Later critics, for example Alice Kuzniar, have viewed him through post-structuralist spectacles: Hölderlin instates Derridian *différance*. His poems are the sites of constantly deferred meanings; he refuses to let 'utterance be reduced to pure content' (Kuzniar 1987: 5). The exemplary poet produced a body of work of exemplary openness.

Modern commentators have tended to call Hölderlin's madness schizophrenia. Others have suggested he faked madness in order to avoid arrest for treason, at a time when large numbers of students were being rounded up for sympathising with French revolutionary principles (Rosen 1998: 125). Lukács, in his essay of 1934, implied that it was the result of what was for Hölderlin a world-historical conflict. There was in Germany simply no audience, no plebian mass, to which Hölderlin's more revolutionary Jacobin statements, as Lukács saw them, for instance in *Hyperion*, could be addressed (Lukács 1968 [1934]: 138 etc.).[4] There is certainly a sense in which Rousseauian, revolutionary ideals and *Naturphilosphie* come together in Hölderlin. Diotima, in her farewell letter to Hyperion, writes:

> And if I should become a plant, would the loss be so great? I shall still exist. How could I vanish from the sphere of life wherein the eternal love, which is common to all, joins all natures? How could I sever myself from the union which links all beings?
>
> (cited in Lukács 1968 [1934]: 150)

For Lukács, Hölderlin's nostalgia for a Hellenic golden age was both the expression of his revolutionary hopes, and, through an effect of contrast, an indictment of the present. Hölderlin's Hellenism embodied a recognition of the failure of his generation's hopes; for Lukács, the failure of Hölderlin's private aspirations was 'the inevitable consequence of [a] great general failure'. Hölderlin was above all an elegaic poet, and in elegy, according to Schiller's definition, 'the sorrow must result only from an enthusiasm roused by the ideal' (Lukács 1968 [1934]: 151). Thus the reader too experiences the gap and sense of loss. Lukács aimed to show that only through grasping this historical contradiction might we come to a 'correct' understanding of Hölderlin. However, he does not offer it as an easy understanding, in the sense of a straightforward, discursive elucidation. Lukács not only helps us see that the work is the product of specific historical contingency, he also clarifies an important aspect of Hölderlin's claim to greatness: he was too genuine a poet not always to echo 'the momentary and concrete occasion of his experience, he has no need therefore to rehearse . . . in abstract terms the ultimate bases of the individual experience he expresses' (Lukács 1968 [1934]: 146).

Heidegger – politically Lukács's polar opposite; in the year Lukács wrote his essay Heidegger was appointed to his Freiburg post by the Nazis[5] – was close to Lukács in this respect. For Heidegger, too, Hölderlin was far from being a metaphysical poet. Metaphysical interpretations, Heidegger told the audience of his lectures on *The Ister* in 1942, cannot help us comprehend Hölderlin's poetry. His rivers, for example, are not symbolic images of something higher or deeper, in such a way that the superior and true comes to be identified with the spiritual and non-corporeal; in Hölderlin's mind is no such distinction between sensuous and non-sensuous, the sensible and the intelligible (it can indeed be disturbing, as Charles Rosen has noted, to realise that he really did accept the literal existence of the ancient gods (Rosen 1998:123)). Hölderlin is concerned to preserve the river's enigmatic quality. Heidegger quotes the final lines of the poem: 'Yet what that one does, the river, / Nobody knows' (Heidegger 1996 [1984]: 16–18, and see Hölderlin 2007: 256–7). Heidegger uses the word *Rätsel*, which can mean 'riddle' as well as 'enigma'; but this does not mean the river is like a puzzle to be solved, but rather something we should bring closer to us *as* an enigma (Heidegger 1996 [1984]: 34–5); Heidegger implies that the poetry similarly calls on us in this way. The river, like the poem itself, is a kind of dwelling place for human beings, yet one that is hard to appropriate; with Hölderlin, it is allowed to remain foreign. It flows into the future. The river is the journeying itself: the journeying of becoming 'homely', or the place arrived at in and through the journeying. It is 'the locality of the dwelling of human beings as historical upon the earth' (Heidegger 1996 [1984]: 33). Such too might the analyst's and the patient's journeying become, along the flow of their words.

I shall extract a couple of further related themes from Heidegger's work on Hölderlin, which does more than any other commentary to suggest the quality of attention that reading him encourages. For Heidegger, metaphysical misreading is linked to another central topic in his 'dialogue with Hölderlin':

Hölderlin held open the possibility of a thinking that would oppose the instrumental, performative, calculative thinking of modernity, a thinking that might transcend the technological. In the mid-1960s, late in his life, Heidegger was insisting that this opposition must be undertaken on home ground, not in some distant or abstract conceptual realm:

> a reversal can only be prepared in the world where the modern technological world originated, and . . . it cannot happen by any takeover by Zen Buddhism or any other Eastern experiences of the world. There is need for re-thinking which is to be carried out with the help of the European tradition and of a new appropriation of that tradition. Thinking itself can be transformed only by a thinking which has the same origin and calling . . .
>
> (Heidegger, cited in Wolin 1993: 113)

In the 1942 lectures he spoke of how for calculative thinking a thing exists only in terms of what it does, its performance; it is thus securely framed within space and time, which are understood as ordered and calculable, so much so that we are likely to take them for granted. But Hölderlin's poetry – perhaps indeed all poetry – can open us to other ways of experiencing locality, time and journeying.

In a long digression on Sophocles's *Antigone*, which Hölderlin translated, and which according to Heidegger radiates throughout his poetry (Heidegger 1996 [1984]: 51), Heidegger ponders *das Unheimliche*, the un-at-home and uncanny, and the uncanniness of human beings which consists in their capacity for catastrophe, which can turn them away from their own essence. We are beings of risk, capable of being mistaken, and of seeking the homely only to find it refuses itself to us (Heidegger 1996 [1984]: 74–7). Poeticising, Heidegger infers from his reading of *Antigone*, is revealing 'that which is always already revealed . . . and is the nearest of all that is near' (Heidegger 1996 [1984]: 119–20); 'becoming homely in being unhomely', the 'unhomely being homely of human beings upon the earth', is worthy of poeticising (Heidegger 1996 [1984]: 120–1). He had in mind the choral ode from *Antigone*, which like *The Ister* starts with a call to the rising sun; it was perhaps the ode's dwelling on the enigma of the everyday that, as Heidegger said, meant it spoke ever anew to Hölderlin.

For Heidegger, Hölderlin's poetry requires that we transform the ways in which we think and experience: that we go beyond a thinking based on symbols, representations and images. Hölderlin, wrote Heidegger, means us to understand that to dwell poetically upon the earth, which is what we must do, we must bear it, suffer it, rather than attempt to grasp or appropriate it. If we are lucky, we may be struck by the truth of Hölderlin's poetry, but first have to allow ourselves to ponder it, even from afar. Heidegger concluded his 1942 lectures with a quotation from the hymn *The Journey*. In Hamburger's translation:

If someone tries to grasp it by stealth, he holds
A dream in his hand, and him who uses force
To make himself its peer, it punishes.
Yet often it takes by surprise
A man whose mind it has hardly entered.

Zum Traume wirds ihm, will es Einer
Beschleichen und straft den, der
Ihm gleichen will mit Gewalt;
Oft überraschet es einen,
Der eben kaum es gedacht hat.

(Hölderlin 2007: 188–9)

Hölderlin's 'openness', comparable to Goya's, is a result of historical contingency as much as strategy: Hölderlin was a revolutionary in an inhospitable climate. In this and other respects, he is like his contemporary William Blake; the similarity of spirit between the lines cited above and Blake's *Eternity's Sunrise* will not go unnoticed. Hölderlin constantly, with constancy, spoke of crisis, with acute consciousness of the disparity between mind and world. For Lukács he was caught between Kant and Hegel, and made his theoretical contribution, through his philosophising with Hegel, to the elaboration of the dialectic. In *Hyperion*, Hölderlin cited the Athenian philosopher Heraclitus's insight, so crucial for Hegel, that there is a 'one differentiated from itself' (Hölderlin 1965 [1797, 1799]: 93), as the founding moment of all philosophy, the point of departure for thought;[6] hence, Lukács concluded that for Hölderlin philosophy is identical with dialectic (Lukács 1968 [1934]: 151). More recent commentators would go further in resisting the closure that the Hegelian/Marxian dialectic, for all its continuously unfolding quality, might imply. For 'With every inflection Hölderlin's voice recants itself, reinstates difference, and . . . holds teleological narrative drive in suspension' (Kuzniar 1987: 196). Hölderlin's, and the Romantic generation's, 'radically new, unprecedented way of structuring the future' (Kuzniar 1987: 199) opens a new problematic of 'dwelling' in the present. Reading him is an induction into analytic dwelling.

Laplanche ended his book with a startling and terrifying image of Hölderlin on the brink of madness; it echoes the visual language of Goya.

We should . . . envisage him racing the cone of shadow cast by the earth, at the very moment it reaches him – not fleeing it but fixing directly onto the sun. Only you'd need completely to invert this image, as in a photographic negative in which the sun is black.

(Laplanche 1961: 133; see also Kuzniar 1987: 155 on
light–dark imagery in the poems)

Staying with Hamburger's translations of Hölderlin, with their respect for the darkness, I begin to learn to bear the sense of catastrophe that hovers over the moments of bliss. I have to accept the limits of my grasp. There is always another impenetrable text in a foreign language, a lived, breathed idiom.

Novalis

Here is Laplanche's colleague Jean-Bertrand Pontalis:

> Wherever I open Novalis's collected *Fragments*, what do I find? Flashes of thought shooting across the horizon at incredible speed and lighting it up. As if the Rimbaud of *Les Illuminations*, the Leonardo of the *Notebooks*, as if quickness of intelligence, poetic *éclat* and infinite curiosity had managed to fuse into one.
>
> These fragments are the polar opposite of a system and even of a work. They expose the illusion of a 'beautiful whole' – unless each fragment can be said to add up to a whole.
>
> Novalis stays as close as possible to the mind's productions, he sticks to the moment at which the idea, with unerring directness and the utmost impatience to get itself said, bursts out into words – its surging, its lighting up. There's no question of asking it to wait, that particular idea, image, sensation which has sprung up without warning from who knows where, which has precipitated itself in you, and demands, now, immediately, to stand on its own two feet, regardless.
>
> In his most boring book, Freud laboriously analysed the 'technique' of the joke, of the *Witz*, while Novalis *is* the *Witz*, the rocket, the spark, the grain of pollen swept along by the wind. 'Sometimes the analyst's interpretations, when they seek neither to explain nor to understand, are like lightning flashes ripping open a heavy mass of cloud, lightning flashes electrifying the night sky.'
>
> (Pontalis 2002: 22–3)

(And so, we might add, can be the utterances of the patient.)

Another writer, Arthur Versluis, reacting to Novalis from something closer to a New Age perspective, uses similar imagery to Pontalis's. He speaks of

> meanings often so ethereal that they excite a flash of insight only to be lost with the onset of more discursive thought . . . in reading the *Fragments* one encounters spaces across which the mind leaps, thereby attaining a flash of recognition unavailable to one reading continuous, unbroken prose . . . There is a void within many of these aphorisms, and many times the reader must complete the thought . . . If Novalis's works sometimes appear inaccessible, it is often because one has not arced across that inner synapse . . .
>
> (Versluis 1989: 20–1)

Novalis's 'observations are wary and elusive as deer: one only catches fleeting glimpses' (Versluis 1989: 16–17).

Like Hölderlin's, Novalis's writing is one of 'sustained deviation and displacement per se' (Kuzniar 1987: 194). Certainly, reading the *Fragments* is rarely the same experience twice, and it is a mixed experience. Sometimes he seems to speak with great immediacy and a sense of modernity: 'We are here outside the times of the universally valid Forms' (Novalis 1989: 69 (no. 234)). At other times he can go dead, and appear to be stuck in an irredeemably mystical, Christian neo-Platonist past, fit only for a Victorian keepsake book. But there is something about Novalis that will not let the reader override the possibility that it may be he who has gone dead or deaf. The experience is akin to that which Marion Milner described in relation to her own internal world and its mysterious 'answering activity', on days when 'answer came there none' (Milner 1987a: 56 ff.). When Novalis does come alive, it feels that I am as key to the process as the words and thoughts he 'objectively' wrote. Form, content and reading process weave together. It is quite possible to look for a 'model of mind' in Novalis, but it is the feeling of being caught up in a dynamic process, in which any sought-after model is elusive, that can really take hold. As Alice Kuzniar has written,

> For Novalis, the task of the reader is not qualitatively different from his own task as writer; it is the temporal continuation of his work. Meaning cannot be excavated the more the reader probes into the text. On the contrary, the text requires extension and extrapolation: 'Der wahre Leser muß der erweiterte Autor seyn' [The true reader must be the extended author].
>
> (Kuzniar 1987: 94–5)

The critic Glyn Hughes sums up: 'behind the sometimes vague rhetoric and the conditioned imagery of the period is a profoundly disturbing modern figure, attempting nothing less than a total reordering of experience.' Fichte's philosophical system, with its emphasis on the creative power of the ego, helped Novalis to 'unleash the questionings of his own mind'. His aim became 'to achieve in language what logic has left undone' (Hughes 1979: 77–8), and his vision reached beyond the realm of Platonic *Idea* into the day-to-day.

'Novalis', Georg Philipp Friedrich von Hardenberg, was born in 1772 and died before he was 30 of tuberculosis. A man of practical abilities, both technical and administrative, he worked as an inspector of the salt mines in his native Saxony. He was educated, to an even greater extent than Coleridge, in what we would now call science, in physics, chemistry, geology and astronomy. His approach to science was to regard it both as the exercise of observation and reasoning and, following Fichte, as another way of dreaming the world. Novalis felt, however, that Fichte was too concerned with rational consciousness, which 'left gaps which human experience cries aloud to fill' (Hughes 1979: 63); the major gap, for Novalis, was the experience of love.

Fichte's concept of the Not-I, the *Nicht-Ich*, felt utterly inadequate to a young man whose most powerful and terrible experience was the death in 1797 of his 15-year-old fiancée Sophie von Kühn; the events of 1797 are the subject of Penelope Fitzgerald's evocative, allusive *The Blue Flower* (Fitzgerald 2002 [1995]). The *Nicht-Ich* became, within what Novalis called his *Liebesreligion*, his religion of love, the *Du*, the 'thou'. This 'thou' was not merely a neutral other, but an equal to the 'I'.[7] Novalis speaks in order to engage the reader personally and as an equal.

Von Hardenberg became Novalis in 1798, adopting the name for his book *Blüthenstaub* (*Pollen*), a collection of the Fragments that had first begun to appear that year in the Schlegels' seminal journal *Athenäum*. The idea of the Fragment was formulated by Friedrich Schlegel after he had been impressed by Chamfort's *Pensées, Maximes et Anecdotes* following its publication in 1795; as a literary form it was to have a brief and spectacular flowering, from 1798 to 1800, the lifespan of the *Athenäum* itself (Gasché 1991: viii). Hughes, using that imagery of sparks and explosions that had continued vigour in the hands of Pontalis and Versluis, theorised the Fragment thus:

> the fragmentary form . . . conveys not so much want of system as the potential of the subject, which it deliberately leaves open-ended. The nature of [the author's] thought lies in its constant flux and in the daring of its associative leaps, the mind exploding with ideas, sparks flying from its own incandescence.
>
> (Hughes 1979: 51)

For both Friedrich Schlegel and Novalis, the fragment was 'something more allusive, more open-ended than the rather sententious aphorisms of the eighteenth century' (Hughes 1979: 64); Novalis, in addition, was wary that the fragment should not become just another literary manner, a game of clever paradoxes, commenting that 'Friedrich goes in for poetic trifling with speculation' (Hughes 1979: 51). As a strategy out of the impasse he cultivated his own version of Schlegel's *Witz* (Hughes 1979: 67). In Novalis's hands, *Witz*, 'the principle of combinatory art', is not quite translatable as 'wit': it is more embodied, something emerging from the profoundly felt or dreamt, like an epiphany or a *Capricho*. Novalis's fragments, wrote Hughes, 'are more confessional, more speculative, depth-charges rather than constructs'; Novalis himself described them in a letter to Schlegel as 'fragments of the continuing dialogue with myself – cuttings (in a horticultural sense)' (Hughes 1979: 64). He *was* the *Witz*.

Novalis's *Witz*, in Hughes's characterisation, also allows associative leaps not merely for their own sakes but in order to suggest 'infinite abundance', to open out new recognitions and bring together scattered insights (Hughes 1979: 53). Here was the poem in its most radically open-ended form. 'The recognition of its own finite nature points forward to the unattainable infinite . . . The poem is no longer a finished statement, but an insight into a dynamically expanding range of possibilities' (Hughes 1979: 56). The writing itself is a performative, time- and contingency-bound, always provisional act; as Kuzniar has put it, 'Novalis refuses to sustain the notion that writing could ever prefigure an atemporal moment. For him a writing which would claim to do such a thing would err. The absolute could then command the arrest of the poet's pen' (Kuzniar 1987: 121).

After Sophie von Kühn's death, Novalis wrote to a friend: 'I shall retreat into myself more and more. Thus the path to the hereafter will become familiar. The chasm which separates us will become narrower and narrower' (cited in Versluis 1989: 10). It is perhaps not surprising that the earliest Fragments, like this one published in the first issue of *Athenäum*, should have a grief-stricken, other-worldly ring:

> The external world is the world of shadows; it projects its shadows into the kingdom of light. Now indeed everything within us seems dark, lonely and without form; but how different all will appear when this darkness has gone and the shadow-body has passed away.
>
> (cited in Hughes 1979: 65)

But other imperatives were at work too. There was *Wollust*, which could mean both joy in life and that which, like *jouissance*, can produce ecstasy. There was the idea of 'magic idealism', deriving from Fichte: for Novalis magic, of which we all potentially capable, was 'the art of using the world of the senses in one's own way' (Fragment of 1798, cited in Hughes 1979: 66). There was also Novalis's own excitability, and excitability had a particular status in the 1790s: in contemporary (Brownian) medicine it was called *Reiz*, a sort of life-force. Novalis the young writer, excited by writing, sought to generate *Reiz* in the reader too; he courted 'incomprehensibility as stimulus (*Reiz*)' (Calhoon 1992: 19). As he put it himself in another Fragment:

> In praise of the mysterious state. The unknown is that which attracts one towards knowing. The known attracts no more. The absolutely unknown is equivalent to absolute attraction. Practically I [*sic*]. The possibility of knowledge is itself the highest attraction – the absolute unknown. The unknown Beyond in the sciences. Mystification.
>
> (Novalis 1989: 116 (no. 480))

Reiz, to put it in a more modern idiom, was stimulus toward the emergence of desire, the desire above all to go on desiring. Such perhaps was the 'Romanticisation of the world' which Novalis proposed in probably the most famous of all the Fragments:

> The world must become romanticised. So one finds the original sense renewed. Romanticisation is nothing but a qualitative exponentiation. The

lower self becomes identified with the better self in this operation. In the same way we ourselves are such a qualitative exponential series. This operation is still totally unknown. In it I give the common sense a higher sense, the quotidian a longing, homesick aspect, the familiar the majesty of the unfamiliar, the finite an infinite shine – hence I romanticise it. – The inverse is the operation for the higher, unfamiliar, mystic and infinite. – this becomes, through these combinations, logarithmic – it becomes a familiar expression. Romantic philosophy. Novel language. Lingua romana. Higher exchange and reduction.

(Novalis 1989: 56 (no. 162))

It means 'The art of estranging in a pleasant way ("die Kunst, auf eine *angenehme* Art zu *befremden*"), making a subject strange and yet familiar and alluring, that is romantic poetics' (Novalis 1989: 109 (no. 446)).

The Fragment for Novalis was to be unlike the riddle in so far as it was irreducible, not open to being worked out or solved. 'Many books do not need to be reviewed, for they contain the interpretation already in themselves [*Sie enhalten schon die Recension mit*]' (Kuzniar 1987: 123). Novalis produced Fragments in their hundreds. They might be compared to William Blake's *Proverbs of Hell*, written in the early 1790s; they are generally lighter in spirit, but no less challenging. For Hughes they are simply 'the most breathtaking of all the products of German Romanticism', the fruit of 'the astonishing breadth and agility of [Novalis's] mind, the daring and beauty of his analogies, the creativity and novelty of his language . . .' (Hughes 1979: 65). An album of Fragments and extracts from Fragments follows: enigmatic, philosophical, humane. Perhaps those I have chosen tend towards the discursive; I have been unable to resist choosing some, and extracts from others, which seem to speak with directness to the concerns of psychoanalysts. Nevertheless, in their compression, they can still qualify as *scriptible*, and tap deeply into the reader's own creative, meaning-making capacities.

The first are from *Pollen, Blüthenstaub*:

> a word forms a nodal point in an unending contextual chain: every individual is the central point of an emanational system . . . the fragment, like the pollen grain . . . wafted in the wind, is received elsewhere than at its place of origin and excites further reflection . . . everything is spermatic (*Alles is Samenkorn*).

(cited in Kuzniar 1987: 99)

> Affiliations are contiguous and unpredictable, not predetermined, codifiable, and continuous. Links in the chain are forged by chance.

(cited in Kuzniar 1987: 84)

Every word has its peculiar meaning, its secondary meanings, its false and totally arbitrary meanings. Etymology is diverse, genetic, pragmatic, as the need requires it.

(cited in Kuzniar 1987: 95)

The impulse towards association is the impulse towards organization . . .

(Novalis 1989: 31 (no. 36))

The fewer the axioms, the higher the science.

(Novalis 1989: 35 (no. 54))

The more ignorant one is by nature, the more one's capacity for knowledge. Each new perception makes a more profound and living impression . . .

(Novalis 1989: 35–6 (no. 58))

The most ingenious insight is discerning the proper employment of insight.

(Novalis 1989: 39 (no. 81))

These are from *New Fragments*:

One is alone with whomever, whatever one loves.

(Novalis 1989: 57 (no. 168))

How little people have cultivated multiplicity – have cultivated silent total watchfulness of all which is in and about them, in each instant educated. Bonnet's observation: Watchfulness is the mother of genius.

(Novalis 1989: 64 (no. 202))

Even chance is not unfathomable – it has its regularity.

(Novalis 1989: 67 (no. 224))

Play is experimenting with chance.

(Novalis 1989: 67 (no. 225))

All that is visible rests on the invisible – the audible upon the inaudible – the felt upon the unfelt. Perhaps thinking rests on unthinking.

(Novalis 1989: 70 (no. 240))

What is man? A consummate trope of the spirit. All true communication is also sensory imagery – and so aren't the lover's caresses the highest communication?

(Novalis 1989: 74 (no. 263))

Individuality in nature is wholly infinite . . .

(Novalis 1989: 79 (no. 290))

And these from *The Encyclopaedia*:

All illusion is as essential as truth, just as the body is essential to the soul. Error is the indispensable instrument of truth. With error I make truth – the complete employment of error – the complete repossession of truth . . .

(Novalis 1989: 87 (no. 332))

To search after originality is a more learned, yet crude, egotism. Whoever doesn't treat each strange thought as his own, and each of his own thoughts as an alien thought, is no true scholar . . . For the true scholar there is nothing familiar and nothing strange. All is familiar and alien at once to him . . .

(Novalis 1989: 84 (no. 316))

To think is to speak. To speak and to do or to make are only modifications of the same operation. God spoke, and it was light, and it was.

(Novalis 1989: 84 (no. 320))

Contrasts are inverse analogies.

(Novalis 1989: 85 (no. 321))

On illness, music and listening:

Each illness is a musical problem – the healing a musical solution . . .

(Novalis 1989: 98 (no. 385))

Medicine must become something wholly different. The teaching of the art of living and of the nature of life . . . The completed physics will be the universal teaching of the art of living . . .

(Novalis 1989: 98 (no. 386))

The body is the product of and also the modification of sensation – a function of soul and world . . .

(Novalis 1989: 99 (no. 390))

The next two Fragments chime with some of Christopher Bollas's thinking (Bollas 2007, 2009):

The temper of a word points to musical proportions in the soul. The acoustics of the soul are still dark and obscure, but perhaps of a very momentous scope. Harmonic and disharmonic oscillations.

(Novalis 1989: 99–100 (no. 396))

Doesn't language also have its treble, bass and tenor notes? Nor also its measure, nor its keynote – nor meaningful stops and tempo? Are not the diverse genre diverse Instruments?

(Novalis 1989: 105 (no. 420))

The dream teaches us a remarkable way of intruding the faculty of our soul into each object – each in itself instantly transformed.

(Novalis 1989: 102 (no. 404))

It is peculiar that the association of ecstasy, religion, and the ferocity of the people has not long since been made, considering their inner kinship and the familiarity of the tendencies.

(Novalis 1989: 102 (no. 408))

If thoughts can't be made perceptible (and voluntary) to you, then do the reverse, making external things intentionally perceivable – which is tantamount to this: if ideas of external things aren't possible, make external things thoughts. If you can't make a thought independent from you, detached – and strange to you – in other words, making the soul externally manifested – then proceed to attempt the opposite with external things – and exchange these mentally.

Both operations are idealistic. Whoever has both completely in his grasp is a magical idealist. Shouldn't the completion of both operations be dependent upon one another?

(Novalis 1989: 120–1 (no. 497))

Alice Kuzniar noted that the verb *schweben*, the root of the adjective in Freud's *gleichschwebende Aufmerksamkeit*, evenly suspended attention, recurs throughout Novalis's writing; it is a token of his refusal to alight on one element in an unending analogy. 'Should there exist a higher sphere than mere being or chaos', Novalis wrote, 'it would be poised between being and non-being – hovering between the two [*das Schweben zwischen beyden*] – ineffable. And here we have the concept of life'. Novalis never let his poetic voice stay in one mode for long. In his novel *Heinrich von Ofterdingen* 'intimations are short and characters are labile' (Kuzniar 1987: 99); the work approximates to what Friedrich Schlegel called the enigmatic portrayal of an enigma. *Heinrich von Ofterdingen* has a dreamlike quality, in which there are 'so many correspondences with the invisible that the world of the senses is increasingly overlaid by them'; Novalis was, as Hughes says, almost obsessed by analogies and their symbolism (Hughes 1979: 74). The novel's mysterious Blue Flower ultimately stands for all these correspondences and analogies; it came to be an emblem of Romanticism itself. It moves from realism to dream, and future to past and back again, disrupting temporal sequence and expectation. 'Joyce shows the shadows of Agamemnon or Ulysses looming behind the citizenry in the bars of Dublin; Novalis sets deities and personified natural forces alongside human representatives' (Hughes 1979: 76–7). The mysterious, unknowable nature of these deities and forces points to a constitutive, 'originary lack and awareness of the fragmentary', which 'prompts the longing for completion and propels the novel forward; it generates the narrative': the art of estranging in a pleasant manner (Kuzniar 1987: 119).

Heinrich reads a book in a cave; he does not understand the language but enjoys the pictures; perhaps he sees himself in the protagonist. What he reads has neither beginning nor end. He does not know how to interpret the tales of the stranger, and he is unable to put their effect on him into words; he 'surmises there must be many words he does not know' (Kuzniar 1987: 103). The reader too is thus left in the lurch. Unanswered questions raise themselves in the reader's mind, which probably echo those in Heinrich's, although he does not articulate them: does the story he is reading prefigure his own life, or is he re-enacting an old story?

> Will the illuminated manuscript have been Heinrich's autobiography? . . . This episode precludes, though, the very act of closure it invites by virtue of this very unending mirroring not only between the episode and its text but also between Heinrich as reader and ourselves . . . Because both texts lack closure, their reception becomes all important. However our readings are destined to be unending . . .
>
> (Kuzniar 1987: 131–2)

Novalis's work – we have not touched on the remarkable poetry, the *Hymns to the Night* and *Spiritual Songs*, or the fragmentary novel *The Disciples at Sais* – was characterised by both spontaneity and restraint. He can get hold of us because, like Goya, he is the 'impersonal author [who] embodies a multiplicity of readers' (Kuzniar 1987: 123). His Romanticism is not confessional, not that of the explicit autobiography. In this way too his work is 'in the place of the analyst'. For 'The whole of Novalis's writings is informed by a poetics that links strangeness with familiarity, mystery with understanding, and repression with pleasure, justifying ultimately the kind of authority that turns knowledge into enigma in the first place' (Calhoon 1992: 19).

Chapter 5

Baudelaire and the malaise of modernity

Enigmatic first encounters

How the poet Baudelaire can accost us, all unawares, and hook us in. He slips his arm under ours, like the enigmatic Miss Scalpel in the prose poem *Mademoiselle Bistouri*. Like Miss Scalpel, Baudelaire leads us into a world that is decentring and profoundly personal, ripe with suggestion, menace and aching melancholy, full of dark humour and contradiction, and subject to its own unanswerable logic.

Miss Scalpel mistakes, or pretends to mistake, the curious narrator for a doctor, and invites him to go along with her. He accepts – for he is, he tells us, a 'passionate lover of mysteries'. Her shabby dwelling turns out to be decorated with engravings of famous doctors. Ignoring his protestations she continues to insist that he too must be a doctor. Finally, she lets him in on a little secret: she would like one of her doctors to visit her fresh from the operating table, still wearing his apron, perhaps with a little blood on it. The prose poem concludes:

> What bizarreries can one not find in a great town, when one knows how to walk about and to look? Life teems with innocent monsters . . . Lord, have pity, have pity on mad men and women! Oh Creator! Can monsters exist in His eyes Who alone knows why they exist, how they *made themselves*, and how they could *not have helped making themselves*? ('. . . comment ils *se sont faits* et comment ils auraient pu *ne pas se faire*?')
>
> (Petits poèmes en prose, XLVII.
Baudelaire 1975–76: I, 353–6)

Like Mademoiselle Bistouri, Baudelaire can terrify. He rarely seems frightened himself – horrified or despairing, rather, at the same time as unflinchingly curious. He likened this curiosity, his 'taste for horror', to a surgical scalpel, and applied it to himself – 'Oh! Lord! Give me the strength and courage / To look at my heart and body without disgust!' (lines probably written shortly after a suicide attempt; *Les Fleurs du mal*, CXVI. Baudelaire 1975–76: I, 119). He challenges us to do likewise. In his prose poems, published posthumously in 1869 as *Petits poèmes en prose* and later entitled *Le Spleen de Paris* (*Paris Blues*, in a recent translation (Baudelaire 1989)), Baudelaire evolved a new frame within which to exercise his curiosity, and to dwell on the complex and painful human ironies that it exposed. Baudelaire summed up his ambitions in a dedication:

> Which of us has not . . . dreamt of the miracle of a poetic prose, musical without rhythm and rhyme, supple and jolting enough to adapt itself to the lyrical movements of the soul, the undulations of dreams, sudden leaps of consciousness?
>
> (Baudelaire 1975–76: I, 275–6)

Transgressing genre distinctions, or amounting to a new genre in their own right, the prose poems defy categorisation; it is indeed this fundamental uncertainty of definition which is constitutive (Stephens 1999). In their density and compression (a large number of the fifty pieces in his *Petits poèmes en prose* are half a page or less in length, and the longest is only just over five pages), they have resonances well beyond the immediate circumstances of their making, although they register these too, in layered and oblique ways.

For example, underpinning the 'dialogic' appeal of 'Mademoiselle Bistouri' to a nineteenth-century, metropolitan audience is an awareness, tacitly shared by writer and readers, of the prestige of the medical profession in its expanding public health role, particularly among prostitutes; at one point the narrator jokingly counters Mademoiselle Bistouri by telling her he will return 'after the doctor has been'. For the post-Freudian reader, Mademoiselle Bistouri is also a kind of proto- and anti-Dora. She compels the narrator to recognise the power of the transference. She absolutely insists on his authority as the one presumed to know; at one point she even elicits from him a wish to take her history; her apparent state of misrecognition is the driving force of the piece. Yet how *méconnaissante* is she really? In her insistence on mistaking his identity and refusal to treat him as a mere unknown quantity, she also comprehensively undermines him. In another possible reading, she is the lady of the nocturnal margins who turns the tables both on her clients and on the medical profession whose function it is to police her; she constructs the narrator into a doctor in order to practise her own parodic strategy of defiance. Indeed, she seems fully to identify herself with this strategy, to be unable to help living it out; it has become her desire.[1] She is also the enigmatic, alienated and self-alienated figure of the poet himself, who is only just, through his art, able to keep his own head above the waters of madness – Walter Benjamin's 'lyric poet in the era of high capitalism'.

Formal introductions

Charles Baudelaire (1821–67) has long been regarded as the greatest poet of mid-nineteenth century France. Chronologically and in other senses too, he sits between Victor Hugo and Rimbaud. He is a bridge between Romanticism and Modernism, key features of which are heralded in his poetry and his criticism: intensified reflexivity, symbolic correspondences between scents, sounds and colours, the abstract, musical possibilities of language. Of all poets of the period, that is, prior to Rimbaud, Baudelaire is perhaps the most unsettling, with the most to offer and with which to challenge the analytic practitioner: articulations of the disturbing relations of present to past, the courage to name the horrific and shameful, invitations to wander in a world which is both saturated with feeling and populated by watchful, unknowable others. He is the poet of 'the ephemeral human heart' (Lloyd 2002: 142). Useful introductions to his work in English translation are the two bilingual volumes published by Francis Scarfe in the 1980s (Baudelaire 1986, 1989).

Baudelaire grew up in the aftermath of the revolutionary and Napoleonic period. His elderly father died when he was six, in 1827, and his mother, whom he adored up to his death, remarried a man many years her senior the following year. His step-father, Jacques Aupick, was an army major at the time of his marriage, and ended his career as a senator ('Let's shoot General Aupick!' Baudelaire was heard shouting from the top of a barricade in the February Revolution of 1848 (Pichois and Ziegler 1991: 160)). Aupick died in 1857, the year in which Baudelaire was tried for obscenity over *Les Fleurs du mal*, his only, incomparable collection of poetry; Benjamin was probably correct to claim that historically it was the last volume of poetry to have a Europe-wide impact, beyond a single linguistic area (Benjamin 1983 [1955]: 152). Baudelaire's life-long identification with the oppressed and excluded may have had much to do with his own humiliating dependence: from the age of 23, having spent most of his paternal inheritance and amassed large debts, he was subjected by his step-father and his mother to a judicial arrangement whereby he had to collect instalments of his remaining legacy from the family lawyer. He was effectively a legal minor for the rest of his life.[2]

Like very many nineteenth-century European writers, and many psycho-therapists (although perhaps fewer counsellors), Baudelaire's social back-ground was the more affluent end of bourgeoisie. He was both the beneficiary of this background and alienated from it, and his intense awareness of this permeates his writing on many levels; reading him might help the practising therapist to maintain her own reflectiveness about her own and her patients' relation to class, something which is so often overlooked in psychotherapy trainings.

Baudelaire supplemented his allowance by scratching a living as a critic, and he was an early and perceptive commentator on Goya and an ardent supporter of Delacroix, the leading figure among French Romantic painters;

he moved in bohemian and artistic circles alongside Gautier, Flaubert, Courbet and Manet, and died in Paris, of syphilis, in semi-destitution.

Distinctions between poetry and literary, art and music criticism tend to blur in Baudelaire's work. It is highly varied in mood. The poet of the old and outcast is also the poet of escape into a sensual paradise; both aspects found expression in poems associated with his mistress Jeanne Duval. He articulates new and disquieting conditions in which he is constantly seeking his bearings and the last to claim he knows them. He was the poet of the city of Paris and its people, in its and their particularity and transformations, in the years between the revolutions of 1830, 1848 and 1871.[3] Baudelaire's work registers contradiction and violence.

Contextually, when approaching him for the first time, it is also important to acknowledge the continuing authority of the classical tradition in France in the nineteenth century, with its claims to paternal lineage, immutability and stability. The institutions that enshrined these claims – the Académie Française, the Académie des Beaux-Arts, the Comédie Française – were targets for the mockery of the young, but it was the tradition in which all the great names of French Romanticism, Delacroix, Berlioz, Hugo, Lamartine, Gautier, Baudelaire himself, were educated and with which they had to engage – none to greater transformative effect than Baudelaire. The classical tradition was an aspect of the Lacanian 'Big Other', the ever-elusive, ever-present 'they' who must be reckoned with or placated. It survived in degraded form in the paintings and sculptures of (predominantly female) nudes that crowded the annual or biennial Salons, the official exhibitions of the nation's art.

Baudelaire was just too young to have participated in the cultural battles of the Classics and the Romantics of the 1820s and 1830s, and in the turmoil of artistic activity which was stirred up around Victor Hugo and echoed the political revolution of 1830. By the time Baudelaire started publishing, in the mid-1840s, Romanticism, if not quite domesticated, was no longer the hot issue it had been at the time of the great battle of rival partisans at the first night of Hugo's play *Hernani*. Baudelaire's particular debt to Romanticism was in the liberation it offered to explore new territories of subject matter and emotion, with new means. Use of the *mot propre* in poetry, the down-to-earth and specific word, derived from the colloquialisms of art students (Gautier 1874); the *mot propre* brought an emphasis on the visual into French poetry, for the graphic, colourful and telling image. Like Gautier, Baudelaire first found his voice as an art critic. His problem as a would-be poet was imaginatively formulated, with the hindsight of a couple of generations, by Paul Valéry: 'How to be a great poet, but neither a Lamartine nor a Hugo nor a Musset?' (Valéry in his introduction to a 1926 edition of *Les Fleurs du mal*, cited in Benjamin 1999 [1982]: 228) – perhaps not a Hugo, the revered poet of the Parisian crowd, above all.[4]

The metropolis and the new

Baudelaire saw his task, in the mid-1840s, as to breathe new life into Romanticism, or rather perhaps to free it from stultification in the hands of fashionable and mediocre imitators. Following Stendhal's footsteps, he understood Romanticism to mean art that would be open and responsive to the new, to the rapidly changing conditions of the present. In his review of the Salon of 1846, under the heading 'What is Romanticism?', he cited Stendhal: 'There are as many kinds of beauty as there are habitual ways of seeking happiness.' Romanticism consists, Baudelaire wrote, 'not in choice of subject nor in exact truth, but in a way of feeling'. It is 'the most recent, most current, expression of the beautiful'; it *is* modern art. Romanticism is the -ism of the contingent, of that which belongs to the precise, unique conditions of now. It is 'a conception analogous to the morale of the century'. Hence too – and this is of central importance – the heading of his introduction to the review: 'To the bourgeois'. If this leans partly on the older Romantic/bohemian ethic of outraging the bourgeoisie, *épater le bourgeois*, and on his own ambivalent position in relation to his class, Baudelaire was not being sarcastic when he declared to his bourgeois readership, 'you are the majority'. The modern *was* the bourgeois (Baudelaire 1975–76: II, 420–1; 415).

Baudelaire's originality and inventiveness can be found in his readiness to respond to all that was unprecedented and particular in the experience of living in the mid-nineteenth century metropolis. Yet it was experience that also seemed to feel to him somehow outside or post-history, and it was, as such, extremely difficult to evaluate; perhaps the only possible response was a kind of semi-covert, probing irony. This can give rise to a sense of authorial distance which, once the reader gets a hint of it, is unsettling. 'The wonderful envelops us and rains down upon us, like the atmosphere. But we do not see it', Baudelaire wrote at the end of his *Salon* of 1846 (Baudelaire 1975–76: II, 496). His response to the new can seem imbued with a sense of wonder: 'One must always be drunk', he wrote in the prose poem *Enivrez-vous* (XXXIII, Baudelaire 1975–76: I, 337). But it also embraced boredom and banality; was he perhaps also thinking of soot in a dank Paris November when he wrote of the wonderful raining down? 'Since childhood I have felt two contradictory feelings in my heart, horror and ecstasy of life' (Baudelaire 1975–76: I, 703). He claimed that he was – at least on rare 'fine days of the spirit', that is, days in which crushing awareness of mediocrity did not reign – in love with 'the bitter or heady flavour of the wine of Life' (Baudelaire 1975–76: II, 724, cited in Lloyd 2002: 226). He wrote of the 'heroism of modern life': 'how grand and poetic we are in our cravates and patent leather boots'. But his frock-coated bourgeois of the 1840s are very far from the revolutionary, modern-antique heroes envisaged by the painter David in the 1790s, resolutely reaching out towards a future that would also be a return to the finest human achievements of the classical past. As an art critic, Baudelaire proclaimed the 'genius of the future'; but such an artist would be precisely one who could 'seize the epic side of life today and get us to see and understand . . . how grand and poetic we are', etc. (Baudelaire 1975–76: II, 407).[5] One must always be prepared, in reading him, for things to be double- if not multiple-edged. Baudelaire limbers us up; we must maintain our mental agility.

No Hegelian, he was profoundly sceptical about 'progress', and this was not a mere intellectual posture; the idea simply did not make any sense to him (see, for example, Baudelaire 1975–76: I, 663 and II, 580–1). At the end of his review of the *Salon* of 1845 he wrote, 'to the wind that will be blowing tomorrow no one turns an ear'; this ambiguous sentence seems to suggest both that the future cannot be anticipated, and that, on the contrary, we know it only too well and don't want to know it. He immediately went on to suggest that it is right under our noses, in the present: 'and yet the heroism *of modern life* surrounds and crowds in upon us. Our true feelings suffocate us enough for us to recognise them' (Baudelaire 1975–76: II, 407). These suffocating 'true feelings' included an experience of anomie, boredom, emptiness, jangling irritability, and a restless search for distraction and relief in the face of a pressing lack: spleen and ennui. This, as many following Baudelaire have argued, is the defining condition of the industrial and post-industrial era, and translates, in the super-medicalised language of the early twenty-first century, as depressive illness, acute or generalised anxiety disorder, attention deficit hyperactivity disorder.

Like Manet and the Impressionist painters in the 1860s and 1870s, Baudelaire spoke to and helped create a new audience, which he famously addressed in the opening poem of *Les Fleurs du mal*: '– *Hypocrite lecteur*, – *mon semblable*, – *mon frère*!', 'Hypocritical reader, my similar, my brother!' (Baudelaire 1975–76: I, 6). Baudelaire, Walter Benjamin wrote,

> envisaged readers for whom the reading of lyric poetry would present difficulties . . . Will power and the ability to concentrate are not their strong points; what they prefer is sensual pleasures; they are familiar with the 'spleen' which kills interest and receptiveness. It is strange to come across a lyric poet who addresses himself to this, the least rewarding type of audience . . .
>
> (Benjamin 1983 [1955]: 109–10)

But he found his readers because, in this rare instance, lyric poetry was in rapport with their experience; they were readers for whom the structure of experience itself had changed (Benjamin 1983 [1955]: 109–10). Baudelaire will not let us forget the reality of changes in the cultural structuring of experience.

What he faced was, broadly speaking, experience reshaped by laissez-faire capitalism. This flourished later and more rapidly in France than in England; its ethic was famously summed up by King Louis-Philippe's minister François

Guizot: *Enrichissez-vous!* ('Get rich!' Is there an ironic echo in Baudelaire's later *Enivrez-vous* – 'Get drunk'? *Petits poèmes en prose*, XXXIII). The American poet, critic and anarchist Kenneth Rexroth put the position starkly. Baudelaire, he wrote, is 'the poet of the society analysed in Capital . . . His subject was the world of primitive accumulation, of the ruthless destruction of all values but the cash nexus by the new industrial and financial system – of bankers and their mistresses in sultry boudoirs; of the craze for diabolism, drugs, flagellation, barbarism; of gin-soaked poor dying in gutters, prostitutes dying under bridges, tubercular and syphilitic intellectuals; of the immense, incurable loneliness of the metropolis; of the birth of human self-alienation, as Marx called it – Baudelaire called it vaporisation of the ego – of the Communist manifesto; and of revolution and revolution betrayed' (Rexroth 1986 [1968]: 173).

Benjamin, less florid, wrote of 'the impenetrable obscurity of mass existence' (Benjamin 1983 [1955]: 64). It was an obscurity born of new social relations, and the creation of new social classes, subclasses and underclasses. For Baudelaire 'the gloomy majesty [*la noire majesté*] of this most disquieting of capitals' (Baudelaire 1975–76: II, 667, cited in Benjamin 1999 [1982]: 231) was characteristic not just of its architecture but of its crowd. 'The city is full of strange sights and sounds, and its streets are thronged with queer people, such as are never seen in our own land, but which remain indelibly stamped upon the visitor's memory', wrote an American visitor to Paris in 1869 (McCabe 1869: 16). Or, as a modern critic has put it:

> The swarming crowds that live in the metropolis, thronging it in such numbers that they resemble more the uniformity of insects than the individuality of humans, fill the air with their dreams, dreams that hinge precisely on their being seen as individuals . . .
>
> (Lloyd 2002: 160)

The effect was that *dépaysment*, the apprehension of strangeness and otherness, and doubt as to the evidence of one's senses, which Surrealism, with Paris its international headquarters, courted in the twentieth century.[6]

Flânerie and free association

In his excursions in the city Baudelaire developed a persona which masked and expressed both his distance and his involvement: the *flâneur*, the man of the crowd, an apparently aimless walker of the streets. *Flânerie* was a free-associative wandering, a way of bearing lostness and disconnection at the same time as allowing experiences and a hope for meanings in. Historically, the *flâneur* owed his existence to Rousseau, Balzac and Nerval (Hazan 2010: 316 ff.).[7] In Baudelaire's world he was also related to the figure of the Dandy, whose ancestors were Byron and Beau Brummell; he stalked Baudelaire's later writing. The Baudelairian *flâneur* was a kind of aristocrat distinguished not by title or lands but by the possession and cultivation of imagination. Imagination, in a sense as elevated and dangerous as that which Coleridge conceived for it, was for Baudelaire the 'queen of the faculties' (Baudelaire 1975–76: II, 585; 619–23), a kind of protected zone of the human spirit, all that stood between Baudelaire, with his profoundly personal version of Catholicism, and Original Sin, man's essential bestiality. Yet it was far from straightforwardly redemptive: the exercise of imagination could lead to a heightened awareness of man's irredeemable nature. Obstinacy and determination to work, veiled by an appearance of leisureliness, imperturbability and *sang-froid*, were the artist's only resources and imagination's indispensable adjuncts (see Lloyd 2002: 199). All were required to maintain an openness to the tragic, extraordinary and miraculous in the everyday, which was the *flâneur*'s vocation (as it needs to be the psychoanalyst's).

The *flâneur* must catch experience on the hoof; he must convey a sense that his utterances are a kind of live performance in which the unexpected can happen. 'I saw him composing verses on the run while he was out on the streets; I never saw him seated before a ream of paper', wrote the poet Ernest Prarond on the period around 1845 (Séché 1928: 84, cited in Benjamin 1999 [1982]: 273). Baudelaire's friend Charles Asselineau recalled that he would ' "cook" his thought in the oven of flânerie and conversation' (cited in Hazan 2010: 334–5). The *flâneur*/dandy was engaged in an internal drama: Baudelaire described Delacroix, his contemporary template for a dandy, as like 'the crater of a volcano artistically hidden by bouquets of flowers' (Baudelaire 1975–76: II, 758); he must internally confront and manage the flux and mutability of his own being. He might indeed develop a multiplicity of guises, and this is reflected within and around Baudelaire's texts in the multiplicity of echoes they set up. Through 'imagination', he must remain open to all that which, internally and externally, is mysterious and replete with feeling, and hold himself together in the process. Then, 'All of a sudden, Baudelaire draws back from what is most familiar to him and eyes it in horror . . . He *draws back from himself*; he looks upon himself as something quite new and prodigiously interesting, although a little unclean . . .' (Desjardins 1887: 18, cited in Benjamin 1999 [1982]: 306). He can prepare the analytic practitioner to face his or her own multiplicity.

Present and past

In the 1850s, after the coup d'état in which Louis-Napoléon, Bonaparte's nephew, proclaimed himself the emperor Napoleon III, Paris underwent the most dramatic and rapid of its nineteenth-century transformations. Baron Haussmann's demolition of much of the surviving medieval centre allowed new boulevards to be opened up, for commercial, sanitary and military purposes: they allowed the rapid movement of troops across the city in case of insurrection. Alongside these developments came the further growth of the suburbs, beyond the 1840s fortifications, and new, unprecedentedly bright nocturnal illumination.

The first line of *Mademoiselle Bistouri* announces that the poet's uneasy encounter takes place at the edge of the city, under gas light. The American visitor of 1869, James Dabney McCabe, fresh from the 'plain and practical' New World, was similarly struck by the light. He produced a guidebook resplendently entitled *Paris by Sunlight and Gaslight: A Work Descriptive of the Mysteries and Miseries, the Virtues, the Vices, the Splendors, and the Crimes of the City of Paris.*

> You pass so rapidly from the bright, merry life of the Paris of today to the crumbling, mysterious monuments of the Paris of centuries ago, that you seem to be living in two different ages of the world; and then to come suddenly out of some palace in whose gorgeous halls kings have revelled, into some dirty, dark quarter where bitter poverty stares you in the face at every step, and appals you with its terrors, is a change sufficiently marked to make any man doubt the evidence of his senses . . .
>
> (McCabe 1869: 17–18)

The passage precisely catches disorienting experiences which Baudelaire registered and to which he can help us remain alert: present and past exist side by side and interpenetrate; behind bright façades can lurk decay, estrangement, terror, deprivation. The Australian critic Rosemary Lloyd is acute to this. 'Past and present collide in the city, memories cling to it like mud . . .' (Lloyd 2002: 160). The wanderer in Paris could not fail to be struck by what the light revealed and failed to disperse, and this included a gnawing sense of private as well as public and historic pasts. Baudelaire's Paris is a city of 'myriad relations' (Baudelaire 1975–76: I, 276, cited in Benjamin 1983 [1955]: 119); 'I have more memories', he wrote, 'than if I were a thousand years old' (*Les Fleurs du mal*, LXXVI. Baudelaire 1975–76: I, 73).[8]

Identification and compassion 'defined his political position throughout his life' (Hazan 2010: 338), with the old and desititute, drunks, rag-pickers and prostitutes. Baudelaire the *flâneur* followed in the footsteps of Goya in Bordeaux or Géricault in London. The narrator of the prose poem *Le Vieux Saltimbanque* feels his throat seized by 'the terrible hand of hysteria' at the sight of a broken-down street acrobat amidst the joy and clamour of a public holiday (*Petits poèmes en prose*, XIV, Baudelaire 1975–76: I, 295–7). In the poem *Les petites vieilles* old women who remind him of marionettes or wounded animals evoke the multiple figures of their former selves: 'mothers whose hearts could bleed, courtesans or saints, whose names, once, were on everyone's lips' (*Les Fleurs du mal*, XCI; Baudelaire 1975–76: I, 89–91). Baudelaire's poetry draws on epiphanic moments of perception 'when time is perceived not as one-directional arrow, but as a series of layers like those in a cliff built by millennia of accumulated sediments' (Lloyd 2002: 226). The city figures in Baudelaire as a palimpsest, a parchment which has layers of writing inscribed on it. 'The city whose labyrinthine streets – both those that now shape Haussmann's Paris and those destroyed to make that vision possible – figure a spider's web of associations across space and time' (Lloyd 2002: 225).[9]

Andromaque, je pense à vous! – 'Andromache, I think of you!' – declares the poet in the opening line of *Le Cygne* (*The Swan*, *Les Fleurs du mal*, LXXXIX. Baudelaire 1975–76: I, 85–7). The thought of Homer's Andromache, the widow of the Trojan hero Hector, who was killed by Achilles, has suddenly fertilised the poet's memory (*A fécondé soudain ma mémoire fertile*) as he walks across the brand-new Place du Carrousel. *Le vieux Paris n'est plus* – 'the old Paris is no more'; he recalls the ramshackle collection of run-down houses and fragments of ruined buildings which used to stand there (*tout ce camp de baraques, / Ces tas de chapiteaux ébauchés et de fûts*). Without Baudelaire having to spell it out, these evoke a classical past and might, for readers of an older Romantic generation, have recalled a particular alley that had occupied the site of the Carrousel, the Impasse du Doyenné, the semi-slum in which Gautier, Nerval and their friends had taken up bohemian residence around 1830. He is reminded, too, of once having seen a swan that had escaped from its menagerie, 'brushing the dry paving with its webbed feet, dragging its white plumage along the rough ground' (*de ses pieds palmés frottant le pavé sec, / Sur le sol raboteux traînant son blanc plumage*), vainly searching for water from a dried-up stream and pining for the lake of its birth. As Lloyd comments, 'the passer-by [reader] cannot escape the ghosts of the past, summoned up by associations as unpredictable and intricate as the bond linking Andromache and the swan' (Lloyd 2002: 160). For Baudelaire himself, and his modern readers, the bond would include that between widowed mother (with her new, martial, husband) and stranded poet son.

This persistence of the past can be sensed, physically sensed, as we register the form and rhythms of the verse. Baudelaire's use of the classical alexandrine, with its twelve syllables and six beats, can work to bring together the cultural and the personal, a sense of a past going deeply back in time and the startlingly, physically present. The juxtaposition can shock and jar. Consider this ear-splitting line, at the start of *À une passante* (*To a woman passer-by*, *Les Fleurs du mal*, XCIII. Baudelaire 1975–76: I, 92–3):

La rue assourdissante autour de moi hurlait.

(The deafening street bellowed around me.)

Or this, which has a different resonance, and opens the poem *Recueillement* (*Meditation* or *Introspection*, from the third, 1868, edition of *Les Fleurs du mal*. Baudelaire 1975–76: I, 140–1):

Sois sage, ô ma Douleur, et tiens-toi plus tranquille

(A translation might be: 'Be good, oh my Sorrow, try not to fidget.')

A private experience of chronic pain finds expression in ordinary speech – the speaker might be trying to soothe a fretful child – framed in a metre typically reserved, in the work of the great seventeenth-century dramatists Corneille or Racine, for heroic and public resolve or grief (that, for example, of Racine's *Andromaque*); the effect is reinforced by the old-fashioned capitalisation and personification of *Douleur*. The poise and rocking balance of the metre contrasts with a pressing ache, and echoes the rise and fall of its intensity, but in the end does little to assuage it. Like the reference to Andromache in the first line of *Le Cygne*, the classical alexandrine in Baudelaire works to register the past's inescapable power, for good or ill, to bind and give shape to present experience, together with regret at the passing of time and the impossibility of retrieving or reliving it. All poetry exploits the sound of the language and the physical experience of voicing it aloud – the alliterations, the fricatives, the nasals, the rhymes and para-rhymes. Few poets have so knowingly brought these resources together within the template of a time-hallowed form to achieve Baudelaire's searing intensity:

> *Comme un sanglot coupé par un sang écumeux / Le chant du coq au loin déchirait l'air brumeux*
>
> (Like a sob cut short by frothing blood, the cock's crow in the distance tore the foggy air)
>
> (From *Le Crépiscule du matin*, *Les Fleurs du mal*, CIII. Baudelaire 1975–76: I, 103–4; see also Benjamin 1983 [1955]: 99)

Mourning and proximity

Baudelaire reminds us that the past must, finally, be mourned. *Nous célébrons tous quelque enterrement* – 'we are all at some funeral' – he wrote in 1846, in the concluding section 'On the heroism of modern life'. Patterned waistcoats and cravats aside, colour had all but disappeared from men's fashions by the 1840s: it was the generation of the black frock coat.

> Is it not the necessary dress of our suffering epoch, which even carries on its thin black shoulders the symbol of perpetual mourning? Note well that the black suit and frock coat not only have their political beauty, which is the expression of universal equality, but also their poetic beauty, the expression of the public soul: an immense procession of undertakers, political undertakers, amorous undertakers, bourgeois undertakers . . .
>
> (Baudelaire 1975–76: II, 494)

Mourning is the defining condition of the times; 'spleen' and 'ennui', modern equivalents of melancholy, full of ennervation and boredom, are its symptoms. As mourners we merge together, like the figures processing behind the coffin in Gustave Courbet's great painting of 1849–50 of a rural funeral, *The Burial at Ornans* (Courbet was among Baudelaire's friends and painted his portrait).

Such merging produced profound ambivalence. The city brought new forms of proximity and non-communication: 'Before buses, railroads, and trams became fully established during the nineteenth century, people were never put in the position of having to stare at one another for minutes or even hours on end without exchanging a word' (Benjamin 1983 [1955]: 151). The opposing forces of attraction and repulsion are a driving tension in Baudelaire's poetry and criticism:

> If he succumbed to the force by which he was drawn to them and, as a *flâneur*, was made one of them, he was nevertheless unable to rid himself of a sense of their essentially inhuman make-up. He becomes their accomplice even as he dissociates himself from them. He becomes deeply involved with them, only to relegate them to oblivion with a single glance of contempt. There is something compelling about this ambivalence where he cautiously admits to it . . .
>
> (Benjamin 1983 [1955]: 128)

'Oh you I could have loved, oh you who knew it!' (*Ô toi que j'eusse aimée, ô toi qui le savais!*) concludes the poem *À une passante* (*To a woman passer-by*) (*Les Fleurs du mal*, XCIII. Baudelaire 1975–76: I, 92–3). Proximity produces desire and complicity alongside estrangement and disgust. Baudelaire brings, in *Mademoiselle Bistouri*, for example, an acute and uncomfortable awareness, protest as we might, of our inescapable implication with the strangers and the strangeness we glimpse in passing. The beautiful passer-by who catches the black frock-coated observer's attention is herself in mourning, like Andromache, *en grand deuil*. We are enforced and ambivalent participants, facing our common losses, past and future, a state of affairs, Baudelaire might remind us, which prevails in the consulting room too.

Free reading, free listening

Le Cygne invites participation (Lloyd 2002: 21). In the last two lines of the poem the reader is invited to continue with his/her own list of the dejected and abandoned: 'sailors forgotten on an island, prisoners, the defeated . . . and many others still!' This final line, with its 'many others still', is 'a handing over of the baton to us as readers to contribute our own allegories of exile'. For, as Rosemary Lloyd writes, 'the fleeting beauty that marks the modern cannot be written in bronze' (Lloyd 2002: 21), or in the marble or enamel favoured by Baudelaire's older contemporary Gautier. Baudelaire's response to the transient is to embrace it, rather than to seek to manage the anxiety it engenders by trying to arrest it and cast it in definitive form. In the process he encourages an awareness of our own common mutability. Reading Baudelaire, and writing about him, it is indeed hard not to feel that one is also wandering, as with a patient, in a crowd of signs, experiences, ideas and sensations, so fertile in associative possibilities is the ground he treads.

Baudelaire's poetic strategy is indeed to awaken us to our own associative and identificatory capacities, just as the little river and the thought of Andromache stirred the poet's fertile memory in *Le Cygne*. He softens us up, then allows us no rest. In the poem *Brumes et pluies* (*Mist and Rain*, *Les Fleurs du mal*, CI. Baudelaire 1975–76: I, 100–1), as Lloyd points out, he gathers together

> a series of images – the pitcher, the cat, the bell – and sounds – the dripping gutter, the smoking log, the ticking clock – that lack logical connections in the same way that cards in the Tarot pack appear in no logical order but are able to suggest multiple possibilities without defining any.
>
> (Lloyd 2002: 185)

His writing, furthermore,

> draws so much on patterns of sound, on echoes across his production as a whole, on the connotations as well as the denotations of words, that it frequently seems, if not to defy translation, at least to throw the power of translation into question.
>
> (Lloyd 2002: 232)

Lloyd goes on to recommend a kind of 'multiple reading', the original plus several different translations (Lloyd 2002: 232). The imagery of *Le Cygne* consists in shapes that 'are not made neat and tidy for us. They may lie as heavy as rocks, but they can shift into countless patterns, like the fragments in a kaleidoscope' (Lloyd 2002: 21). The kaleidoscope effect extends both across Baudelaire's œuvre, and beyond it in time, into intertextuality. The swan of *Le Cygne* echoes the mocked, ungainly bird in *L'Albatros* (*Les Fleurs du mal*, III. Baudelaire 1975–76: I, 9–10) and the great antarctic seabird of Coleridge's *Ancient Mariner*. Baudelaire sensitises us to echoes.

Correspondences, symbols and allegory

The poem *Correspondances* (*Les Fleurs du mal*, IV. Baudelaire 1975–76: I, 11) might at first seem to offer itself as a kind of key to the rest of the volume, an invitation to a free-associative reading in which one image suggests others and the world presents itself as allegorical web. Baudelaire quotes from it in an essay on Wagner: he uses his own verses as confirmations and premonitions of the richness of thought and feeling generated by Wagner's music, and as a way of establishing a sense of kinship with him. At the same time the poet's and the reader's implication is more profound, more complex and unfathomable than a mere unleashing *within* him- or herself of chains of association. The poem announces this clearly:

> Nature is a temple in which living pillars sometimes let slip confused words. Man walks through it, through forests of symbols which observe him as a kindred thing.

> *La Nature est un temple où de vivants piliers / Laissent parfois sortir de confuses paroles;*
> *L'homme y passe à travers des forêts de symboles*
> *Qui l'observent avec des regards familiers.*

Signs read *us*, as in dreams. Yet what is the nature of our relationship to them? If they are kindred or *familiers*, in what sense and to whom? Do the symbols look on like intimate and kindly family members, like loving parents looking out for a child, for example, or malevolently, or with indifference, with the sort of familiarity that might breed contempt? Does the wandering person apprehend them as *familiers*, or is it just that he is a familiar sight to them?

The poem is full of ambiguity, especially when one attempts to translate it into another language. Many different translations might be and have been made. *Confuses paroles* could be rendered as 'barely comprehensible words'; the *regards familiers* might be 'knowing and familiar looks', or simply offhand ones.

The poem will not translate seamlessly. It requires us not only to respect and tolerate its own strangeness, but also to recognise our own struggles with expression and its limitations, subject as it always is to the contingencies and constraints of the conjoined forces of emotion and aesthetics (rhythm, rhyme, para-rhyme, repetition, tone, etc.). Both the poem and our efforts to apprehend it refuse to be still, and this is echoed in the poem's manifest content. This is not mystery and ambiguity for mystery's and ambiguity's sakes. It serves the purpose of throwing into question any certainty about our place in the world as readers of its signs.

The French psychoanalyst Jean-Claude Rolland has noted the pun *cygne* and *signe* (Rolland 2006: 30–1). In the context of analytic listening the pun, he says, might indicate the presence of something unconsciously foreclosed. It is also the *cygne/signe* of a sign itself. A further intertextual association comes to mind, not noted by Rolland, Hölderlin's line 'We are a sign without meaning', *Ein Zeichen sind wir, deutungslos* (cited in Kuzniar 1987: 19). Is the *cygne/signe* then pointing nowhere, a signifier without signified? Perhaps it is, rather, a pointer towards the unending search for meaning itself. Rolland, following Jean Starobinski, reflects on the nature of allegory. The swan in the poem, wrote Starobinski, 'is a figure of loss, privation, vain expectation. The nostalgia which causes it to regret its "native lake" presupposes an insurmountable gap; this is not without analogy with the gap which, in allegory, inserts itself between the signifying "concrete" image and the "abstract" signified entity' (Starobinski 1989: 73, cited in Rolland 2006: 30–1). Reading Baudelaire, more than any poet who preceded him (except perhaps Hölderlin), is to expose oneself to this gap. What may follow is a recognition that the allegorical, for all its consoling promises of connectedness and meaning, has limitations, and that the world is *not* all allegory.

Thus, this central Baudelairian notion of *correspondances* is not just an invitation to close our eyes in confidence that the world's inherent harmony will carry on taking care of itself and of us. Nor is it finally possible, as some critics have claimed, to take off from the theory of *correspondances* to propose a secret architecture in *Les Fleurs du mal.* When Baudelaire wrote, in *Le Cygne*, 'for me, everything becomes allegory', he was perhaps describing a particularly heightened state of sensibility, for at other times allegorical possibility is refused and denied. 'The code says nothing', wrote Rexroth (Rexroth 1986 [1968]: 175),[10] the 'data of remembrance' (Benjamin 1983 [1955]: 142) are always already corrupt and fragmented. We are confronted with the phenomenologically irreducible, with that which lies beyond symbolisation, the Lacanian Real.

Baudelaire can certainly compel us not to look away. Sometimes the horrific and repulsive in his work are transparently symbolic. *Une Charogne (Les Fleurs du mal*, XXIX. Baudelaire 1975–76: I, 312) dwells on an animal carcass putrefying in the sun, which the poet and his lover meet out walking: it is a *momento mori*, inviting an associative contrast with the youth and beauty of the narrator's companion. But the poem also hints at the element of disgust in sexual attraction and this is not so easily catalogued. The prose poem *La Corde* was dedicated, significantly, to Manet, that great refuser of the consolations of the symbol. It describes the act of cutting down the corpse of a child who has hanged himself, and the far from conventionally appalled reactions of the narrator: 'the little monster had used a very thin string which had gone deep into the flesh and now I had to use a pair of thin scissors to look for the string between the two rolls of swollen flesh to free his neck' (*Petits Poèmes en prose*, XXX. Baudelaire 1975–76: I, 330; see also Lloyd 2002: 49). The shocking reminder is of inescapable physicality and the specifics of embodied experience in a world of other bodies. It is that which refuses to be assimilated, to become abstract or mere theory, to 'speak' to us as allegory, even in *confuses paroles*.

At the same time Baudelaire does not lose the reader in the endlessly specific. In the prose poem *La Belle Dorothée* (*Petits Poèmes en prose*, XXV. Baudelaire 1975–76: I, 316–17), for example, there is, as Lloyd points out, 'no pleasure in naming the trees or telling us precisely what kind of crab is in the stew' (Lloyd 2002: 170–1). Baudelaire's conscious effort, which the therapist would do well to emulate, is to refuse stereotype, to keep the reader's (patient's) imaginative response open, not to limit and weigh it down with detail, while trying to insist it remains in touch with the texture and complexity of present, sensory experience.

There are times, however, when this is not possible, when, for example, the passing of time leaves nothing but regret and a sense of the irredeemable in its train: 'poetic memory, once an infinite source of delight, becomes an inexhaustible arsenal of torments' (Lloyd 2002: 224). 'Lovely Spring has lost its perfume' (*Le printemps adorable a perdu son odeur*), Baudelaire wrote, in *Le Goût du néant* (*The Taste of/for Nothingness*), one of the *Spleen* poems in *Les Fleurs du mal* (LXXX. Baudelaire 1975–76: I, 76; see also Benjamin 1983 [1955]: 142–3 and Rolland 2006: 111). Spleen, emptiness, blankness, desolation: Benjamin called it a Sunday feeling. 'The man who has lost his capacity for experiencing feels as if he is dropped from the calendar' (Benjamin 1983 [1955]: 144). Baudelaire's work also opens up for us the terrible experience of melancholia, of loss of experience itself.

The shock of the other

In the 1840s, newspaper readership was growing rapidly, in the first stirrings of modern mass culture. A new literary sub-genre came into vogue, the *physiologie*, the pen-portrait of a social group, type or profession, the bourgeois, artist or lawyer, for example. The *physiologie*, like the 'celebrity culture' of the early twenty-first century, offered the consumer a sense of knowing sophistication; it also masked and reassured against a primitive terror of the other, and the exclusions, the envy and scorn on which its own categories rested. 'What are the dangers of the forest and the prairie', Baudelaire asked, 'compared with the daily shocks and conflicts of civilization? Whether a man grabs his victim on a boulevard or stabs his quarry in unknown woods – does he not remain both here and there the most perfect of all beasts of prey?' (Baudelaire 1975–76: I, 663, cited in Benjamin 1983 [1955]: 39).

The fencer-like Baudelaire, wrote Benjamin, made it his business to parry the shocks of the metropolis and its masses 'with his spiritual and his physical self' (Benjamin 1983 [1955]: 117–18); the photographer Nadar commented on his uneven, cat-like gait, how he seemed to choose 'each stone of the pavement as if he had to avoid crushing an egg' (Benjamin 1999 [1982]: 230). The shock of the city was above all registered in the poetic image. For Benjamin, Baudelaire registered jolts and surprises in the very fabric of his associative and metaphorical language: his similes 'get into the text as disturbing intruders' (Benjamin 1983 [1955]: 98). In an early letter to his mother, he likened the colour of the sky to a pair of blue trousers (cited in Lloyd 2002: 184). Later similes have comparable effects:

Night thickened like a partition

La nuit s'épaississait ainsi qu'une cloison
                    (*Les Fleurs du mal*, XXXVI. Baudelaire 1975–76: I, 37)

We steal a clandestine pleasure in passing, which we squeeze very hard like an old orange

Nous volons au passage un plaisir clandestin
Que nous pressons bien fort comme une vieille orange
                    (*Les Fleurs du mal, Au lecteur*. Baudelaire 1975–76: I, 5)

Your triumphant bosom is a fine wardrobe

Ta gorge triomphante est une belle armoire
                    (*Les Fleurs du mal*, LII. Baudelaire 1975–76: I, 52)

(All the above were noted by Benjamin 1983 [1955]: 98.)

the vague terrors of those horrendous nights which crush the heart like a paper you crumple up

les vagues terreurs de ces affreuses nuits
Qui compriment le cœur comme un papier qu'on froisse
                    (*Les Fleurs du mal*, XLIV. Baudelaire 1975–76: I, 44)

sickly demons in the atmosphere wake up heavily, like businessmen

des démons malsains dans l'atmosphère
S'éveillent lourdement, comme des gens d'affaire
                    (*Les Fleurs du mal*, XCV. Baudelaire 1975–76: I, 94)

Airy Pleasure will flee away towards the horizon like a sylph into the wings of the theatre

Le Plaisir vaporoux fuira vers l'horizon
Ainsi qu'une sylphide au fond de la coulisse
                    (*Les Fleurs du mal*, LXXXV. Baudelaire 1975–76: I, 81)

One critic, Jules Laforgue, commented about this last couplet that 'Hugo, Gautier, and others before him would have made a French, oratorical comparison; he makes a Yankee one . . . (you can see the iron wires and stage machinery)'. Baudelaire's sylph brings us back to earth with a bump; his rough comparisons, 'in the midst of a harmonious period, cause him to put his foot in his plate; obvious, exaggerated comparisons' (Laforgue, cited in Benjamin 1999 [1982]: 244). Desire and its objects are always just out of reach and, when we do get a touch of them, they are ordinary. Yet the sylph exiting stage left also alerts us to the poetry of the prosaic, and the prosaic underpinnings of any attempt to make poetry.

> The seeming inappropriateness of terms . . . that skilful impreciseness of which Racine made such masterly use . . . that air-space, that interval between image and idea, between the word and the thing, is just where there is room for the poetic emotion to come and dwell.
>
> (Gide 1910: 512, cited in Benjamin 1999 [1982]: 307)

Baudelaire, in the words of another twentieth-century commentator, 'understood the clairvoyance of the heart that does not acknowledge all it experiences . . . It is a hesitation, a holding back, a modest gaze' (Rivière, 1911: 21, cited in Benjamin 1999 [1982]: 257). The gap or air-space, like the analyst's 'unsaturated' interpretation, is part of Baudelaire's invitation to us to join in.

Doubles and duplicity

Hypocrite lecteur, mon semblable, mon frère! Insinuatingly, Baudelaire impresses upon us the degree of our duplicity and our unavailability to ourselves and each other. Nowhere is this more demonstrable than in the *Petits Poèmes en prose*. Sonya Stephens, in a brilliant reading (Stephens 1999), shows how the prose poems hinge on a principle of doubling, *dédoublement*: the double as both external and internal other.

The prose poems extend a different invitation from that at the start of *Les Fleurs du mal*.

> We are the readers who are goaded with the accusation that we are too lazy to read more than one or two poems at a sitting, or far less sensitive than the poets or artists whose profession lends such intensity to their experience.
>
> (Lloyd 2002: 48)

But the rug is simultaneously pulled from under our feet: the poet is a creature of 'profound duplicity himself' (Benjamin 1983 [1955]: 26). Prose poems such as *La Fausse monnaie* (*Petits Poèmes en prose*, XXVIII. Baudelaire 1975–76: I, 323–4), in which the narrator is shocked by a friend who gives a beggar a large sum in false coinage, deal with highly duplicitous forms of exchange, which echo those between author, reader and text. There is the 'doubleness of the lyrical space' itself. *La Chambre double* (*Petits Poèmes en prose*, V. Baudelaire 1975–76: I, 2 80–2) is the room in which the poet dreams and which is utterly transformed by the bailiff's knock. The narrative or poetic voice is itself thrown into question. Who is the (split) *je* who speaks in the poems, and invites the reader to respond to the different positions it adopts (Stephens 1999: 64), as for example in *Le Mauvais vitrier*, *The Evil Glazier* (*Petits Poèmes en prose*, IX. Baudelaire 1975–76: I, 285–7)? Here the narrator, in a moment of incomprehensible, diabolic impulsivity, torments a pedlar selling window glass for not providing coloured glass to make the world more beautiful. The *pot de fleurs* which he drops 'like a weapon of war' on to the glazier below is a pun invoking Baudelaire's literary hero Edgar Allan Poe, and *Les Fleurs du mal* (Stephens 2002: 66); there is a further ironic twist in that glaziers were widely held to have created business for themselves by participating in the periodic rioting of 1848–51: window makers as window breakers (Stephens 1999: 70). This, for Stephens, is literature as play and assault. Baudelaire's technique, wrote Benjamin, 'is the technique of the *putsch*' (Benjamin 1983 [1955]: 98–100, cited in Hazan 2010: 338–9).

The *Petits poèmes* exploit comic forms. They combine a dualistic notion developed elsewhere by Baudelaire (Baudelaire 1975–76: II, 535–6) of *le comique signficatif*, which is referential, imitative, and *le comique absolu*, which is grotesque, threatening, potentially transformative, and was particularly evident for Baudelaire in Goya's etchings and English caricature. Both forms of the comic rely on reception: 'it is above all in the one laughing, in the spectator, that the comic comes to life', he wrote (Baudelaire 1975–76: II, 543; Stephens 1999: viii). However, they also depend on the spectator's sense of superiority. The reader is flattered and lured into identification with the poet, the split lyric subject, in his shiftless wanderings in the city, and is then caught repeatedly in disturbing confrontations with an otherness which is also that reader's own. The poems are, Stephens writes in a brilliant metaphor, 'the ultimate *miroir à alouettes* [a mirrored device for trapping larks] for the spectator/reader' (Stephens 1999: 159): the self-regarding reader finds himself enthralled and caught, caught out, implicated in ways that can feel far from merely playful.

Reading the prose poems is also a living demonstration of how that which is marginal, excluded from immediate consciousness, can need to be surprised into awareness, as in an analysis. It is a live experience. Baudelaire tricks and beguiles us into the ever alarming but always also horizonal possibility of meeting ourselves. 'It seems to me that I shall always be comfortable there [or: exactly there] where I am not, and this question of displacement is one which I endlessly debate with my soul' (*Il me semble que je serais toujours bien là où je ne suis pas, et cette question de déménagement en est une que je discute sans cesse avec mon âme*), says the narrator of the prose poem 'Any where out of the world' ([*sic*] *Petits Poèmes en prose*, XLVIII. Baudelaire 1975–76: I, 356–7). The sentence finds its future echo in Lacan's inversion of Descartes's *cogito*: 'I am thinking where I am not, therefore I am where I am not thinking' (*Je pense là où je ne puis dire que je suis*) (Lacan 2007: 430).

The Perverse

Baudelaire also provides, of course, his own critical commentary, taking us under his conversational wing. A friend to whom you have confided one of your likings or passions says ' "That's strange! For it completely goes against your philosophy and all your other passions!" And you reply: "That may be, but that's how it is. I like it; and I probably like it precisely because of the violent contradiction it sets up in my whole being"' (Baudelaire 1975–76: II, 145–6). In 1855 he noted:

> system is a sort of curse that forces us into constantly giving it up it. You have to keep on constructing a new one, and the tediousness of doing this is a cruel punishment. But at the same time my system was always beautiful, large, expansive, commodious, clean and above all well-rounded, or that's how it seemed to me. But some unforeseen and spontaneous by-product of the liveliness of existence was always undermining my puerile and outdated knowledge.
>
> (Baudelaire 1975–76: II, 577; see also Lloyd 2002: 53)

It is not enough, however, for us to settle with the idea, which he himself at times seems to encourage, that what he finally has to offer is merely some sort of sleek if radical reflexiveness. He challenges far more directly, more viscerally than that, not through what he says about himself but through what he shows us of what he is, and we are. 'Baudelaire's writing is often unnerving, as likely to get under our skin like a form of poison ivy as it is to delight us.' Lloyd goes on to frame the challenge thus:

> How does one put up with his misogyny, his bouts of self-destructive selfishness, and his flashes of acidic bad temper? One cannot simply separate out the man and the work in this case, somehow distilling a calm quintessence in verse. It does not happen, or if it does, something vital is lost . . . reading him has to be as much a question of resisting him as of allowing him to take over.
>
> (Lloyd 2002: 9)

'Don't drink and don't smoke. It's bad for your health', wrote Luis Buñuel, certainly one of Baudelaire's spiritual heirs; the great film director had just treated his own 'dear readers' to the most eloquent autobiographical paean to alcohol and tobacco (Buñuel 1984: 48). Baudelaire, tending less to levity than to rage, requires us to face the perverse in ourselves, to 'man's primordial perversity', that which works against and damns us, and at the same time most profoundly expresses and individuates us. *The Imp of the Perverse* was among the stories (or is it an essay? or a prose poem?) by his literary hero Edgar Allan Poe which he translated (*Le Démon de la perversité*), and it is perhaps the passage in all Poe which spoke most forcibly to him. It is about what drives the narrator of the prose poem *Le Mauvais vitrier*. In this awareness of the perverse Baudelaire is resolutely anti-humanist: he is unequivocally against all those flatterers of humanity . . . all those cossetors and comforters who want to send you off to sleep and who repeat in every possible tone of voice, 'I was born good, and you were too, and so were we all, we were all born good!', forgetting, no, pretending to forget, these absurd egalitarians, that we are all touched by evil!

('Etudes sur Poe'. Baudelaire 1975–76 II: 323)

Taking a position

Baudelaire's work is littered with indirect and direct instructions as to how to read his own work and that of others. Often the tasks he implies for us seem deceptively easy. For example, in his review of the Exposition Universelle, the Paris International Exhibition, of 1855, he recalls a story about his contemporary Balzac studying a cottage in a painting of a village in winter. The great novelist wonders what the occupants are doing in there, what they are thinking about, and what their worries may be. Has the harvest been good? No doubt they have debts? Baudelaire concludes, 'I shall find myself appreciating a painting only by dint of the totality of ideas or reveries which it brings to my mind' (Baudelaire 1975–76: II, 579). Yet he will starkly remind us that dream, especially drug-induced, is a source of danger too (see *Les Paradis artificiels*, which includes his great essay on De Quincey: Baudelaire 1975–76: I, 377–520; and Lloyd 2002: 73). He reminds us of the morning after intoxication, the attack on will power. The poem *Rêve Parisien* (dedicated to hard-working Constantin Guys) is a powerful and terrifying statement of this (*Les Fleurs du mal*, CII. Cited in Lloyd 2002: 84–8). We must, somehow, not give up. In his intimate journals, he repeatedly, plaintively, writes instructions to himself: 'Work!' (for example, Baudelaire 1975–76: I, 668, 670, 672). He shows us how to work ourselves, and tries to cajole us into work.[11]

In 1846 he declared that 'the best account of a picture might be a sonnet or an elegy'. If Romanticism consisted in a 'way of feeling', criticism was 'a picture reflected by an intelligent and sensitive mind' (Baudelaire 1975–76: II, 4, 18, 420; Lloyd 2002: 202). Not only the distinction between artist and critic, but also between artist, critic and spectator becomes porous or irrelevant. The kind of critical transposition that Baudelaire proposed and practised is equivalent to the way in which 'a careful reader scribbles notes in the margins of a book' (Baudelaire 1975–76: II, 679) – you, he says, can do the same (see also Lloyd 2002: 206).

Partly he seeks to inculcate in the reader an active, conscious responsiveness. As Lloyd wrote: 'Understanding how to [take up the role of the poet's double and sibling] is in turn dependent on an awareness of how the writing of the poem invites certain interpretations, determines certain images, suggests certain possibilities' (Lloyd 2002: 21) without, however, foreclosing on any of them. We must finally, as he wrote in his essay of 1861 on Wagner, transform our *volupté* into *connaissance*: a critical procedure that might be taken as an object lesson for psychotherapists in a properly reflective use of counter-transference. Listening to Wagner's music for the first time – the overture to *Löhengrin* – Baudelaire fell into a reverie, which he likened to an opium trance, in which a 'reciprocal analogy' between things became clear to him (the music suggested colour, light, images). 'I determined to find out out why, and to transform my pleasure into knowledge' (*Je résolus de m'informer du pourquoi, et de transformer ma volupté en connaissance*) (Baudelaire 1975–76: II, 785–6). *Volupté* could translate as wallowing, bathing, or being pleasurably, self-forgetfully immersed, as in the expression *volupté du travail*, being absorbed in one's work. *Connaissance*, from the verb *connaître*, is an intimate knowing, as against the kind of information- or knowledge-based knowing of *savoir*. Baudelaire wanted to find out what the music did to him, where it came from, how it spoke, what had been in the composer's mind, his history, personality and theories. (What he finds may not surprise: that Wagner's music is an expression of the diabolic as well as the divine, the flesh as well as the spirit, of duality and irredeemable division.)

This Romantic appeal to one's own experience does not imply bland neutrality. From the start of his career Baudelaire's requirement for criticism was that it should be 'passionate, partial and political', that is, he went on, 'made from an exclusive point of view, but one that opens the most horizons'. It should be amusing and poetic, and decidedly not 'cold and algebraic', the kind of criticism which 'under the pretext of explaining everything, has neither hate nor love, and willingly divests itself of any kind of temperament' (Baudelaire 1975–76: II, 418). It means taking a position internally, from which to speak as widely and deeply as possible. In his account of the Exposition Universelle, Baudelaire insisted that to appreciate the startlingly unfamiliar Chinese art that was on display

> critics or spectators must themselves perform a transformation that is close to a miracle and, through a phenomenon of will-power acting on imagination, learn by themselves what gave birth to that curious flowering.
>
> (cited in Lloyd 2002: 192)

The most gifted in this respect might be those solitary travellers who have lived for years in the depths of the woods or out on the prairies. 'No scholarly veil, no university paradox, no pedagogic utopia stands between them and complex truth. They know the admirable, immortal, inevitable rapport between form and function. These people do not criticise: they contemplate, they study.' Beauty, Baudelaire wrote, is always bizarre; who could conceive of a banal beauty? (Baudelaire 1975–76: II, 576–8). He was, as Lloyd has put it, determined 'to find a way of translating the exceptional and the alien, not in order to reduce its quintessential strangeness, but to make that strangeness more approachable' (Lloyd 2002: 192).[12] It is an induction into an analytic attitude.

Supervision with Baudelaire

What more could there be to learn from such a man? What would supervision with Baudelaire[13] be like? 'The world only works through misunderstanding', he noted in his diaries, *Mon Coeur mis à nu* (*My Heart Laid Bare*). 'It is because of universal misunderstanding that everyone agrees. If by some mischance people understood each other they could never agree' (Baudelaire 1975–76: I, 704, cited in Phillips 2005, epigraph). If pre-Lacanian insight such as this can seem cynical or aloof, it is countered elsewhere in his thinking by respect for the individual in her idiosyncrasy: 'Do not scorn anyone's sensibility. Each person's sensibility is their genius' (Baudelaire 1975–76: I, 661).

At one moment he rails against 'universal fatuity' (Baudelaire 1975–76: I, 689), and then he is struck by the 'immense profundity of thought in common expressions'. Of course, he goes on to qualify this: they are 'holes dug out by generations of ants'. His ambivalence confronts us with multiple alternative readings, on none of which can we definitively settle (are these ants of crushable insignificance, or are they to be admired for their drive and wisdom?).

His invitation to transform *volupté* into *connaissance* is echoed in Bion's formulation of the analytic task, the transformation of 'beta' into 'alpha' elements. This, however, as Bion would have agreed, is a fraught and embroiling process, with no guarantee of a happy outcome (Lloyd 2002: 183).

As readers of *Les Fleurs du mal*, we are required to revise our understanding of earlier poems in the light of later ones (see Lloyd 2002: 183). A dream from years ago can be recast; meanings in an analysis are fluid, provisional and open to constant revision. One has to accept this, and listen, constantly. If 'the best response to a picture might be a sonnet or an elegy', so might a response to a patient be a quotation, or a joke, anything that responds to and *meets* the other on a level which is not discursive or evaluative.

He encourages therapists to be alive to deadness, as, for example, André Green has done (Green 1996 [1980]: 163). In his *Salon of 1859* Baudelaire concluded that the 'majority of our landscape painters are liars, precisely because they fail to lie' (Baudelaire 1951: 812) – in other words, they are dead for lack of redeeming imagination (and see Benjamin 1983 [1955]: 151). It is all very well for nature to be 'a storehouse of memories', but there are landscape paintings, just as there are passages of a patient's speech, not to mention analytic interventions, which are dead, mere carriers of Bion's minus-K or minus-L, lacking that which is required for free associative and imaginative activity.

We can feel seduced by Baudelaire, only to find our willingness to be seduced is disallowed. Reading Baudelaire is an exercise in alertness to our patients' (unconscious) manipulations, and to our own readiness to embrace comfort and certainty. He alerts us to the question of who exactly is speaking, and, as creatures of the crowd, to the risk of losing ourselves in identificatory or dissociative chaos. *Moi, c'est tous; Tous, c'est moi. Tourbillon* (Baudelaire 1975–76: 651).

The *miroir à alouettes*, the trap he sets for the spectator/reader (Stephens 1999: 159), is a reminder for therapists of how patients can catch our vulnerabilities, those insufficiently analysed, worked-through and reflected-upon aspects of ourselves. To read Baudelaire, especially the prose poems, is to open oneself to the sickening, vertiginous experience of just how easy it can be to walk into such traps. Kleinians might want to make sense of this phenomenon in terms of the power of unconscious projection and projective identification. The poems also work 'in the place of the analyst': they are lures for our own narcissism, with curative potential, for the doubles in Baudelaire's *petits poèmes* do *not* mirror what we want to see.

We must confront the terror of the 'not-I', of our split selves, and the absolutely incomprehensibly Other. There is no escape from this, even – especially – in sleep, that 'sinister adventure of every evening . . . one could say that men regularly sleep with an audacity which would be incomprehensible if we did not know that it resulted from ignorance of the danger' (Baudelaire 1975–76: I, 654). We are Magritte's 'reckless sleepers'. We must be prepared, although we never can be, to be humbled and demolished, to suffer the most grievous attacks on our (illusory) egos.

He teaches patience, not just through the example of his personal endurance of his own travails, but through the reading experience which his poetry makes available. And, Baudelaire being Baudelaire, this experience contains lessons in the pitfalls of arrogant impatience. 'Lines of verse so perfect, so measured, that at first one hesitates to grant them all their meaning', wrote the great twentieth-century critic Jacques Rivière. 'A hope stirs for a minute – doubt as to their profundity. But one need only wait' (Rivière 1911: 22, cited in Benjamin 1999 [1982]: 257).

Baudelaire *names* it, and can help us not to give up on commitment to do likewise. He can help us maintain the therapeutic space as a whorehouse, where fantasy and wild desire can have an outing.[14] His invitation to *flânerie* is an invitation to the analyst to allow external and internal to interpenetrate, to wander freely if carefully in the world of the person who comes to her, with all its sensations, sights, sounds and smells, its lures, seductions, chance encounters, layers of experience, abjection, squalor and danger. There was, as Hazan has noted, 'nothing passive about Baudelaire's flânerie' (Hazan 2010: 352). We need that active embrace of compassion and despair, so very much Baudelaire's own, to help us face what our patients require us to face with them . . . and much else besides.

Coda

'There is something originally, inaugurally, profoundly wounded in the human relation to the world', said Lacan. 'Life does not want to be healed' (Lacan 1988: 167, 233). Lacan was speaking in a distinctively French idiom which Baudelaire helped shape. Baudelaire rejected the Enlightenment of Rousseau for that of de Sade. He celebrated the artificial, setting it in dialectical tension with the natural, with its drive to cruelty and destruction. Mademoiselle Bistouri, concluded the narrator of the prose poem, had been 'unable to help making herself'. Partly she had constructed her persona herself, through her own fastidious effort; she was also, in the eyes of the dandified *flâneur*, a product of the artificial metropolis, just as he was; the metropolis itself was made and unmade by the same invisible, naturally corrupted human forces. What recourse, then, failing an impossible revolution to drive out corruption, might the poet have? Only, Baudelaire might have echoed Freud, to love and work. 'So when shall I be able to turn the living spectacle of my sad misery into the work of my hands and the love of my eyes?' (*Le Mauvais moine*, *Les Fleurs du mal*, IX. Baudelaire 1975–76: I, 16). For help with such a commitment, especially in its moments of breakdown, Baudelaire might be kept closely alongside.

Chapter 6

Dr Noir, the chevalier Dupin, and John Keats

The dark doctor who is one of the subjects of this chapter was the creation of Alfred de Vigny (1797–1863), a major French Romantic poet from the generation before Baudelaire's. He moved in Victor Hugo's circle in Paris in the 1820s and found success adapting Shakespeare for the French stage. His masterpiece was the play *Chatterton* (1835), based on the tragic life of the English poet; he produced his most remarkable poetry in seclusion in the country near Angoulême during the last decades of his life.

Auguste Dupin's creator, Edgar Allan Poe (1809–49), was born near Boston, Massachusetts. Although he achieved little recognition in his life-time, he single-handedly created a tautened, poetic prose which, in 'one of the most wondrous cases of literary influence in the annals of modern literature' (Harrison 2011: 42), was to leave its mark on Baudelaire and thus on the whole history of modernism. He is credited with inventing the modern detective story; his horror stories (*The Fall of the House of Usher, The Pit and the Pendulum, The Tell-Tale Heart*) and certain of his poems (*The Raven, The Bells*) are part of the common currency of Anglo-Saxon and world literature.

John Keats (1795–1821) belonged to the second generation of English Romantic poets, which included Shelley. Of them all he has perhaps inspired the greatest affection and most consistent admiration among subsequent generations. He was the son of a London ostler (stableman and groom), and in this respect was on the edge of a literary world that was generally classically educated and drawn from higher social echelons. He abandoned the study of medicine for poetry. What is most immediately striking about his verse is its sensual imagery and sensitivity to the natural world; he published for only four years before his early death, in Rome, from tuberculosis. His work was, by and large, poorly received by the literary press of his time.

Vigny and Poe offer fictitious, pre-Freudian accounts of some of the ideal terms of an 'analytic' position. These are illuminating, historically and in terms of theory: Vigny's Dr Noir is partly based on the real-life Dr Esprit Blanche, soul-doctor to the Romantic generation (Murat 2001: 45–6); Poe's Dupin played a famous role in the development of Lacan's thought. Keats, meanwhile, can give courage: he can help therapists and analysts bear the impossibility of maintaining an analytic position. He can help us live with our failures and survive the wounding they can inflict. In the end he did not manage this himself – he died in doubt as to whether he had achieved anything. He can help us accept that we do what we do within our particular and unique idioms. He struggled with classical and class orthodoxies. He understood the importance of discipline better than most, but he can remind us that responsiveness is more important than doing it by the book. And finally, that it is suffering that makes souls.

So far, I have tried to maintain, or at least to keep in mind, certain distinctions. There is art which elicits and requires an analytic attitude in the viewer, which frustrates a search for meanings based on logical or discursive thinking, and which instead insists or nudges us into realising that our attention to it must be free-floating. Only then is there a chance for meaning, often surprising and sometimes unwelcome, to emerge. While such art necessarily draws on cultural clues, it is likely radically to reconfigure or subvert them, or bring them into brand new conjunctions. It invites collaborative engagement and stimulates responsiveness. It challenges us to invent our own ways of reading. It confronts us with our own desire.

Then there are artists who consciously set out with such an attitude themselves, like Baudelaire. There are also those, like Baudelaire again, who provide more or less explicit, if never prescriptive, guides as to the attitude ('passionate, partial, political') required for an approach to their work and that of others (and see further comments below). With Baudelaire in particular it has been hard to maintain these distinctions, so much do the poet and critic dissolve into each other. In this chapter I want to develop a further distinction and play with some late eighteenth- and nineteenth-century personifications, real and fictional, of the holder of this attitude: the proto-analyst or, indeed, the ideal reader, who leads by example. I shall then return to Keats, and discuss the emotional position he tried to develop and maintain, both in relation to the writing of poetry and to the living of his life.

The creatively daydreaming artist is by no means a Romantic invention. In the mid-eighteenth century Diderot pictured himself sitting alone on a bench in the gardens of the Palais-Royal, the hunting ground of prostitutes, 'giving my mind free rein [*tout son libertinage*]. I leave it in charge, at liberty to follow the first sensible or mad idea that presents itself', just like the young rakes who follow one girl then another, 'accosting them all but attaching themselves to none. My thoughts, they are my girls' (Diderot 1967 [1821]: 29).

The nineteenth century developed and elaborated a similar, internally resourceful persona constituted by refusals and self-denials. George Gordon, the 6th Baron Byron, although hardly celebrated for his abstinence, nevertheless stands near a genealogical source: he is the model dandy, distinguished by his *sang froid*, incisiveness of perception and fearless willingness to name things as he finds them. For Ruskin, Byron 'spoke without exaggeration, without mystery, without enormity, and without mercy'; Berlioz adored Byron's extraordinary combination of ruthlessness and extreme tenderness, how he could be 'generous-hearted and without pity' (MacCarthy 2003: 551).[1] The dandy is always by definition painstakingly self-cultivated. He is thus also both a real and a fictional character, both a person and a representation, a ready-made transferential object. 'Part of Byron's magic lay in his detachment, the powerful sense of mysteries undisclosed', and in a sense of his 'somnambulant passions' (MacCarthy 2003: 523, 329). Sharply aware of the power of the erotic, he was in possession of passions of his own, yet he was also dispassionate and refused to be pinned down. 'If a writer should be quite consistent / How could he possibly show things existent?' he wrote in *Don Juan* (Byron 1970: 841), expressing a viewpoint in strong contradistinction to Augustan niceties. Byron's 'paradoxical nature, his mobility of thinking, the multiplicity of voices in his writing' (MacCarthy 2003: xiii) were necessary requirements. Byron was 'everywhere and nowhere' ('I am there where I am not', wrote Lacan); he was 'the man "of no country", having given up England, who finds himself a floating global citizen' (MacCarthy 2003: xiii). Behind the cliché of the Romantic artist as rebellious outsider was the serious (proto-analytic) task of finding a position, a viewpoint, or, indeed, accepting the position of having no position.

The Romantic artist might thus be defined as such by the need to position and reposition, mythologise and demythologise, identify and disidentify himself. This is pictured variously and repeatedly in the art of the late eighteenth and early nineteenth centuries, from Goya's etching of a sleeping etcher, to Gérard de Nerval's autobiographical lover negotiating a world of hallucination in *Aurélia* (Nerval 1972). The nineteenth century also dreamed the opposite of this figure, his malign reduction to absurdity: deprived of great events and beset by boredom, he becomes the etiolated aesthete, as satirised by Charles Dickens, for example, in the person of Harold Skimpole in *Bleak House*, or by Wilkie Collins in the sadistic Mr Fairlie in *The Woman in White*. He is the pseudo- or anti-therapist, for whom detachment has become sadistic disengagement.

Another contemporary aspect of this persona is the figure of the doctor, whose prestige and institutional power were growing rapidly from around the 1770s (Goldstein 2001 [1987]). There is Goya's moving self-portrait with Dr Arrieta of 1820: Goya represents the soberly but impeccably dressed Dr Arrieta (no bloodied apron here) stubbornly cradling his sick, resistant patient from behind, in an act of cool-headed holding, which is also an act of faith. In the late eighteenth century and the first decades of the nineteenth, the great British and French alienists Francis Willis (of madness of King George fame), the founding father of French psychiatry Philippe Pinel, and his major followers Jean-Etienne Dominique Esquirol and Etienne Georget, developed a benign, listening stance. Esquirol spoke clearly for this ethic. While humane restraint may occasionally be necessary to prevent injury,

> The doctor who treats a maniac must never seek to inspire fear in him
> . . . The doctor needs to be a comforting figure for his patients; he must
> skillfully find opportunities to show himself benevolent and protective,
> he must maintain a loving but grave tone, ally kindness with firmness,
> command esteem. By means of this conduct he will gain the patient's
> confidence, without which there can be no cure; his bearing, his look, his
> words, his tone of voice, his gestures, even his silence, act on the mind
> (*l'esprit*) or the heart of the maniac.
>
> (Esquirol 1838: II, 34)

Others, such as the father-and-son team Esprit and Emile Blanche, while insisting on their own self-restraint and a similar attitude of kindly benevolence, *douce bienveillance*, were not unusual in cultivating a more intimidating firmness as an essential therapeutic tool (Murat 2001: 25–6, 39–40, 56), a crude early intuition perhaps of what psychoanalysis later understood to be the centrality of therapeutic boundaries in treatment. In their private clinic in Montmartre, and later in the Paris suburb of Passy, the Drs Blanche welcomed their charges into the family, Gérard de Nerval among them. The opium-addicted Coleridge had similarly been cared for, kindly but firmly, in the family house of his long-suffering friend the physician James Gillman in Highgate (Holmes 1999: 426 ff.).

The figure whom Mademoiselle Bistouri presumes to be a doctor in Baudelaire's prose poem is a satirical play on medicine's contemporary claims to constitute itself as a kind of philosophical master-discipline. He is, to say the least, an ambiguous figure, and this ambiguity itself contributes to the way the poem requires a kind of readerly analytic attitude. On one hand, his motives and behaviour are dubious and as complex as the reader's possible readings: the possibility that he is merely a sexual *flâneur* cannot escape the reader, while Mademoiselle Bistouri supposes (or she, or the narrator, want us to suppose that she supposes) that he is a member of the prestigious medical profession because he is 'so kindly towards women'; he finally loses his 'professional' composure altogether and swears at her (Baudelaire 1975–76: I, 354). On the other hand, he is half-way towards representing a holder of an analytic attitude: he evinces a sense of wonder and an openness to the unknown, and the prose poem presents him as a transferential object to its heroine and, in so far as we cannot know what to make of this slippery narrator, to its reader too.

The dandy/doctor develops, in nineteenth-century fiction, another, less refractive facet: he becomes the aristocratic philosopher/detective. The practices and attitudes of the real-life Dr Blanche feed into the character of Dr Noir in Alfred de Vigny's novel *Stello* (1963 [1832]), Noir who tolerates, and inflicts, boredom and silence, but not sentimentality. Edgar Allan Poe offers Auguste Dupin, the first fully fledged detective in Western fiction, whose lateral mode of thinking adumbrates that of the working psychoanalyst.

Dr Noir

The novel best known as *Stello* (discussed below in its fine translation by Irving Massey) was published in 1832 in the early years of the July Monarchy. It echoed and contributed to contemporary debate, stimulated by the sense of elation and liberation among sections of the educated young following the 1830 Revolution, about the role of the artist and the relation of art to political and social life. The novel's original title, *Consultations du Docteur Noir: Stello ou les Diables bleus* (*Consultations with Doctor Noir. Stello or the Blue Devils*), privileges the doctor rather than the figure of Stello, the confused poet who seeks the doctor's help. Like Baudelaire's prose poems, the book defies conventional categorisation, as contemporaries noted: a reviewer for the London-based *Foreign Quarterly Review* wrote warmly that it was 'a production altogether *sui generis* . . . [a] clever but whimsical literary *nondescript*' (Anon. 1833: 513). In addition to an introductory 'consultation', the book consists of three separate episodes, in each of which Doctor Noir tells his patient a cautionary tale about the place of a poet in hostile socio-political circumstances: *Histoire d'une puce enragée* (*The Tale of the Mad Flea*), featuring Nicolas Gilbert, 1750–80, poet and satirist of the later years of the Ancien Régime, *Histoire de Kitty Bell* (*The Story of Kitty Bell*), about the fate of Thomas Chatterton in the reign of George III, and, the longest, *Une histoire de la Terreur* (*A Tale of the Terror*), about André Chenier, trenchant poet of moderate revolutionary views who was sent to the guillotine by Robespierre in 1794.

Stello is a young man blessed by circumstance, with aspirations as a poet, who seems to have come to the end of his tether with fruitless self-analysis. On certain days, following periods of unusual liveliness and bonhomie, he grows irritable, volatile, melancholy, anxious, despairing, full of spleen, with 'all the devils of migraine' sawing, drilling and hammering into his cranial bumps. His head sinks on his chest 'under the weight of his relentless depression'. It is in this condition, lying fully dressed on a couch, that Doctor Noir discovers him (Vigny 1963 [1832]: 3–6). 'Ah! thank God', cries Stello, setting out on a histrionic monologue that will last for two and half pages, '. . . it's you, a doctor of the soul, not one of those who are hardly even doctors of the body; you, who see to the bottom of everything, where other men see only superficial forms!' Stello having exhausted himself and concluded with a groan, the Doctor remains 'as cold as the statue of the Czar at Saint Petersburg in winter', and announces that Stello has the 'Blue Devils'. Stello is desperately seeking personal salvation in a dream of devoting his talents to a political cause, but he has no idea how to realise this; Doctor Noir, who shows himself to have a somewhat conservative agenda, aims through his stories to cure Stello of this 'temptation' (Vigny 1963 [1832]: 7). I shall not go into the stories, in each of which Noir himself plays a central role and demonstrates his superior powers of reasoning. I shall, rather, attempt to provide a sketch of his therapeutic persona.

That Doctor Noir is a sort of Mephistophelean transference figure for Stello is suggested by the fact that we discover little about him, not even his first name, and that he seems able to transcend time: he is an ageless presence, virtually unchanged from 1770 to 1832, although we do find out that he has learned from experience. He has had privileged access to Louis XVI and his court, to William Beckford Senior, the famous late eighteenth-century Mayor of London, and to Saint-Just and Robespierre. The Doctor, like one of his modern incarnations, familiar to generations of British TV viewers, passes through time and history unscathed. Partly he has such right of passage simply by virtue of being a doctor (see, for example, Vigny 1963 [1832]: 136), such is the prestige of his profession, which Vigny sees no need to underline, except in so far as he has Doctor Noir declare, quite early in the novel, 'The Abbé has made way for the Doctor, as if this society, becoming materialist, had decided that the care of the soul would have to depend henceforth on the care of the body' (Vigny 1963 [1832]: 44). Vigny confirms the extent to which medicine had established itself as medicine of the soul, but still not, in 1832, so unproblematically that this could pass totally without comment.

The 'harsh soul doctor' of 'inexorable reasoning' (Vigny 1963 [1832]: 34) is regarded by his patient as 'cold-blooded', 'impassive' (Vigny 1963 [1832]: 7), 'implacable' (Vigny 1963 [1832]: 54), 'callous' (Vigny 1963 [1832]: 89) and 'inflexible' (Vigny 1963 [1832]: 167). The struggling Stello calls him 'you black Doctor, with your ineluctable . . . bleak truths' (Vigny 1963 [1832]: 33, 67). He is a 'doleful, dour, deep Doctor', not 'capable of emotion' (Vigny 1963 [1832]: 51). Lying back in his armchair 'in his usual fashion', Doctor Noir is indeed an 'imperturbable inquisitor' (Vigny 1963 [1832]: 174). He prides himself on his 'sangfroid' (Vigny 1963 [1832]: 26), and he has, he says of himself, got over 'that common distemper, the philanthropic mania' (Vigny 1963 [1832]: 29) from which Stello suffers. He is resigned, Bion-like, to being on the receiving end, declaring at one point that 'everyone was thoroughly dissatisfied with me, as often happens' (Vigny 1963 [1832]: 120). He recommends that the 'solitary thinker observes an *armed* neutrality that mobilizes at need' (Vigny 1963 [1832]: 180), such as he models himself.

He has shown himself in the past to be vulnerable and human, of course: meeting the self-possessed Kitty Bell he finds himself 'at a loss what to think, do, or say next'. He says of himself, in response to Stello's complaints, 'Whatever opinion you may have conceived of me as a result of my hard-headed reasoning and the harshness of my analytic method, I assure you that I have a very kind heart; I just don't let the world know about it.' If he allowed Kitty Bell to see it in 1770, he has since, he says, corrected his mistake (Vigny 1963 [1832]: 42–3). He practises keeping his own reflective capacities alive, even though, at this particular juncture in the novel, he is hurrying towards Robespierre's house and danger:

All the while I was reviewing the scenes I had just witnessed. I concentrated my attention on them, I summarized them, I set them up in perspective. I had already begun that labour of philosophical optics to which I subject all my experiences.

(Vigny 1963 [1832]: 121)

The philosopher-doctor seeks to brings about the disillusion of his patient. Throughout the book he insists on his present relationship with Stello, and comments on his sense of Stello's current state: 'with what paradox are you infatuated now, if you please?' (Vigny 1963 [1832]: 174). Free of philanthropic mania and maintaining his armed neutrality, he refuses to pity his patient or interfere in his life: 'I care very little about your actions' (Vigny 1832 [1963]: 175), he tells him. He challenges his sentimentality – 'you wear your heart on your sleeve' (Vigny 1963 [1832]: 69) – and exposes its lameness; he confronts Stello's attempts to evade responsibility, pointing out, for example, that 'one is always a good master when one isn't the master' (Vigny 1963 [1832]: 85), and he explores his patient's relationship to authority (Vigny 1963 [1832]: 173).

In his commitment to introducing Stello to reality he talks with him about envy (Vigny 1963 [1832]: 167), and splitting and its infantile roots: 'the theories of well-meaning children who see everything in black and white, dream of nothing but angels or demons . . .' (Vigny 1963 [1832]: 78). He shows Stello his omnipotence. Where, he asks, does the temptation to 'flout the conditions of our being' come from? 'It comes from every child's desire to try out the other's game, never doubting his own limitless ability.' He confronts him with his self-delusion: 'You're fooling yourself . . . that idea [of limitless ability] has preoccupied you for a long time; you have been cherishing it; you love it; you fondle and caress it with secret devotion.' Noir's overarching aim is to free Stello of the lure of 'external things', to enable him to develop his own ability to reflect, and through the treatment to inure him against 'that . . . weakness when the spirit tires of studying itself, of living upon its own essence, and being fully and gloriously nourished thereby in its solitude' (Vigny 1963 [1832]: 70; here his words seem to carry an echo of Kierkegaard). At the same time Doctor Noir (and Vigny) might seem to be promoting a kind of narcissistic, solipsistic position. Yet in charting the real fate of the poets Gilbert and Chatterton, and getting behind the by then well-established cliché of the Romantic solitary in his garret, Vigny/Noir is far from seeking to instill self-pity. In encouraging and cajoling Stello to follow the conditions of his own being, Doctor Noir seeks to connect him to the strength inherent in his own desire.

How, though, is this to come about? By tracing 'the course of the idea which has led us to this point; the idea must be followed as one follows a winding stream' (Vigny 1963 [1832]: 69). This in turn requires the calm and discipline which Doctor Noir imposes upon Stello during the lengthy consultation. Such

calm is in stark contrast to a 'sick man's delirium', that, for example of the
leaders of the Terror in 1794, who 'didn't have the strength to stop to think
amidst it all'. For 'Thought, as I understand it, that calm, hallowed, strong
and penetrating faculty, is something of which they were no longer capable.
It does not descend into a soul that abhors itself' (Vigny 1963 [1832]: 82). 'I
do not find the circumstances right for thought', Bion is alleged to have said
at a large group conference (Symington 1986a: 278); in similarly Bionic vein,
Noir notes the role played by hatred and guilt in attacking thought.

Doctor Noir is, it follows, fiercely against that great enemy of free
association and thought, synthesis. In the following passage he is speaking
about two opposing 'pure ideologues', the revolutionary 'Terrorist' of 1794
Saint-Just, and the radical Catholic philosopher Joseph de Maistre (whose work
was to leave its mark on Baudelaire). In both equally he hears, as Baudelaire
was to hear, 'the cry of the carnivorous animal behind the human voice'. Both
are constructors of systems:

> In their anxiety to connect everything, at all costs, to a cause, a theory, a
> Synthesis from which everything can be derived and by which everything
> will be explained, I perceive a perennial weakness in men; like children
> walking in the dark, they are seized with terror because they cannot see
> the bottom of the abyss which neither God the Creator nor God the Saviour
> wanted us to see. Therefore it seems to me that the very men who think
> themselves most secure, because they construct the vastest systems, are
> the weakest, and the most terrified of Analysis, the sight of which they
> cannot bear, because it rests content with positive consequences, and
> observes only through the shadowy haze in which Heaven has chosen to
> enfold it, the *Cause* – the eternally undefinable *Cause* . . . Analysis is the
> whole destiny of the eternally ignorant human soul. Analysis is a plumb-
> line. Cast deep into the ocean, it terrifies and disheartens the weak, but it
> reassures and guides the brave who grasp it firmly.
>
> (Vigny 1963 [1832]: 134–5)

Doctor Noir's practice, and that which he finally recommends to Stello,
is a practice of Imagination, which, anticipating Baudelaire's famous phrase
(*l'imagination, cette reine des facultés*) by some thirty years, he calls 'the
greatest and the rarest of the faculties': 'allow the imagination which may
inhabit you its free and independent flight.' For 'The Imagination lives only
by virtue of the spontaneous emotions peculiar to the temperament and the
idiosyncrasies of the individual' (Vigny 1963 [1832]: 178, 180).

Noir's final 'prescription' for Stello is somewhat anti-climactic, a plea for
a sort of art-for-art's sake position, which is echoed in Théophile Gautier's
famous, near-contemporary preface to his novel *Mademoiselle de Maupin* in
1834: Stello must separate the poetic from the political life. Might *Stello*,
though, still reward interrogation as to whether it is *scriptible* or *lisible*? Is it

merely a kind of illustrated lecture, or is it able to engage the reader differently
– even, as a 'literary non-descript', to begin to do what Baudelaire's *Petits
poèmes en prose* do? The penultimate paragraph, addressed directly to the
reader, would at first sight seem to point to clunking *lisibilité*: 'Doesn't Stello
seem something like *feeling*? And Doctor Noir like *reason*?' This conclusion,
with its offer of a simple key, does not really do the novel justice, however.
Its very banality might work to kick-start the reader into reconsidering the
story and engaging with the more gnomic and challenging of the doctor's
utterances, such as his emphatically capitalized remark, towards the end, that
'HOPE IS THE GREATEST MADNESS' (Vigny 1963 [1832]: 181). Perhaps
the novel's final words encourage this more open-ended engagement, which
might put the reader too in the place of Doctor Noir's patient: 'if my head and
heart had been disputing the same question, they would not have spoken
differently' (Vigny 1963 [1832]: 183).[2]

The chevalier Dupin

Edgar Allan Poe certainly lends himself to reading in terms of the uncertainties
and slippages he engenders in the reader. As a recent critic has observed, Poe's
tales 'of Mystery and Imagination' 'question the notion of identity itself' (Renza
2008: xxxiv), within the context of an expanding culture of individualism in
the United States: 'it makes critical sense to construe Poe's many ambiguous
representations of identity (or is it representations of ambiguous identities?)
as a well-disguised effect of the period's impersonalising, capitalist ideology'
(Renza 2008: xxxiii–xxxiv). *The Tell-Tale Heart*, for example,

> stages a scene in which we readers interchangeably double as the tale's
> ostensible victim and victimizer . . . Using whatever cognitive mode is at
> our disposal, we cannot help but think we know [the murderous narrator's]
> mind . . . Yet Poe's tale simultaneously treats *us* as knowable for thinking
> to know its narrator in this last way. *We readers* in effect become the 'eye'
> that the tale would metaphorically fix or kill.
>
> (Renza 2008: xxxiii)

But it is on the character of Auguste Dupin that I want to focus as it develops
in three stories, *The Murders in the Rue Morgue* (1841), *The Mystery of
Marie Rogêt* (1842–43) and *The Purloined Letter* (1844) (Poe 2008: 78–186).
Dupin – in later stories he becomes the chevalier – is a 'young gentleman' of
'excellent – indeed of an illustrious family' who has been reduced to genteel
poverty (Poe 2008: 81–2). With his odd but distinctive green glasses (for his
too is a sort of 'labour of philosophical optics' [Vigny 1963 [1832]: 121]) he
is unmoved by the seductions of a merely technical expertise and is uniquely
able to 'see' what is under his nose. For 'If it is any point requiring reflection
. . . we shall examine it to better purpose in the dark', as Dupin states at the

start of *The Purloined Letter* (Poe 2008: 167). The anonymous narrator says that his design in the three stories is to depict Dupin's character and idiosyncrasy: his 'habits of moody reverie', his combination of 'frankness' and an 'indolent humour'. Historical precursors of Freud's Baker Street contemporaries Holmes and Watson, Dupin and his narrator occupy 'chambers in the Faubourg Saint Germain' where they 'slumber tranquilly in the present, weaving the dull world around us into dreams' (Poe 2008: 116–17). In *The Murders in the Rue Morgue*, the first of the trio of stories, the setting is decidedly 'gothick': the mansion is 'time-eaten and grotesque', probably haunted, and is 'tottering to its fall' like the House of Usher, 'in a retired and desolate portion' of the Faubourg. All this, the narrator says, was in keeping with 'the rather fantastic gloom of our common temper'. The pair live in seclusion and would, we are told, probably have been considered, like many an analyst, 'harmless madmen' had anyone known about them. Dupin is 'enamoured of the night for her own sake'; by day, behind 'massy shutters' and in the light of a couple of perfumed tapers, the pair 'busied our souls in dreams'. At night they roam the streets of the Paris of Poe's imagination (he never went there), 'seeking, amid the wild lights and shadows of the populous city, that infinity of mental excitement which quiet observation can afford' (Poe 2008: 82–3). How the twenty-something Baudelaire, reading Poe's stories in the 1840s, must have resonated to them and felt himself recognised, as if by a double.[3]

In a lengthy interview with the hapless Prefect of Police, Dupin shows himself to be the perfect (psycho)analyst: 'sitting steadily in his accustomed armchair, Dupin was the embodiment of respectful attention'; shielded by his green glasses, 'he slept not the less soundly, because silently . . .' (Poe 2008: 120). Poe is interested above all in the nature of Dupin's 'analytic abilities'. They are founded in the application of reason and can, as he painstakingly shows us, be elucidated; however, the qualities of mind which distinguish the analyst are not so reducible, and Poe insists on this in the opening words of *The Murders in the Rue Morgue*:

> The mental features discoursed of as the analytical, are, in themselves, but little susceptible of analysis. We appreciate them only in their effects . . . the analyst [glories] in that moral activity which *disentangles* . . . He is fond of enigmas, of conundrums, of hieroglyphics . . . His results, brought about by the very soul and essence of method, have, in truth, the whole air of intuition.
>
> (Poe 2008: 78–9)

Poe is explicit that it is this attitude and its holder that is his primary interest; a little essay of two or three pages follows this opening, and Poe concludes it by announcing that the 'narrative which follows will appear to the reader somewhat in the light of a commentary on the propositions just advanced' (Poe 2008: 81).

Among Dupin's most important assets is a readiness, in 'undertakings where mind struggles with mind' (Poe 2008: 80), to enter into trial identification, 'an identification of the reasoner's intellect with that of his opponent', as the narrator puts it in *The Purloined Letter* (Poe 2008: 176–7). He gives the example of an evenly balanced game of draughts played by equally skilled players, in which the eventual winner must find some additional 'acumen': 'the analyst throws himself into the spirit of his opponent, identifies himself therewith . . .' (Poe 2008: 79). Similarly in whist:

> it is in matters beyond the limits of mere rule that the skill of the analyst is evinced. He makes, in silence, a host of observations and inferences . . . the difference in the extent of the information attained, lies not so much in the validity of the inference as in the quality of the observation. The necessary knowledge is that of *what* to observe. Our player confines himself not at all; nor, because the game is the object, does he reject deductions from things external to the game . . . A casual or inadvertent word; the accidental dropping or turning of a card, with the accompanying anxiety or carelessness in regard to its concealment . . . embarrassment, hesitation, eagerness or trepidation – all afford, to his apparently intuitive perception, indications of the true state of affairs.
>
> (Poe 2008: 80–1)

He practises a kind of enquiring empathy or mirroring, which gives rise to what psychoanalysis would later call counter-transference: 'I fashion the expression of my face, as accurately as possible, in accordance with the expression of his', says Dupin, 'and then wait to see what thoughts or sentiments arise in my mind or heart, as if to match or correspond with the expression' (Poe 2008: 176–7).

Probably drawing on Coleridge's distinction between fancy and imagination, Poe/the narrator is at pains (*The Murders in the Rue Morgue*) to distance the analytic from the merely mechanical or mathematical:

> The analytical power should not be confounded with simple ingenuity . . . Between ingenuity and the analytic ability there exists a difference far greater, indeed, than that between the fancy and the imagination, but of a character very strictly analogous. It will be found, in fact, that the ingenious are always fanciful, and the *truly* imaginative never otherwise than analytic.
>
> (Poe 2008: 80)

Dupin is acute to the limits of mechanical reason. In *The Purloined Letter* he praises his adversary, the Minister, whom he has succeeded in outwitting, for being both mathematician and poet: 'As poet *and* mathematician he would reason well; as mere mathematician he could not have reasoned at all . . .'

(Poe 2008: 179). As mere mathematician, the guilty Minister would have been at the mercy of the police, with their standard and well-tried (evidence-based) methods. They twice conduct the most methodical search for the missing letter, with minute attention to visible detail, and possible signs and symptoms of disturbance – a sort of diagnostic mania. In failing thus to find the letter they are caught, in Dupin's view, by their own ingenuity, which leads them to two mistakes: a failure of identification with the Minister's way of thinking, and a refusal to consider anything other than 'their *own* ideas of ingenuity'. 'They have no variation of principle in their investigations; at best, when urged by some unusual emergency . . . they extend or exaggerate their old modes of *practice*, without touching their principles' (Poe 2008: 178). They are entrapped in their own cleverness, and imagination is a casualty; they fall, as they do again in *The Mystery of Marie Rogêt*, into 'one of the infinite series of mistakes which arise in the path of Reason through her propensity for seeking the truth in *detail*' (Poe 2008: 166). They are (*The Murders in the Rue Morgue*) too close up, like the great Parisian criminal-turned-police-chief Vidocq, who

> without educated thought, . . . erred continuously by the very intensity of his investigations. He impaired his vision by holding the object too close. He might see, perhaps, one or two points with unusual clearness, but in so doing, he, necessarily, lost sight of the matter as a whole. Thus there is such a thing as being too profound. Truth is not always in a well. In fact, as regards the more important knowledge, I do believe that she is invariably superficial
>
> (Poe 2008: 94)

Dupin values peripheral vision and suggests that it is better when, for example, looking at a star to do so by glances, 'in a sidelong way, by turning towards it the exterior portions of the retina (more susceptible to feeble impressions of light than the interior)'. He understands, like the great astronomers William and Caroline Herschel, that seeing is an art (Holmes 2008: 115–16). 'By undue profundity we perplex and enfeeble thought; and it is possible to make even Venus herself vanish from the firmament by a scrutiny too sustained, too concentrated, too direct' (Poe 2008: 94–5). He is careful to maintain a common-sensical perspective so that he does not make the mistake of being 'too deep or two shallow for the matter in hand'. For one can (*Marie Rogêt*) be 'too cunning to be profound'. He satirises the prefect's 'wisdom'; it has 'no *stamen*. It is all head and no body, like the pictures of the goddess Laverna [the Roman goddess of thieves] – or, at best, all head and shoulders, like a codfish' (Poe 2008: 115). Such disembodied wisdom, dissociated from libido, like that satirised in Goya's *The Sleep of Reason* (which produces monsters), is not true imagination.

One of the errors into which, for Dupin, this over-profundity and cunning lead the inquirer is to underestimate the unprecedented in the ordinary. The police are misled into thinking that the mystery of the disappearance of Marie Rogêt will be easy to resolve, because such disappearances, followed by the discovery of a corpse, are common, ordinary. For precisely this reason, Dupin says, it should have been considered difficult. The police could easily picture to themselves plenty of modes and motives for the disappearance and death, and assumed that because 'either of these numerous modes and motives *could* have been the actual one . . . one of them *must*'. But the 'ease with which these variable fancies were entertained, and the very plausibility which they assumed', should have been a warning. For

> it is by prominences above the plane of the ordinary, that reason feels her way, if at all, in her search for the true, and that the proper question in cases such as this, is not so much 'what has occurred?', as 'what has occurred that has never occurred before?'
>
> (Poe 2008: 129–30; see also 97)

Conversely, in *The Murders in the Rue Morgue*, the police who tend to be lulled into false confidence by the apparently ordinary can also fall 'into the gross but common error of confounding the unusual with the abstruse' (Poe 2008: 97). Dupin recommends (*Marie Rogêt*) unfocused attention on the wider context. He proposes 'to divert enquiry . . . from the trodden and hitherto unfruitful ground of the event itself, to the contemporary circumstances which surround it'. For 'experience has shown, and a true philosophy will always show, that a vast, perhaps the larger portion, of truth, arises from the seemingly irrelevant'.

He expounds:

> It is through the spirit of this principle, if not precisely through its letter, that modern science resolved to *calculate upon the unforeseen* . . . to collateral, or incidental, or accidental events we are indebted for the most numerous and valuable discoveries . . . [we must] make not only large, but the largest allowances for inventions that shall arise by chance, and quite out of the range of ordinary expectation.
>
> (Poe 2008: 144–5)

He is, 'without a particle of *chicanerie*', a master of free-associative method. In *The Murders in the Rue Morgue* he demonstrates this to the narrator, whose soul he seems to have fathomed, by retracing his steps along a chain of associations which runs: 'Chantilly, Orion, Dr Nichols, Epicurus, Stereotomy, the street stones, fruiterer' (Poe 2008: 85–6). Dupin is aided in this by observation of the narrator's posture, facial expressions and the direction of his glance, which work to confirm to him that he is following the chain correctly. He is mindful of recent conversations between the two of them, and draws on his own knowledge and erudition, as for example when he recalls a conversation on Epicurus and cosmogeny which leads him, encouraged by the narrator's looking up at that moment at the night sky, to Orion.

For Lacan, in his famous seminar on *The Purloined Letter*, it was this aspect of Dupin that was salient. Dupin understood the role, trajectory and displacements of the signifier. *The Purloined Letter* was the fable of this trajectory, and of how 'each subject is transformed by the effects of the signifier . . . how speech invests people with a new reality' (Benevenuto and Kennedy 1986: 99–100). For Lacan Dupin, the exemplary detective/analyst, understood that the signifier for all its displacements always returns to the same place, and that the actions and movements of each of the characters around him were determined by the movements of the letter/signifier.

> If what Freud discovered, and rediscovers even more abruptly, has a meaning, it is that the signifier's displacement determines subjects' acts, destiny, refusals, blindnesses, success, and fate, regardless of their innate gifts and instruction, and irregardless of their character or sex; and that everything pertaining to the psychological pregiven follows willy-nilly the signifier's train, like weapons and baggage.
>
> (Lacan 2007: 21)

All are subject to the Symbolic order in which the signifier places them. For

> the letter is not hidden *in* geometrical space, where the police are looking for it, or in anatomical space, where a literal understanding of psychoanalysis might look for it. It is located 'in' a *symbolic* structure, a structure that can *only* be perceived in its effects, and whose effects are perceived as repetition.
>
> (Johnson 1977: 498)

> how could we find a more beautiful image of the fact that this is the very effect of the unconscious, in the precise sense in which I teach that the unconscious is the fact that man is inhabited by the signifier, than the one Poe himself forges to help us understand Dupin's feat? For, to do so, Poe refers to those toponymic inscriptions which a map, in order not be silent, superimposes on its outline, and which may become the object of a 'game of puzzles' in which one has to find the name chosen by another player. He then notes that the name most likely to foil a novice will be one which the eye often overlooks, but which provides, in large letters spaced out widely across the field of the map, the name of an entire country . . .
>
> (Lacan 2007: 25–6)

The signifier is 'the symbol of an absence'; it 'materialises the agency of death'. It hides from us what is always present in life but never knowable (in Poe's story the contents of the letter is never disclosed); meanwhile, death is under our noses all the time. What, though, of the analyst/detective's own place in the Symbolic?

> The fact that Dupin was previously presented to us as a virtual pauper taking refuge in ethereal pursuits ought rather to lead us to reflect on the deal he cuts for delivery of the letter, promptly assured as it is by the checkbook he produces ... Are we not, in fact, justified in feeling implicated when Dupin is perhaps about to withdraw from the letter's symbolic circuit – we who make ourselves the emissaries of all the purloined letters which, at least for a while, remain *en souffrance* with us in the transference? And is it not the responsibility their transference entails that we neutralize by equating it with the signifier that most thoroughly annihilates every signification; namely money?
>
> (Lacan 2007: 26–7)

Dupin sees, as far as anyone could, the bigger picture; he understands that we are all subject to(o) and inevitably caught up in repetition. The handsome remuneration he receives at the end of *The Purloined Letter* does not work to ensure he is outside and above it all. 'He is ... clearly a participant in the intersubjective triad' (Lacan 2007: 27). His place as an analyst does not, for Lacan, mean that he any more than the rest of us can evade the agency of the signifier.

John Keats

Dupin and Keats might seem very distant relatives. Yet the discipline exercised by Keats in his life is of a related order to Dupin's. Dupin and Keats share a commitment to an 'analytic' reasoning in which genuine thought is that which is open to the peripheral and to a wide, horizontal perspective, which is nurtured by imagination and reverie, and informed by 'binocular' vision: that of both poet *and* mathematician (Poe 2008: 179). Poe had read some of Keats's poetry (Poe 1984), but is unlikely to have been aware of Keats's letter to his brothers of 1817 in which he formulated his famous negative capability; the phrase would have worked to describe aspects of Dupin's analytic attitude. But if, thanks to Lacan, the fictional Dupin emerges as an exemplary 'analytic' practitioner, it is partly because he is fictional; the flesh-and-blood Keats demonstrates that in practice maintaining negative capability is fraught. Nothing can destabilise it more than the real-life encounter with another person, with the exposure to one's own deepest terrors and the rapid closing of defensive doors which can follow. Keats's encounter with Fanny Brawne seems to have had its own destabilising effect on him, as well as prompting him to some of his most compelling poetry, through his renewed efforts to sustain an attitude of negative capability towards his own experience.

Keats's contributions to psychoanalytic thinking have been discussed by Williams and Wadell in terms of an adumbration of a post-Kleinian model of mind: mind as a 'Chamber of Maiden-Thought' and a 'Mansion of Many Appartments'; 'Soul-making' as a model of human capacity for psychic growth (Williams and Wadell 1991: 109 ff.). This Keatsian/post-Kleinian mind famously contains, to quote from the *Ode to Psyche*, 'untrodden regions' full of 'branchèd thoughts', which it is the poet's task to 'fledge' into 'a working brain' (Williams and Wadell 1991: 123–4). Williams and Wadell rightly make much of this, but they also risk offering a solipsistic account in which mind is self-created and self-contained rather than brought into being in and by a pre-existing world of others, with which it intersects. Their account does nevertheless stress Keats's struggle to overcome the illusions of egoistic 'identity'; indeed, a tension between self-creation and the possibility of giving oneself to, or losing oneself in, the other is a propelling force of Keats's poetry.

Keats's poetry also lends itself to discussion in terms of a major thrust of this book: with its ambiguities, uncertainties, and various forms of non-closure, in its sensuality and in the extent to which it can leave the reader unsure as to the identity of the speaker, it can awaken us and prompt us to look deeply within ourselves for a response. *The Eve of St Agnes*, for example – 'part-watchful, part-dreaming' is how Keats's biographer the poet Andrew Motion describes its immediate precursor, 'Hush, hush!' (Motion 1998: 337) – poses a series of open-ended, unanswered questions about sex and adolescent passion. Keats, 'allowing himself the freedom of the poet who has no fixed identity', surrounds these questions with further uncertainties. When, for example, Porphyro melts into Madeline's dream in the poem's final stanza, is it a real or imagined consummation? Is the poem, as Motion asks, 'a celebration of mutual physicality', or, a reading that would support Byron's unflattering view of Keats as a masturbator (MacCarthy 2003: 365 ff.), 'does its manifest inventiveness imply a preference for something solitary?' At the same time, the poem marks the moment at which Keats 'simultaneously buries his conflicting feelings about women, and lifts them into clear view' (Motion 1998: 342–4).

There is the 'punningly dual meaning' (Motion 1998: 505; see also 474) of the famous last phrase of the last line of the sonnet *Bright Star*: 'And so live ever – or else swoon to death.' Does the poet, pillowed upon his lover's breast, mean sexual or literal death? If it is a sexual death, then the alternative, to live forever, would be condemnation to eternal frustration. The reader is allowed no resolution, for these meanings are not alternatives: condemned to life, we must face the both the transience of sex and the inevitability of death.

Similarly, *La Belle Dame sans Merci* in Motion's reading 'creates surfaces of beguiling simplicity, through which readers peer into states of great emotional complexity'. The poem's starker implication, overlooked by generations of commentators, is that the ailing knight-at-arms has been active in choosing his fate: he 'provokes his own suffering, so that he can become one of those who know that love is an illness . . .'. Keats, Motion suggests, deeply troubled by his feelings for Fanny and the shadow of the early loss of his mother, was also drawn to positioning himself in this way (Motion 1998: 374–6; see also 42). One might take this further. Perhaps those generations of readers, specifically male readers, have been tricked by the poet into concluding that it is the *Belle Dame* who, as an archetypal *femme fatale*, provides the driving force of the poem's narrative. A dawning suspicion that the knight's predicament is of his own making has the added unsettling potential to confront the reader with his own contrary, death-driven attempts to master his suffering.

The famous closing couplet of the *Ode to a Grecian Urn* – 'Beauty is truth, truth beauty, – that is all / Ye know on earth, and all ye need to know' – does not, in fact, work as a concluding explanation. The lines do not merely offer an acceptance, which seems to be voiced by the urn itself, that human knowledge has its limits, that we see through a glass darkly. Actually, as Motion points out, they deny or contradict some of what has gone before: they do not summarise 'the moods and inquiries of the poem', they are not, the earlier verses of the poem would suggest, all that mankind knows or needs to know. The reader may be jolted into realising that art and philosophy are both like life and, in the final analysis, inadequate to it. For to

> fulfil himself as a beauty-loving and truth-telling poet, Keats must remain faithful to the world of experience, and suffer the historical process which constantly threatens to extinguish his ideal, rather than opt for a world of substitutes and abstractions.
>
> (Motion 1998: 394)

Substitutes and abstractions can, in the words of the ode, 'tease us out of thought' (Motion 1998: 394). And thought itself is often 'shadowy'. Likewise, what distinguishes Psyche, in the *Ode to Psyche*, is a lack of fixity, and this ode too ends on a note of openness and lively ambiguity. Keats's tribute to the goddess is necessarily incomplete precisely because it is an artifice, something which Keats's lines, full of surprise and brio, 'consciously artful . . . packed with ambivalences', do not allow the reader to forget (Motion 1998: 388–9).

But it is through a review of the attitudes he brought to his vocation as a poet that I want to try to reach towards a conclusion. Keats completed most of a medical training, at a time when medicine, as he himself understood, was at a revolutionary stage of its development (Motion 1998: 46);[4] in abandoning medicine for poetry he still hoped to be 'doing the world some good' (Motion 1998: xxv, 318). His whole orientation as a poet might be described as a desire to address suffering. This is how Motion summed it up:

> While we read his work and notice its consoling luxuries, its healthy and unhealthy airs, its medicinal flowers, its systems of nervous sensibilities, its working brains, its ethereal flights, its emphasis on 'sensation', its fluctuating temperatures, its marvellous chemical transformations, and its restorative sleeps, we realise that these things are not just incidental details, but the components of a selfless and moral imagination.
>
> (Motion 1998: 46)

But if, as Keats wrote in *The Fall of Hyperion*, 'a poet is sage; / A humanist, physician to all men', the poet's role was not to soothe, but to demonstrate, as he put it in his great journal-letter to his brother and sister-in-law of early 1819, 'how necessary a World of Pains and troubles is to school an Intelligence and make it a soul. A Place where the heart must feel and suffer in a thousand diverse ways!' 'Apollo', wrote Motion, 'was always his tutelary spirit' (Motion 1998: 131–2).

Informing this vision was his first-hand experience of suffering, as a surgeon's assistant at Guy's Hospital in 1815, as nurse first to his dying mother and then to his younger brother Tom and, in the last years of his brief life, as a sufferer himself, of the pains of love and the rampages of tuberculosis. Throughout his mature work he insisted on the sensuous, corporeal base to all thought and experience: thoughts are functions of sensations. This was an insight 'felt in the pulses', to borrow his own phrase, rather than just than a dead outgrowth of eighteenth-century 'sensationalist' philosophy. There was also his awareness of social suffering and the results of political repression, sharpened by his contact with Leigh Hunt and the radical journal *The Examiner*, and his friendships within Hunt's circle. Motion has demonstrated Keats's indebtedness to Hunt: *Endymion*, his first attempt at a lengthy, sustained poetic statement, took shape under the influence of Hunt's attacks on the restored Bourbon monarchy in France and the British government's support for it, and of Hunt's poem *Rimini*, based on Dante's *Inferno*, in which it is not the lovers Paolo and Francesca who are seen as sinful so much as the society that stifled them and their development. The 'beauty' of the famous opening lines of *Endymion* ('A thing of beauty is a joy forever') can, alongside the holiness of the Heart's affections (Keats 1958: I, 184), 'wipe away all slime / Left by men-slugs and human serpentry' (Keats 1988: 129). Keats, in Motion's words, links beauty's

> opportunities for self-forgetting to its role in promoting intellectual and human growth. As the imagination treats what the senses absorb or feel, it organises a journey from subjectivity to objectivity . . . Keats offers the opening lines of his poem as an article of faith in the power of poetry to function as a distinctly liberalising force.
>
> (Motion 1998: 163)

Keats's idealism is of an order that links it to Wordsworth's, in the Preface to *Lyrical Ballads*, and Shelley's, in the *Defence of Poetry*. There was also the impact of William Hazlitt, whose essays and lectures were much admired in Hunt's circle (Motion 1998: 124). Of special importance was Hazlitt's long early essay *Principles of Human Action* of 1805, in which, following in the Unitarian tradition of Rational Dissent, he made a powerful philosophical case for 'disinterestedness' against a prevailing (then as now) Hobbsean and Malthusian view that self-interest was the primary motivating factor in human conduct (Paulin 2003). In this essay, written when he was 26, in the year of Trafalgar and Austerlitz, Hazlitt argued that it is, on the contrary, imaginative sympathy that moves and binds us together. For '. . . the human mind . . . is naturally interested in the welfare of others in the same way, and from the same direct motives, by which it is impelled to the pursuit of our own interest' (Hazlitt 1969 [1805]: 1). One's future self, his argument goes, is as remote and unknowable as any other person; the way in which we seek our future welfare or self-interest is the same as that with which we would try to identify other people's welfare. The key is imagination: because 'That which is future, which does not yet exist can excite no interest in itself, nor act upon the mind in any way but by means of the imagination' (Hazlitt 1969 [1805]: 22). Thus, self-interested and other-interested actions, since they have a common source in imagination, are indistinguishable (Barbalet 2009: 200):

> The imagination, by means of which I alone can anticipate future objects, or be interested in them, must carry me out of myself into the feelings of others by one and the same process by which I am thrown forward as it were into my future being, and interested in it.
>
> (Hazlitt 1969 [1805]: 3)

In the final analysis clear distinctions between self and other are not sustainable. Partly Hazlitt's reasoning is that the concept of an ongoing self is based on a linguistic confusion, a 'nominal abstraction', which seems to justify an imaginative projection of present self into the future (Barbalet 2009: 201); for one modern commentator, who also sees the essay as an important contribution to modern sociological action theory, this linguistic argument grounds the notion of selfhood in history: the *Oxford English Dictionary* dates modern usage of the concept of self to the late sixteenth and early seventeenth centuries (Barbalet 2009: 203), and thus, as the liberal, oppositional Hazlitt was aware when he wrote the essay, to the beginnings of capitalism. More-over, for Hazlitt, 'the individual is never the same for two moments together' (Hazlitt 1969 [1805]: 85); all individuals are aggregates, 'and aggregates of dissimilar things' (Hazlitt 1969 [1805]: 87). Part of the clinching, concluding argument of this astonishingly prescient and undervalued essay concerns sex: far from being the ultimate, biologically driven expression of innate self-interest, it is anticipatory or imaginative sympathy with the *other's* desire which is the foundation of sexual passion (Hazlitt 1969 [1805]: 129): 'physical desire is mediated by other-directed sympathy' (Barbalet 2009: 206).

Hazlitt was never among Keats's close friends; yet all this, together with Hazlitt's lectures on literature in early 1818, particularly on Shakespeare, which Keats attended (Motion 1998: 227), confirmed and fed into his intuitions about creativity, identity and identification. These were certainly further stimulated by his reading and discussions of another highly evolved contemporary theory of creative activity, Coleridge's 'negative belief', in which a 'suspended state' of imagination, a radical letting thought be, might be brought about by a 'suspension of the Act of Comparison' (Holmes 1999: 130; see also Chapter 1, above).

In December 1817 Keats wrote the letter to his brothers George and Tom, which contains his statement on negative capability:

> several things dovetailed in my mind, & at once it struck me, what quality went to form a Man of Achievement especially in Literature & which Shakespeare posessed [sic] so enormously – I mean *Negative Capability*, that is when man is capable of being in uncertainties, Mysteries, doubts, without any irritable reaching after fact & reason . . .
>
> (Keats 1958: I, 193)

Keats extended Hazlitt's 'disinterestedness' to include both a necessary preparedness, through tolerance of uncertainty and doubt, to enter imaginatively into the world of another, with, in addition, a renunciation of designs upon the reader. A couple of months later he was writing to John Reynolds of his suspicion of poets who, like Wordsworth or Hunt at times, bully the reader 'into a certain Philosophy engendered in the whims of an Egotist':

> We hate poetry that has a palpable design upon us – and if we do not agree, seems to put its hand in its breeches pocket. Poetry should be great & unobtrusive, a thing which enters into one's soul, and does not startle or amaze it with itself but with its subject . . . we need not be teazed with grandeur & merit – when we can have them uncontaminated & unobtrusive.
>
> (Keats 1958: I, 223–5; see also Motion 1998: 229)

Or indeed unsaturated, like an interpretation as far as possible free of egotistical designs, driven rather by the analyst's commitment 'to feel his way through to whatever is the patient's experience of the moment' (Alvarez 1992: 6). Such an interpretation might only become possible once themes in the patient's experience and the analyst's experience had begun to 'dovetail' in the analyst's mind.

Keats's aspiration towards transparency of utterance found fruition in the late odes; they have few parallels in English literature (Plumly 2008: 362–3).

He came to view his identity, as a poet and a person, as depending on his having no fixed identity (Motion 1998: 355). In a letter to Richard Woodhouse of 27 October 1818 he once more contrasted the 'egotistical sublime', into which he felt Wordsworth had been seduced, with the idea of the 'chameleon poet':

> the poetical Character itself . . . is not itself – it has no self – it is everything and nothing – It has no character – it enjoys light and shade; it lives in gusto, be it foul or fair, high or low, rich or poor, mean or elevated . . . What shocks the virtuous philosoper [*sic*], delights the camelon [*sic*] Poet. It does no harm from its relish of the dark side of things any more than from its taste for the bright one . . . the poet . . . is certainly the most unpoetical of all God's Creatures . . .

In the same letter he went on to underline the blurred distinction between self and others, a distinction which the Wordsworthian 'egotistical sublime' would seek to preserve.

> It is a wretched thing to confess; but it is a very fact that not one word I ever utter can be taken for granted as an opinion growing out of my identical nature – how can it, when I have no nature? When I am in a room with People if I ever am free from speculating on creations of my own brain, then not myself goes home to myself: but the identity of everyone in the room begins to press upon me that, I am in a very little time anhilated [*sic*] – not only among Men: it would be the same in a Nursery of children: I know not whether I make myself wholly understood . . .
>
> (Keats 1958: I, 387; letter cited in Motion 1998: 318)[5]

In his journal-letter to George of February to May 1819, Keats wrote of his idle 'state of effeminacy' (anticipating his own *Ode to Indolence* of later in the year[6]) in which 'Neither Poetry, nor ambition, nor Love have any alertness of countenance as they pass me by'; they seemed to him more like figures on a Greek vase 'whom no one but myself could distinguish in their disguisement'. He called this state his 'only happiness', continuing, with a metaphor later adapted up by Bion: 'I am however young writing at random – straining at particles of light in the midst of a great darkness – without knowing the bearing of any one assertion of any one opinion' (Keats 1958: II, 78–9, 80, and Motion 1998: 359).

Keats was developing the discovery he had made for himself on his walking tour of Scotland with Charles Brown in 1818; through abandoning preconceived judgements and being prepared to register 'contraries' in a single moment, he found the most active engagement for his imagination (Motion 1998: 274), with all the human, Hazlittian implications of the term: the discovery, for example, of a horrified empathy for the dire plight of the rural poor. Losing his bearings, he was able to begin to find them.

The ideal creative state was, he wrote in a letter to Reynolds in February 1818, a 'delicious diligent Indolence'. This now explicitly connects with a vision of the interpersonal and social. Keats linked the image of a spider's web, stretched and suspended from a very few leaves and twigs, with the idea that man too might be content

> with as few points to tip with the fine Webb of his Soul . . . but the Minds of Mortals are so different and bent on such diverse Journeys that it may at first appear impossible for any common taste and fellowship to exist between two and three under these suppositions – It is however quite the contrary – Minds would leave each other in contrary directions, traverse each other in Numberless points, and at last greet each other at the Journeys end.

In what might be taken as a motto for the analyst, he went on to formulate the mildest of injunctions:

> Man should not dispute or assert but whisper results to his neighbour . . . thus . . . every human might become great, and Humanity instead of being a wide heath of Furse and Briars with here and there a remote Oak or Pine, would become a grand Democracy of Forest Trees . . . The receiver and the giver are equal in their benefits. [Let us, he concluded, in furtherance of this bold social vision] not therefore go hurrying about and collecting honey-bee like, buzzing here and there and impatiently from a knowledge of what is to be arrived at; but let us open our leaves like a flower and be passive and receptive.
>
> (Keats 1958: I, 231–2; Motion 1998: 232–3)

Motion has summed this up eloquently: 'delicious diligent Indolence' is thus 'nothing to do with inertia, everything to do with openness; nothing to do with self-effacement, everything to do with immersion'. Keats thus 'broadens the notion of negative capability to admit issues of responsibility as well as responsiveness' (Motion 1998: 232–3).

'Men should bear with each other', Keats told another of his friends in January 1819 (Motion 998: 227). Negative capability was an orientation to the other and to life. As such it 'must be able to withstand the disorienting, painful, catastrophic implications of . . . experiences of psychic tumult' (Williams and Wadell 1991: 188). For negative capability, in the nature of things, could not and cannot always be relied upon. That it might ever be a state one could occupy permanently is a fine aspiration and an illusion. Furthermore, it is inherently unstable, in perpetual need of renegotiation and recreation. Neither is it a merely passive state of reverie, something one abandons oneself to; it also has an active element, and involves both responsiveness and responsibility; there is the possibility, the requirement, to 'direct one's dream', as Gérard de Nerval put it, instead of merely undergoing it (cited in Béguin 1939: 377). Keats came to this distinction in *The Fall of Hyperion*; but on the way he had been thrown about, in a shifting disequilibrium, between responsible masculine reason, a questing imagination, and the corrective of feminine ('effeminate') fancy and dream; the offsetting of one term by the other had constantly, with endless frustration, to be corrected and counter-corrected.

In a close reading of *Endymion, Hyperion, The Fall of Hyperion* and the late odes, the critic Joel Faflak has tracked Keats's halting, disrupted coming-to-terms – if this is an adequate phrase – with constitutive instability and interminability. That it is possible to chart his failures and his travails in this way is one of the great, humanising rewards of reading him; he gives form to his very failure to find expression for the ineffable. What is more, in the accumulation of mythic figments that are part and parcel of this process he introduces himself to himself, or, as Faflak puts it, to 'identity's interminable pathology: the aesthetic residue of the subject's unconscious life perpetually recycled, the abject of the subject which *is* the subject' (Faflak 2008: 230). He brings the reader face to face with the abysmal as well as the exhilarating nature of his own discovery: 'That which is creative must create itself' (cited in Motion 1998: 212). It is also the mark of a particular daring.

The main reference points in Faflak's reading are Nietzsche, gender, the psychosomatic body and psychoanalysis. For Faflak, quoting from *The Birth of Tragedy*, what Keats 'reads' in himself is Nietzsche's 'hidden [Dionysian] substratum of suffering and of knowledge' revealed beneath the contemplative Apollonian surface of poetry's 'beauty and meditation' (Faflak 2008: 200, citing Nietzsche 1967: 46). Wordsworth, as Keats himself felt, finally stopped short. Keats, on the other hand, '[in] Nietzschian fashion . . . *does* dare to explore. He confronts poetry's radically self-making nature by reading within the giant forms of his unconscious . . .' (Faflak 2008: 200). Faflak takes his argument so far as to see Keats offering 'the sustained development of the clinical setting of the psychoanalytic scene as dialogic encounter between two subjects who struggle to articulate this suffering as it is transferentially displaced between them', in which Apollonian contemplation of a dark Dionysian core reveals only what Shelley, in his essay 'On Life', called 'the dark abyss of – how little we know' (Faflak 2008: 200, citing Shelley 2002: 508).

Negative capability is the unconscious of a masculine 'cold philosophy' ('Lamia'), of rationalism, and of the 'consequitive reasoning' (Keats 1958: I, 185) Keats so distrusted; it is, Faflak writes, a feminine 'transgression of masculine signification'. Yet Keats is 'perpetually "tolled back"' to the ' "sole self" of the poet's egotistical consciousness', against which, nevertheless, the banished psychosomatic body can still demonstrate its ability to mesmerise masculine reason: 'My heart aches, and a drowsy numbness pains / My sense', opens the *Ode to a Nightingale*. In Faflak's subtle analysis, feminine 'fancy', in the *Ode to a Nightingale*, 'both constitutes and trangresses the boundaries of masculine vision', leaving the poet 'caught in a no-man's land of gender's ambivalent "waking dream"' (Faflak 2008: 203). Hence, what has been seen as his 'stylistic cross-dressing': he borrowed from women's romance at a time when Regency culture was growing anxious about its own masculinity (Wolfson 1995: 91, cited in Faflak 2008: 206). Keats substitutes 'the developmental logic of reason . . . [for] the psychsomatic field or "Vale" of the psyche's dark internal functioning, staged indeterminately between the masculine and the feminine' (Faflak 2008: 206).

Endymion was Keats's first long verse narrative. He described it in his preface as 'a feverish attempt rather than a deed accomplished'. Its value, for all his disappointment with it, lay in what it allowed him to find out rather than in what it achieved, for it was also, as Motion writes, a 'giant "chamber of thought"' in which, at its most expansive, thoughts are 'groped for and then sensuously extrapolated', a 'high-temperature forcing house' (Motion 1998: 212).

Endymion (who had also been the subject of a painting by Girodet in 1791, which startlingly introduced a dreamy androgyny into the resolutely masculine discourse of the school of David[7]) is a 'brain-sick shepherd-prince' on Mount Latmos. The moon goddess falls in love with him and leads him, confused and ennervated, through 'cloudy fantasms'. A solitary dreamer, Endymion/the poet is intoxicated with the idea of perfection and omniscience, addicted to it, in a 'melancholic dis-ease . . . which the text's therapy cannot overcome' (Faflak 2008: 208). For Faflak, *Endymion* was an attempt 'to read the unconscious as transformative and transcendental'; Endymion's longing for a promised awakening to the unconscious's essential truth ends in the 'traumatic realisation that this dream exists "no more"' (Faflak 2008: 200). Keats moves, we might say, from a position analogous to Novalis's to one comparable to Hölderlin's. At one point Peona, the Greek spirit of vengeance and retribution who is among mythical figures who put in an appearance, places Endymion 'On her own couch' to try to help him read 'the troubled sea of the mind' (Faflak 2008: 207). It is a free-associative enterprise which both Endymion and the text would finally seem to resist. In the end, Endymion is carried off by the moon goddess to live with her for eternity, in an unsatisfactory and feverishly reached conclusion. It is in no sense a resolution to the struggle between competing forces, the terms of which Keats has nevertheless set out. Endymion was unable to hold on to that which had been intimated in the *Ode to a Grecian Urn*: the possibility that 'to transcend Reason's curse of individuation is to lose one's identity in a moment both liberating and terrifying, neither potently masculine nor cripplingly feminine' (Faflak 2008: 204). Faflak sums up: 'uncomfortable with feminine unreason, the text appears equally uneasy about a masculine reason that would gender away what seems integral to its own identity' (Faflak 2008: 208).

The uncompleted *Hyperion* once more takes up the quest for self-awareness (Hölderlin's novel *Hyperion* developed a parallel theme). It is an epic striving for an Apollonian vision set against the trauma of the destruction of the power of the old gods: Saturn mourns his fallen realm and with the Titans looks for help from Hyperion, the still surviving sun god. The poem breaks off at the point at which the young Apollo appears, the god of music, poetry and knowledge, who was of course also associated with medicine and healing. The poem's striving is, however, thwarted and disrupted, 'unsettled by the mind's "Creations and destroyings"' (Faflak 2008: 208).

Only through a readiness to grieve (Faflak 2008: 218–19, 220) might the poet/Apollo 'die into life'. In the much shorter *The Fall of Hyperion*, the poet walks in a dream through a garden to a forbidding shrine; only those people may approach 'to whom the miseries of the world/Are misery, and will not let them rest'. Now the curse of individuation, the 'habitual self' from which Endymion was seeking release, is exposed to 'the abyss of its own unreason' (Faflak 2008: 208–9). Faflak draws on Nietzsche's distinction between (poetic) Apollo who reads the unconscious through its surface, symbolic appearance and (unpoetic) Dionysus who 'surrenders to this symbolism's dark irrationality'; *The Fall* attempts to hold the two in a tension that 'the poet is compelled to speak'. He meets Moneta, a goddess in mourning for Saturn's 'wither'd race'. But *is* he a poet or merely a dreamer? This is the question Moneta and *The Fall* pose. The speaker's negative capability, in *The Fall*, is his 'capacity to witness and comprehend'; in the pale, shrouded figure of Moneta, Stanley Plumly writes, Keats's memory is made alive – of his mother and Tom. His struggle is to allow memories to live in himself and thus, as in the poem, 'see past the face . . . into the mind . . . with its "electral changing misery", its "wide hollows" . . . To see as a poet, as a true dreamer, is to see as a healer and knower' (Plumly 2008: 181–2).

Yet to speak one's dreams is to continue to risk.

> To *not* tell one's dreams is to remain unconscious of their irrationality and to live one's life as if one's soul were a 'clod'; *to* tell is to enter into the dream of life, a perpetual reading of its unconscious. *The Fall* figures this struggle between telling and not telling as the primal scene of poetry's self-making power.
>
> (Faflak 2008: 201)

In *Hyperion*, Keats is unable to accept that immortality, that of Hyperion/ Apollo, is the same as interminability; *The Fall*, in contrast, in a closing phrase that never seems to lose its power to stop the reader short, embraces the interminability of the unconscious: 'On he flared.'

The light of the sun god, instead of banishing the night like detached, enlightening Reason, flares through the darkness, fuelled and consumed from within. For 'Keats's texts struggle *beyond* the Freudian ken of a therapeutic cure to explore identity's interminable pathology . . . Keats' psychoanalysis is the interminable exploration of the psyche's darkness as the negative capability of what the subject cannot know or say about himself' (Faflak 2008: 230–1). This recognition of our essential, Nietzschian, unknowability is the discovery of interminability; and with it comes the transparency of speech, the transcending of individuality, of *The Fall of Hyperion* and the late odes: that supra-personal state that has the potential, on rare Baudelairian 'fine days of the spirit', to connect both patient and analyst to something beyond the ken of both.

Stanley Plumly, writing like Andrew Motion as a fellow poet, has put it like this:

> The place in his poetry that Keats has come to, in his final days as a writer, is a practice of form in which the eye and the ear are indistinguishable – as they are, for example, in *To Autumn*. Indeed, the synaesthetic eye, the painter's eye, in this great ode acts as might a first-person pronoun, the entity to whom the poem is happening; but because this eye is essentially a lens – a sentient, capacious yet focusing lens – it affects a certain neutrality, an 'objectivity'. The profound shift in point of view in the *The Fall* – from apparent objectivity in the first version to apparent subjectivity in the second – changes completely the announced entity to whom the poem is happening, and changes the story, too. Keats's dream-speakers, regardless of 'point of view', make shibboleths of the distinctions between subjective and objective voices.
>
> (Plumly 2008: 176–7)

'Posthumous' Keats suffered from a persistent myth that grew up before he had died and gathered force in the nineteenth century and into the twentieth: that if it was not superficial Fanny Brawne who caused his decline, it was a combination of his Tory critics and his own sensitivity (Plumly 2008). This story was accompanied by a related myth, now debunked thanks to Motion and other historians, that the childlike Keats was blissfully apolitical. He certainly was not: from his earliest contacts with Leigh Hunt and other radicals his verse resonates with allusions to repressive government at home and post-Waterloo reaction in Europe. Perhaps both myths thrived because they helped assuage the terror of an increasingly technologised and alienated society: the terror being of the anticipated disaster that will ensue if we cultivate openness to our Dionysian substrata, as Keats or Goya did, and to the mind of the other. The present book aims to add its voice in counter-warning: to regard immersion in the radical poetry and painting of the post-Enlightenment as interesting but somehow marginal to the serious, 'scientific' practice of psychotherapy might be to deprive ourselves of a vital resource in the struggle against all that which, including from within psychotherapy itself, does violence to the complexity of the human. Among all the other available agents of illness and madness, mechanistic misrepresentations of each other under the banner of therapeutic certainty can work to make us iller and madder: trainings in advanced self-alienation (see Miller 2006).

It will be no surprise to discover that the nineteenth century also came up with representations and personifications of this shadow side of the clinic: Mary Shelley's unfortunate Dr Frankenstein is a seminal figure, and perhaps it is not coincidental that the author was a woman. The victim of one of the most sinister if less celebrated medical practitioners in European fiction is possibly also a woman – at least the narrative seems to imply that she is. The French writer Philippe-Auguste Villiers de l'Isle-Adam, in a powerful contribution to the Romantic Gothic updated for the times, published a little story in 1877 entitled 'The Treatment of Dr Tristan'. The social and political context was the early years of the Third Republic, following France's humiliating defeat in the Franco-Prussian war. The new Republic aimed, among its many projects for national reinvigoration, to extend the reach of public health in ways consistent with the most up-to-date scientific and psychological principles, with doctors in the vanguard (Thomson 2004: 19–34 ff.).

Villiers's Dr Tristan Chavassus is, it would appear, a specialist in aural hallucinations. Where Lacan suggested deafening oneself in one ear the better to attend to the unconscious (Lacan 2007: 394), Chavassus recommends both: he is a destroyer of listening, both external internal. He belongs within a chain of heroic pioneers of modern, progressive rationalism satirized by Villiers: Thomas Alva Edison, for example, inventor of the new Eve, an 'electro-human machine' offering 'the frisson of first love', and a certain chemist who has patented a process for analysing the last breaths of the dying. Dr Chavassus considers hearing to be merely prurient (in its active sense) or a source of injury (its passive sense): his métier is helping people who are 'all ears' or 'can't help over-hearing', or who have been sent away 'with a flea in the ear'. But his real specialism is curing those who hear voices, like Joan of Arc. No more 'heroic inspirations' to fear, no more patriotic flutterings of the heart, no more siren appeals to great tomorrows. The doctor will make sure that the sufferer's ear drums are as muted 'as any serious and rational drum ought to be these days'. In effect, he deafens his patients, by repeatedly bellowing the word 'Humanity' into one ear and fragments of certain 'obsolete' words such as 'Generosity!', 'Faith!', 'Disinterestedness!', 'Immortal Soul', into the other. An electric current passed between the ears completes the cure. The patient leaves, writes Villiers, overwhelmed with gratitude, bathed in 'Good Sense', well-being and indifference (Villiers de l'Isle-Adam 1980: 264–9).

Conclusion

In the Ca' Rezzonico museum in Venice there is an unusual and intriguing fresco by Giandomenico Tiepolo. It was made in 1791 (that recurrent decade) and it is called *The New World*. It shows a small crowd, mostly seen from the rear, some in carnival costume. They are waiting their turns to look inside a tent containing a peep-show, a popular entertainment like the phantasmagoria. A man with his back to us, in a tricorn hat, stands on a box and manipulates a long stick which, unseen to us and to the waiting Venetian crowd, moves transparent or semi-transparent panels inside the tent. These panels would have been set in line with painted scenes on them, and would have created a sense of three-dimensional depth and movement to viewers who, one by one, squint through a peep-hole. Light, itself constantly changing, enters through the top of the tent. The man may also be able to drop down new panels so that the scene, whatever it is, changes. He is a master-of-ceremonies like the figure in the tricorn hat in Goya's *Madhouse*. There is a sense of wonder and anticipation, faintly tinged with carnival menace.

Film historians have interpreted the image as announcing the art form of the future, the art of moving pictures which would be able to show the world in all its detailed, unpredictable, surprising contingency – the world of Benjamin's 'optical unconscious'. It also chimes with contemporary cultural developments, the fascination with the fleeting, unpre-ordained and unrepeatable, that which escapes preconception, in Goya's drawings, or Hoffmann's fantastic and dreamlike tales (the subtitle of one of these, *The Golden Vase*, is *A Tale of Modern Times*). The picture speaks to an amazed and anxious fascination with the unknown, that which is not semiotically predetermined but which is nevertheless right under our noses, the familiar made both more articulate and more mysterious once it is noticed – just that with which free association can connect us. It is also a fascination with the Dionysian, with that which we can glimpse but never know or master, the Freudian dream's navel. This is tellingly expressed in the scene in Luis Buñuel's *Belle de Jour* in which Catherine Deneuve looks into a little box, the contents of which, like what is going on in Tiepolo's tent, is never revealed.[1] 'There is something censored in what one believes to be evidence', wrote Yves

Bonnefoy (Bonnefoy 2006: 48); in this understanding the impulse to seek evidence, for therapeutic efficacy, for example, would be akin to the irresistible desire to look into the box, as if into a primal scene which would disclose *it*, the Lacanian *objet* (*petit*) *a*, the secret, the final piece of the jigsaw.

There can be joy too in this encounter with the unknowable, if it is an embrace and not just a quest, and this is an important aspect of Romanticism which is not easy to put into words: a youthful and maybe, for most of us, only occasionally or rarely felt sense of life's possibilities, accompanied by a feeling of emotional achievement; a brave sense of having few illusions and little to lose, which might allow one to meet the other person in all her or his foreignness; a sense of the present moment as alive and unfolding (the figures in Goya's madhouses or Théodore Géricault's portraits of the insane, it might be argued, are at the opposite pole of this, isolated and deadened, or suffering because their minds are elsewhere, caught up in repetition and fancy).

Tiepolo's *New World* hints at the other side, the hidden content of what Bonnefoy christened *le grand rêve*. To an extent, Enlightenment itself was a critique of 'the great dream' as religious, faith-based construct in which the post-Renaissance world could be conceived and experienced as the product of god-given harmony and order. Enlightenment was an attempt to reveal and redress that which this world-view masked, to open eyes not only to the mysteries and happenstances of the material and visible world, but also to the inhumanities and abuses it contained. Where, for example, do we find images of the destitute or the imprisoned in Rome at the time of Raphael? The lack of visual representation of the mad before roughly the mid-eighteenth century has often been commented on.

In a sense, however, Enlightenment was also its own *grand rêve*, and it is this that was coming into view around the period of its late eighteenth-century crisis. It was what Romantics recognised – the recognition defines them *as* Romantics – as the great dream of Reason, which can seek to over-ride experience, and worse. 'The philosophy which put the fear of death into infamy in the eighteenth century . . . chose to serve that very infamy under Napoleon', wrote Adorno and Horkheimer (1989 [1944]: xii). Among its fruits were brand new forms of human misery and oppression, all of its own creation. Enlightenment was double-edged. Here is Coleridge in 1818, rousing himself in support of Sir Robert Peel's bill to regulate the hours of child labourers in the cotton factories, enlightened legislation pitted against what Coleridge called the 'so-called' enlightenment science of political economy, in which human beings might be managed as abstractions, in terms of accountancy and profit. Coleridge wrote:

> It is a science which begins with *abstractions*, in order to exclude whatever is not subject to a technical calculation: in the face of all experience, it assumes these as the *whole* of human nature – and then on an impossible hypothesis builds up the most inhuman edifice, a

Temple of Tescalipoca! (Tezcatlipoca was the Atzec god, whose throne was built of human skulls.)

(cited in Holmes 1999: 476)

A 'so-called' science is one that starts with abstraction rather than doubt, and this can lead to atrocity, as has been demonstrated over and over again since Coleridge's day. The present book urges a continuing wary scepticism towards this persisting aspect of Enlightenment, to which belong reductionist therapeutic practices in which emotional pain is translated into the abstract language of medical disorder, all the more easily to be 'managed'. Therapeutic regimes, like cotton mills, are of course products of complex webs of vested interest, which social scientists and historians of psychiatry have analysed in detail (Goldstein, for example, has charted a lineage from Monomania to Attention Deficit Disorder. Goldstein 2001 [1987]: 398–406; see also Leader 2008); and we are all, post-Foucauldians not excepted, inevitably caught up in our own interests, allegiances and networks of power. This should not absolve us, however, from the work of thoughtful analysis towards which the Romantics can point us.

If Enlightenment survived and adapted itself to its great crisis, this also led, in the nineteenth century, to a major cultural parting of the ways, the effects of which are still with us. On one hand was the 'new confinement' identified by Foucault, the medicalisation and technologisation of emotion and experience (Foucault 1971 [1961]). On the other hand, in a refusal to be confined, was the Romantic and psychoanalytic discovery of a madness at the core. Slavov Žižek has summed up the Romantic break with Enlightenment and its light–dark metaphor in terms that Goya would have understood:

the subject is no longer the Light of Reason opposed to the nontransparent, impenetrable Stuff (of Nature, Tradition . . .); his very kernel, the gesture that opens up the space for the Light of Logos, is absolute negativity, the 'night of the world', the point of utter madness in which fantasmatic apparitions of 'partial objects' err around . . . the true question . . . is how the subject is able to climb out of madness and to reach 'normalcy'. . .

(Žižek 1998, cited in Faflak 2008: 210–11)

Such is the question, with appropriate scare quotes, which analyst and patient continue to peer into, carefully, session by session, consultation by consultation, redefining 'normalcy' in the process.

Notes

Introduction

1   indeed, it requires a strong imagination as well as an accurate psycho-analytical understanding in order to be able to conceive the possibility & to picture out the reality, of the passion of those Times for Jupiter, Apollo &c/& the nature of the Faith (for a Faith it was – it vanished indeed at the Cock-crowing of a deliberate Question, in most men; but in the ordinary unchecked stream of Thought it moved on, as naturally as Contraband & Legal Goods in the same Vessel, when no Revenue Officers are on the Track.) Having as usual, thro' a Labyrinth of Parentheses wandered out of the Possibility of connecting my sentence grammatically tho' logically I have never let go of the Thought, I am to memorandum a striking instance of this gross confusion of this Paganizing of Christianity.

(Coleridge 1961: para 2670)

Freud's first use of the word psychoanalysis was in 1896, first in French, then in German (Jones 1953: I, 269).

2   Every enthusiast for the period will have his or her own beacons. The present writer was stimulated to expand his Romantic horizons by a review by the poet Michael Hofmann of translations of Hölderlin's poetry by Michael Hamburger. Hofmann bracketed Hölderlin with Shelley, Novalis, Kleist and Büchner, all prime movers in Romanticism's 'incredible ferment'. He also listed some Romantic themes:

youth, love, friendship, generation conflict, sibling relationships, world- and self-intoxication ... a revitalised appreciation of the classics, idealist philosophy, revolution, spirituality and the death of religion, a volatile interest in the inner and outer world (all sorts of fads and '-isms'), a proclivity for associations, amalgamations, movements, new magazines, publishing ventures and experiments in social living.

(Hofmann 2004)

I Psychoanalysis and Romanticism: crisis, mourning and the mysteries of the ordinary

1   Freud was dismissive of Schubert's book in *The Interpretation of Dreams*. Yet he was also frank in his acknowledgement that 'the psychical achievements of dreams received readier and warmer recognition during the intellectual period which has now been left behind, when the human mind was dominated by philosophy and not by the exact natural sciences' (Freud, S. 1900: 63). Henri Ellenberger went further: '... there is hardly a single concept of Freud or Jung that had not been anticipated by the philosophy of nature and Romantic medicine' (Ellenberger 1970: 205).

2 1735–88. The cultural ambience of 'Brownismus' in late eighteenth-century Germany, by modern standards a brutal therapeutic regimen, is wonderfully evoked in Penelope Fitzgerald's novel *The Blue Flower* (Fitzgerald 2002 [1995]).

3 Freud indeed acknowledged Romantic accounts of dream as

> a liberation of the spirit from the power of external nature, a freeing of the soul from the bonds of the senses, and similar remarks by the younger Fichte and others, all of which represent dreams as an elevation of mental life to a higher level
>
> (Freud, S. 1900: 63)

and he deplored their mysticism.

4 'Painting is a science, and should be pursued as an enquiry into the laws of nature. Why, then, may not landscape painting be considered as a branch of natural philosophy, of which pictures are but the experiments?' At the same time painting, for Constable, was 'but another word for feeling' (cited in Thornes 1999: 51).

5 Lacan's view, in 1953, was that psychoanalysis belongs on the side of art provided 'art' is understood in its medieval sense, in which arithmetic, geometry, music and grammar were included among the 'liberal arts'. He agreed with Freud that psychoanalysis is closer to scientific than religious discourse, although it is a 'practice . . . with a scientific vocation' rather than a science. By 1977 he had come to feel that psychoanalysis 'has no scientific status – it merely waits and hopes for it. Psychoanalysis is a delusion – a delusion which is expected to produce a science . . .' (cited in Evans 1996: 174).

6 Lionel Trilling, for one, saw origins and parallels for psychoanlysis in Diderot's novel of 1762 *Le Neveu de Rameau*, with the urbane narrator 'Diderot' representing ego and the undomesticated nephew of Rameau id (Trilling 1979 [1950]: 34–5).

7 At the other end of our period, the poet Alfred de Musset satirised the problem of a definition in fictional letters between two provincials, Dupuis and Cotonet (worthy precursors of Flaubert's Bouvard and Pécuchet).

> Until 1830 we believed romanticism was imitation of the Germans, to whom we added the English, on advice given to us . . . From 1830 to 31, we believed that romanticism was the historical mode . . . from 1833 to 1834, we believed that romanticism meant not shaving and wearing waistcoats with large lapels starched stiff . . .
>
> (Furst 1980: 47–8)

For detailed historical discussions of the development of the meaning of the word 'Romantic' across Europe, see Eichner 1972.

8 In Germany shortly after the turn of the eighteenth/nineteenth centuries, Hölderlin voiced a parallel idea, in blunter terms: 'Cruelly God hates all-knowing minds' (cited in Kuzniar 1987: 149). Edgar Allan Poe expressed it some four decades later in terms of forming 'a vague and half-formed conception of the meaning . . . I seemed to be on the verge of comprehension, without power to comprehend – as men, at times, find themselves on the brink of remembrance, without being able in the end, to remember' (Poe 2008: 104). Baudelaire modelled the modern artist on the child, who with 'involuntary, joyful receptivity . . . sees everything in its *newness*, he is always *drunk*' (Baudelaire 1975–76: II, 684, 690).

9 Freud, of course, acknowledged this history: 'even before the time of psycho-analysis, hypnotic experiments, and especially post-hypnotic suggestion, had tangibly demonstrated the existence and mode of operation of the mental unconscious' (Freud, S. 1915: 168–9).

10 A *Märchen* was a kind of fairy-story, an old narrative form involving supernatural subjects which was revived by the Romantics.

11 It was on this increasingly populated and popular borderline, where expanding town met country, that the Impressionist painters were to make their first experiments in the 1860s (see House 2004).

12 Wordsworth gave voice to this Romantic impulse, if sentimentally: 'man is dear to man; the poorest poor / Long for some moments in a weary life / When they can know and feel that they have been / . . . kind to such / As needed kindness, for this single cause, / That we have all of us one human heart' (Wordsworth 2000: 53).

13 In 1967, following the publication of Michel Foucault's *History of Madness* (Foucault 1971 [1961]), Jacques Derrida pointed to the sheer impossibility of Reason sustaining a dialogue – that on which Foucault rested his historical argument – with Unreason (Derrida 1967).

14 The figure of Théroigne de Méricourt is exemplary, a mythic bogey-woman in a later nineteenth-century bourgeois imaginary. A former *demi-mondaine*, in 1792 Théroigne de Méricourt became a fervent revolutionary and warrior feminist of the 'amazon batallions'. She lost her mind during the Terror and was incarcerated as a famous case of melancholic insanity under Etienne Esquirol, a founder of the modern asylum (see Roudinesco, 1989, and Esquirol 1838: I, 220–2).

2 The analytic attitude: an overview

1 *Gleichschwebend*: 'simultaneously with its connotation of equal distribution, it also has the meaning of revolving or circling . . . Another possibility, which emphasises the psychological balance rather than the motion, would be "poised attention"' (Reik 1948: 157). Thus wrote Theoedor Reik. Reik was dismissive of A.A. Brill's 'mediocre' translation of the word as 'mobile attention': Pavlova, he wrote, is mobile, but this does not give a good picture of her activity on stage (Reik 1948: 157, n1). The Romance languages have gone for the equally suspended or the floating: '*attention en égal suspens*' (Bourguignon *et al.* 1989: 148–89) or '*également flottante*', '*atención parejamente flotante*', '*attenzione ugualmente fluttuante*', '*atenção equiflutuante*' (Laplanche and Pontalis 1988: 43).

2 'I dressed his wounds, God cured him.' The saying is attributed to the French surgeon Ambroise Paré (*c.*1517–90).

3 For an excellent critical comparison of Freudian, Lacanian, Kleinian and Winnicottian frames of reference, see White 2006.

4 The influence of phenomenology on psychotherapy practice is more openly acknowledged in humanist circles; see Ernesto Spinelli's *The Interpreted World* (Spinelli 1989). A dilute form of phenomenology seems to underlie Carl Rogers's 'core conditions' (see Rogers 1967 [1961]).

5 Although there were great differences between him and Laing, and although he would probably not have wanted to describe himself as a phenomenologist (or an anything), Peter Lomas might be mentioned in this context: for his commitment to doubt and ordinariness, opposition to dogma, and emphasis on the personal element in therapy (Ingleby 1999: 140), all of which was summed up in the title of a collection of essays published in his honour in 1999, *Committed Uncertainty in Psychotherapy* (King (ed.) 1999).

6 Bion was referring to a comment Freud made to Lou Andreas-Salomé in a letter of 1916, which, interestingly, concerns writing: 'I know that in writing I have to blind myself artificially in order to focus all the light on one dark spot . . .' (letter 25 May 1916; Freud, S. 1916: 45).

7 'Bion was a gnarled and quirky writer, not . . . because he could not help but being, but because . . . he was obsessed with truth. If we allow that by art, Donald

Barthelme [author of the paragraph that follows] means what Bion means by "aesthetic truth", the following might describe Bion's quandary and quest:

> However much the writer might long to be, in his work, simple, honest, straightforward, these virtues are no longer available to him. He discovers that in being simple, honest, straightforward, nothing much happens: he speaks the unspeakable, whereas we are looking for the as-yet-unspeakable, the as-yet-unspoken . . . the not knowing is not simple . . . the more problems he takes into account, the more considerations limit his possible initiatives (*New York Times*, February 18, 1982).'
>
> (Boris, 1986: 161)

8 There are, Freud wrote in his 'Recommendations', 'times and places at which one is disturbed by some personal consideration – that is, when one has fallen seriously below the standard of an ideal analyst.' The analyst must 'become aware of those complexes of his own which would be apt to interfere with his grasp of what the patient tells him' (Freud, S. 1912: 112, 115).

9 Jung's views have been developed by post-Jungians, notably Fordham (1969) and Zinkin (1969), although Jungians have never gone so far as Alexander in Alexander, French *et al.* (1946), Greenson (1991 [1967]) or Horner (1987) in privileging the therapeutic efficacy of the 'real relationship' and the 'corrective emotional experience'.

10 Ogden's procedure seems steeped in a sort of Keatsian reverie; Caper's critique echoes Byron, who thought Keats indulged in 'a sort of mental masturbation – he is always f-gg-g his *Imagination*' (MacCarthy 2003: 365 ff.).

11 Thomas Ogden explores similar territory; see, for example, Ogden 1998.

12 Green (2005) offers a fascinating discussion of the analyst as *instigator* of the unconscious message, the phenomenon that 'lies at the bottom of every transference' (Green 2005: 44–5).

3   Goya and the dream of Enlightenment

1 For an excellent discussion of the dilemmas and responses to occupation among members of the Spanish educated classes, see Fraser 2008. See also Carr 1982: 111–15.

2 The art critic Robert Hughes, a passionate writer about Goya, recalled a terrible, possibly life-saving dream from which he awoke in intensive care after a car crash. He was

> the captive of this street gang headed by Goya and his friends, who were a bunch of horrible toughs. For some reason we were in Seville. And they kept taunting me, saying you want to write about me – well, you're never going to get out of here alive.
>
> (Hughes 2002)

3 Bonnefoy also points to the 'Little Giants' and the smiling face of the boy on the shoulders of the other in the foreground: 'this immense head reflects less pleasure in the game than an inexplicable, horrifying ecstasy'. He compares it to faces in pre-Columbian Mexican art, whose smiles can seem to be about ordeals so absolute as to go beyond suffering. 'By means of a mere nothing in the drawing of a mouth Goya darkens the sky of the pastoral idyll, he freezes one with fear, he tips the world of meaning and values into non-meaning, he turns light into a desert . . .' (Bonnefoy 2006: 31).

4 The art historian Nigel Glendinning has noted that the phrase *Yo lo vi* ('I saw it myself') that Goya used as the caption for *Disasters of War* etching no. 44 was a

rhetorical commonplace in the poetry of the period (Glendinning 1977: 70 and n4). To worry over the literal veracity of this, however, or over Goya's assertion, in a letter to his prospective patron, that he witnessed the scene in the madhouse at Zaragoza, might be to miss the point; it would be to position oneself firmly within the terms of Bonnefoy's *grand rêve*, of the Western post-Renaissance tradition, with its massive emphasis on the ocular and its over-riding appeal to the evidence of the external senses. It was precisely this that, in the later eighteenth century and in the work of Goya above all, was starting to break down, a process to be taken further by psychoanalysis. 'I saw this' might equally be said of a hallucination.

5   Important critical context to Goya's response to the intellectuals of the Spanish Enlightenment is provided by the German historian Reinhart Koselleck, who, in the words of his American editor Thomas McCarthy,

> views Enlightenment intellectuals as an uprooted, unrealistic group of onlookers who sowed the seeds of the modern political tensions that first flowered in the French Revolution. He argues that it was the split that developed between state and society during the Enlightenment that fostered the emergence of this intellectual elite divorced from the realities of politics . . . [producing little] centers of moral authority . . . that took little or no notice of the constraints under which politicians must inevitably work. In this way progressive bourgeois philosophy, which seemed to offer the promise of a unified and peaceful world, in fact produced just the opposite.
>
> (Koselleck 1988)

Goya's later work seems to embody a more than half-articulated recognition of this.

6   Here is a psychoanalytic reading of his likely state.

> If we consider that [during his illness of 1793] he was deprived of sight and hearing and motor control, and disoriented further by constant dizziness and inchoate noises, we may suppose that his power of testing reality was debilitated almost to annihilation. A fantastic inner world of confused, monstrous, and terrifying forms, related to his sufferings, broke through from the unconscious. We can imagine this profusion of alarming shapes whirling unseizably through his mind, probably assuming the intensity of hallucinations, and seeming to portend imminent dissolution and death. These nightmares seem to have been strongly sadomasochistic and persecutory; later they became organized around certain themes.
>
> (Wolfenstein 1966: 49)

7   Compare Goya's graphic account of breakdown with the eighteenth-century English poet William Cowper's, his 'alienation from God . . . [in which] Satan plied me close with horrible visions and more horrible voices' (cited in Rosen 1998: 108).

8   Delacroix's 1839 'Tasso in the madhouse' does not quite fit: it is a literary subject, and unlike the other paintings mentioned, it does not base its claims to the viewer's attention on documentary truth ('I saw this').

9   Pinel published a seminal book, *Traité médico-philosophique sur l'aliénation mentale ou la manie*, with the word philosophy in its title, in year IX of the Republic (1800); it was a work of classification, a treatise on the management of a large institution, and a treatment manual. Between this and the appearance in 1838 of the major work of his most influential follower, Jean-Etienne Esquirol, soberly entitled *Des maladies mentales*, the medicalisation of madness, and along

with it the prestige and legal authority of the doctor of the mad, had become more securely established (see Goldstein 2001 [1987]).

10 The first cartoon in Steadman's book is after 'The Dream of Reason', and beneath it he has written 'The tormented Viennese citizen hides his head in his hands, trying vainly to shut out the bats and demons of Freud's odious alchemy' (Steadman 1979: 6). Elsewhere he wonders if it is the artist who needs analysing.

4 Hölderlin, Novalis, word without end

1 There exists a translation by the American writer Frederic Prokosch entitled *Some Poems of Friedrich Hölderlin . . . in German & English, Has German Text with Hölderlins Own Curious Spellings which Transcends Translatability Sometimes* (*sic*). Norfolk, CT: New Directions 1943.

2 Laplanche wrote of the 'lost unknown', and of 'the stabilising function of poetry and myth', a function suggestive of Lacan's *sinthomme*, in the face of the threat of imbalance; of 'the shadow, the negative, the return in the real of a paternal symbol', which appears in the last version of *Empedocles* in the figure of Manes, the aged visionary. For Laplanche, Hölderlin's struggle was 'to wrest from his mother the free use of his desire' (Laplanche 1961: 119 and 101).

3 'I do not take him to be just any poet,' said Heidegger, '. . . for me Hölderlin is the poet who points to the future, who expects god and who therefore may not remain merely an object of Hölderlin research . . .' 'S [interviewer for the news magazine *Der Spiegel* in 1966]: You assign in particular a special task to the Germans? H: Yes, in the sense of a dialogue with Hölderlin' (Wolin 1993: 112, 113).

4 Constantine is doubtful about the extent of Hölderlin's Jacobinism. He embraced the ideals of Liberty, Equality and Fraternity, and was enthusiastic about French revolutionary armies entering Germany in 1792; up to 1799 he seems to have hoped that Swabia might become a republic. But like most German contemporaries he was distressed by the Terror and Jacobin extremism (Constantine 1988: 22–3).

5 For thorough discussions of Heidegger's relationship to National Socialism, see Wolin 1993.

6 'The great saying εν διαφερον εαυτω (the one differentiated in itself) of Heraclitus, could be found only by a Greek, for it is the very being of Beauty, and before that was found there was no philosophy . . .' (Hölderlin 1965 [1797,1799]: 93).

7 In *Die Christenheit oder Europa*, written in 1801, while Napoleon was returning from Egypt and about to overthrow the Directory, Novalis, in line with other Romantics, anticipated a new Jerusalem. The book is a poetic vision expressed with prophetic assurance. There are signs, he wrote, 'that a new age is about to be born, a new church, a new humanity, a new history, where Christianity will mediate between political powers and usher in perpetual peace' (Hughes 1979: 70).

5 Baudelaire and the malaise of modernity

1 The variety, quirks, individuality, perversity, and courage of Baudelaire's women 'are there above all to force the reader to contemplate them, to meditate on them, and to extend that meditation into an exploration of self and world' (Lloyd 2002: 113).

2 Psychoanalytically minded commentators were quick to register the Oedipal dimensions of Baudelaire's struggles. They have tended to take somewhat reductionist positions; Baudelaire's case may have seemed almost too good to be true. The classic example is René Laforgue's *The Defeat of Baudelaire* of 1932,

deplored by Albert Béguin (Laforgue 1932, Dracoulides 1953 and Wolff 1981 are further essays in this vein). There were also commentators from within the psychoanalytic mainstream ready to resist such reductionism. Ella Freeman Sharpe, author of one of the best psychoanalytic books on dreams (Sharpe 1988 [1937]), reviewed Laforgue in balanced terms (Sharpe 1932: 376–7). 'Out of the initial misery of looking on, with its stimulus to hatred and jealousy, there emerged finally in [Baudelaire's] style the sublimation of balance, synthesis, and unity, characteristic of all great art. Psycho-analysis has not yet fathomed the secrets of that metamorphosis.' Laforgue's contribution, Sharpe felt, was towards the dawning of a day 'when children will not be left to battle alone with traumas beyond their powers of adjustment' (Sharpe 1932: 378).

3   The discordancy of the 1830 and 1840s, for example, was

> underscored by the fact that the prisons of La Roquette and Mazas were built with the same gusto with which Liberty Trees were planted everywhere. Bonapartist propaganda was harshly suppressed, but the ashes of Napoleon were brought home . . . The centre of Paris was cleared and its streets opened up, but the city itself was strangled in a belt of fortifications.
> (Reynaud 1922: 287–8, cited in Benjamin 1999 [1982]: 304; see also Hazan 2010)

4   Sainte-Beuve suggested Baudelaire defend himself at his trial in 1857 along these lines:

> In the field of poetry everything was taken. Lamartine had taken the skies, Hugo the earth . . . Musset the dazzling life of passion and orgy . . . Théophile Gautier, Spain and its vibrant colours. What then remained? What Baudelaire has taken. It was as though he had no choice in the matter . . .
> (cited in Benjamin 1999 [1982]: 273)

5   The painter who was to come closest to fulfilling this vision, although Baudelaire never directly championed him as such, was his friend Edouard Manet (how, perhaps, given the endemic irony of the proclamation, could he have championed him? Instead, he praised a minor draughtsman called Constantin Guys).

6   Wordsworth had evoked similar experiences of 'the huge fermenting mass of humankind' in *The Prelude*: 'How oft, amid those overflowing streets, / Have I gone forward with the crowd, and said / Unto myself "The face of everyone / That passes by me is a mystery."' He went on to catalogue a teeming population of beggars, hawkers and street entertainers (Wordsworth 2000: 483 ff.).

7   There is a superb account of the history and cult of the *flâneur* in Eric Hazan's *The Invention of Paris* (Hazan 2010: 315–39). Hazan does not mention Freud, a *flâneur* himself during the period in which he was studying at the Salpêtrière under Charcot. In a letter to Martha of October 1885 Freud recounted a stroll along the Champs-Elysées, where 'Elegant ladies walk . . . with expressions suggesting that they deny the existence in this world of anyone but themselves and their husbands or are at least graciously trying to ignore it. . . . On the benches sit wet nurses feeding their babies, and nursemaids to whom the children dash screaming after they have had a quarrel . . .' Three days later, interestingly, he was somewhere 'off the map' (where had he been?) which he had sent Martha. 'I found myself surrounded by the most frantic Paris hubbub until I worked my way through to the well-known Boulevards and the Rue Richelieu . . . The yelling of the newspaper vendors was deafening' (Letter from Freud to Martha Bernays, 19 October 1885, in Freud, E.L. 1961: 171–4).

8   Lloyd is reminded of Proust's metaphor from Chapter 3 of *Le temps retrouvé*: 'as though men were perched upon living stilts which keep on growing, reaching the

height of church-towers, until walking becomes difficult and dangerous and, at last, they fall' (Lloyd 2002: 225).

9   'In bourgeois society . . . the past dominates the present . . . In bourgeois society capital is independent and has individuality, while the living person is dependent and has no individuality', wrote Marx and Engels in the Communist Manifesto in 1848 (Marx and Engels 2004 [1848]: 237).

10   Lloyd takes a similar view. Early in the poet's evolution, as traced in *Les Fleurs du mal*, 'sensation and emotion prevail over understanding. The careful architecture of *Les Fleurs du mal* invites us to read [a given poem] in the context of those immediately before and after it', but also with poems that may come much later in the book. Later, the

> tendency to read nature as an allegorical dictionary, together with Nature's powers over the poet's senses, are presented in a far bleaker light. Here what Nature seems to offer is not the possibility of ultimately understanding existence but rather a series of terrifying images of decay and death. In that light 'Correspondances' becomes on re-reading a poem that is much more ambivalent, much less triumphant than when we first encounter it.
>
> (Lloyd 2002: 183)

11   In his notebook Baudelaire wrote: 'At every moment we are crushed by the idea and the sensation of time. And there are only two ways of escaping this nightmare – two ways to forget it: Pleasure and Work. Pleasure drains us. Work fortifies us. The choice is ours' (Baudelaire 1975–76: I, 669, cited in Lloyd 2002: 222).

12   'If we want to keep Racine, we must keep him at a distance – make him strange', wrote Roland Barthes (Barthes 1970: 149).

13   A phrase suggested by Brett Kahr.

14   I thank Percival Mars for this truly Baudelairian observation.

6   Dr Noir, the chevalier Dupin, and John Keats

1   The French sculptor Antoine-Augustin Préault, in what was probably by then becoming a studio cliché, characterised himself in the 1840s as an eagle who, unlike lesser creatures, is able to look at the sun without blinking (Snell 1982: 238 n2).

2   The novel, described in the last chapter as 'the first consultation', was not, in fact, the last word: in a second consultation, the historical novel *Daphné*, which concerns the Emperor Julian (The Apostate), the Doctor transports Stello back to fourth-century Antioch in order to help Stello understand the hazards of introducing pure idealism into popular religion. It is the first consultation, however, that establishes the Doctor's persona; the second adds little to it.

3   '[H]e was like me . . . I saw, with horror and delight, not only topics I'd dreamt of, but *sentences* I'd thought of, and that he had written twenty years before!' Thus wrote Baudelaire in a letter to the art critic Théophile Thoré in 1864 (cited in Hazan 2010 (2002): 329 n25).

4   Contemporary medicine embraced Bichât's anatomical chart of life and death,

> surgical insights of the heirs of John Hunter, the zoonomic speculations of Erasmus Darwin, the evolutionary studies of Cuvier and Lamarck, the chemical research of Lavoisier, Davy, and Saussure, the analysis of specific poisons by Orfila, Vauquelin, and Berzelius . . . the fraught implications for pathology and subspecial diversity of Alexander von Humboldt's South American journeys, the experiments with induced 'suspended animation' during surgery of Hickman, the stethoscope of Laënnec and microscope lenses

of Brewster and Wollaston, the revelation of electromagnetic principles by Oersted and Faraday, the linkage of psychology and biology by Cabanis, the study of brain anatomy by Charles Bell, and the attempt to map the geography of the nervous system and the personality by Gall and Spurzheim.

All these initiatives and developments, Hermione de Almeida has written, also belong to specifically 'Romantic medicine and its high concern with the issues of life'. They express medicine's 'comprehensive participation in the Romantic movement and its fundamental aspiration to know life and read its meaning with all the radical specificity possible to human thought and discourse – and sight' (Almeida 1991: 3–4).

5   Keats's willingness to efface himself, and even risk losing himself in identification, in fact drew on Wordsworth as well as Hazlitt, the Wordsworth who wrote in the preface to *Lyrical Ballads* that

> it will be the wish of the Poet to bring his feelings near to those of the persons whose feelings he describes, nay, for short spaces of time perhaps, to let himself slip into an entire delusion, and even confound and identify his own feelings with theirs.

(Wordsworth 2000: 604)

6   There are important precedents: Thompson's *Ode to Indolence*, Wordsworth's *Vernal Ode* (Motion 1998: 359). If both Thompson and Wordsworth were attuned to indolence's creative potential, Keats, perceiving its underground, active, questing dimension, asserts that it is the absolutely necessary precondition for creative, imaginative activity.

7   Anne Louis Girodet de Roussy-Trioson, 1791, 'Endymion – Effet de lune', Paris, Louvre.

Conclusion

1   I am grateful to Frank Gray for these observations.

Bibliography

Abrams, M.H. (1953) *The Mirror and the Lamp: Romantic Theory and the Critical Tradition*. Oxford: Oxford University Press.

Ackroyd, P. (1995) *Blake*. London: Sinclair-Stevenson.

—— (2009) *Poe: A Life Cut Short*. London: Vintage Books.

Adorno, T. and Horkheimer, M. (1989 [1944]) *Dialectic of Enlightenment*. (Translated by Cumming, J.) London: Verso.

Alexander, F., French, T.M. *et al.* (1946) *Psychoanalytic Therapy: Principles and Application*. New York: Ronald Press.

Almeida, H. de (1991) *Romantic Medicine and John Keats*. Oxford: Oxford University Press.

Alvarez, A. (1992) *Live Company: Psychoanalytic Psychotherapy with Autistic, Borderline, Deprived and Abused Children*. London: Routledge.

Anon. (1833) review of Vigny, *Les Consultations du Docteur Noir*: The Foreign *Quarterly Review*, Vol. 11. London: Treuttel and Würtz, and Richter.

Appignanesi, L. (2008) *Mad, Bad and Sad: A History of Women and the Mind Doctors from 1800 to the Present*. London: Virago.

Appignanesi, L. and Forrester, J. (1992) *Freud's Women*. London: Weidenfeld and Nicolson.

Aron, L. (1996) *A Meeting of Minds: Mutuality in Psychoanalysis*. Hillsdale, NJ, and London: The Analytic Press.

Audi, R. (ed.) (1999) *The Cambridge Dictionary of Philosophy* (2nd edition). Cambridge: Cambridge University Press.

Bacon, R. (2006) 'Borderline Practices', unpublished paper delivered to Psychotherapy Sussex, November.

Bakhtin, M. (1981) *The Dialogic Imagination: Four Essays*. Austin, TX: University of Texas Press.

Balint, E. (1993) 'The Analyst's Field of Observation', in *Before I was I*. London: Free Association Books.

Barbalet, J. (2009) 'Disinterestedness and Self Formation: Principles of Action in William Hazlitt'. *European Journal of Social Theory*, 12(2). London: Sage.

Barham, P. (1993) *Schizophrenia and Human Value*. London: Free Association Books.

Barrès, M. (1926) *La Folie de Charles Baudelaire*. Paris: publisher unknown.

Barthes, R. (1970) *S\Z*. Paris: Editions du Seuil.

Baudelaire, C. (1975–76), *Oeuvres complètes*. 2 vols. (Texte établi, présenté et annoté par Pichois, C.). Paris: Librairie Gallimard, Bibliothèque de la Pléiade.

—— (1986) *Baudelaire: The Complete Verse.* (With an introduction and translations by Scarfe, F.) London: Anvil Press Poetry.

—— (1989) *Baudelaire: The Poems in Prose.* (With an introduction and translations by Scarfe, F.) London: Anvil Press Poetry.

—— (1995 [1861]) 'The Painter of Modern Life', in *The Painter of Modern Life and Other Essays (Arts and Letters).* (Translated by Mayne, J.) London: Phaidon Press.

—— (1997) *Baudelaire in English.* (Edited by Clark, C. and Sykes, R.) London: Penguin Books.

Béguin, A. (1938) *L'âme romantique et le rêve.* Paris: Librairie José Corti.

Bell, M. (2005) *The German Tradition of Psychology in Literature and Thought, 1700–1840.* Cambridge: Cambridge University Press.

Bellenger, S. (ed.) (2005) *Girodet 1767–1824.* Catalogue of exhibition, Musée du Louvre, Paris 2005–06. Paris: Gallimard/Musée du Louvre.

Benjamin, W. (1969 [1936]) 'The Work of Art in the Age of Mechanical Reproduction', in *Illuminations.* (Translated by Zohn, H.) New York: Schocken Books.

—— (1979 [1931]) 'A Small History of Photography', in *One-Way Street.* London: New Left Books.

—— (1983 [1955]) *Charles Baudelaire: A Lyric Poet in the Era of High Capitalism.* (Translated by Zohn, H.) London: Verso.

—— (1999 [1982]) *The Arcades Project.* (Translated by Eiland, H. and McLaughlin, K.) Cambridge, MA and London: The Belknap Press of Harvard University Press.

Berlin, I. (1979 [1956]) *The Age of Enlightenment.* Oxford: Oxford University Press.

Bernheimer, C. and Kahane, C. (eds) (1985) *In Dora's Case: Freud-Hysteria-Feminism.* London: Virago.

Bion, W.R. (1962) 'The Psycho-Analytic Study of Thinking'. *International Journal of Psycho-Analysis*, 43: 306–10.

—— (1967) 'Notes on Memory and Desire', in Spillius (Bott) 1988, Vol. 2, 17–21.

—— (1984a [1962]) *Learning from Experience.* London: Karnac.

—— (1984b [1970]) *Attention and Interpretation.* London: Karnac.

—— (1989) [1961]) *Experiences in Groups and Other Papers.* London and New York: Tavistock/Routledge.

—— (1990) *Brazilian Lectures: 1973 São Paulo; 1974 Rio de Janeiro/São Paulo.* London: Karnac Books.

Bird, W. (2004) 'Oh Monstrous Lamp! The Special Effects in Goya's "A scene from 'El Hechizado por Fuerza'" in the National Gallery, London'. *Apollo*, March.

Blake, W. (1988) *The Complete Poetry and Prose of William Blake.* (Edited by Erdman, D.V., commentary by Bloom, H.) New York: Anchor Books.

Bollas, C. (1987) *The Unthought Known.* New York: Columbia University Press.

—— (1999) *The Mystery of Things.* London: Routledge.

—— (2002) *Free Association* (Ideas in Psychoanalysis). London: Icon.

—— (2007) *The Freudian Moment.* London: Karnac.

—— (2009) *The Infinite Question.* Hove and New York: Routledge.

Bonnefoy, Y. (2004) *Goya, Baudelaire et la poésie* (Entretien avec Starobinski, J., suivi d'études de Jackson, J.E. et Griener, P.) Geneva: La Dogana.

—— (2006) *Goya, les peintures noires.* Bordeaux: William Blake & Co.

Boris, H.N. (1986) 'Bion Re-visited'. *Contemporary Psychoanalysis*, 22: 159–84.

Bourguignon, A., Cotet, P., Laplanche, J. and Robert, F. (1989) *Traduire Freud*. Paris: Presses Universitaires de France.

Boyd Whyte, I. (2010) 'Modernity, Architecture, and the City', in Becker, L., Wadley, N., Elliott, D. and Boyd Whyte, I., *Modern Times: Responding to Chaos: Drawings and Films Selected by Lutz Becker*. Catalogue of exhibition. Cambridge: Kettle's Yard, University of Cambridge.

Britton, R. (1994) 'Publication Anxiety: Conflict between Communication and Affiliation'. *International Journal of Psycho-Analysis*, 75: 1213–34.

Brookner, A. (2001) *Romanticism and its Discontents*. London: Penguin Books.

Brousse, M.-H. (2007) 'Art, the Avant-Garde and Psychoanalysis'. (Transcribed by Schneider, M.). *Lacanian Compass: Psychoanalytic Newsletter of Lacanian Orientation*. 3 October, 1(11). Available at: http://lacaniancompass.files.wordpress.com.2011/05/lacaniancompass111.pdf.

Brown, J., and Galassi, S.G. (2006) *Goya's Last Works*. New Haven, CT and London: Yale University Press.

Bryson, N. (1983) *Word and Image: French Painting of the Ancien Régime*. Cambridge: Cambridge University Press.

Büchner, G. (1993) *Complete Plays, Lenz and Other Writings*. (Translated with an introduction and notes by Reddick, J.). London: Penguin.

Buñuel, L. (1984) *My Last Breath*. (Translated by Israel, A.) London: Jonathan Cape.

Butler, M. (1981) *Romantics, Rebels and Reactionaries: English Literature and its Background 1760–1830*. Oxford: Oxford University Press.

Byron, G. (1970) *Complete Poetical Works*. (Edited by Page, F., new edition revised by Jump, J.) Oxford: Oxford University Press.

Calhoon, K. (1992) *Fatherland: Novalis, Freud, and the Discipline of Romance*. Detroit, MI: Wayne State University Press.

Caper, R. (1998) *A Mind of One's Own*. London: Routledge.

Carr, R. (1982) *Spain, 1808–1875*. Oxford: Oxford University Press.

Casement, P. (1990 [1985]) *On Learning from the Patient*. London: Routledge.

Chaplin, S. and Faflak, J. (2011) *The Romanticism Handbook*. London and New York: Continuum.

Charpentier, J. (1921) 'La Poésie britannique et Baudelaire'. *Mercure de France*, 147, 1 May.

Cixous, H. (1976) 'The Laugh of the Medusa'. *Signs*, 1: 875–9.

—— (1994) (ed. Sellers, S.) *The Hélène Cixous Reader*. London: Routledge.

Clubbe, J. (1997) 'Between Empire and Exile: Byron and Napoleon, 1814–1816'. *Napoleonic Scholarship: The Journal of the International Napoleonic Society*, 1(1), April. Montreal, Quebec: The International Napoleonic Society.

Coburn, W.J. (2009) 'Attitudes in Psychoanalytic Complexity: An Alternative to Postmodernism in Psychoanalysis', in Frie and Orange (2009).

Coleridge, S.T. (1961) *The Notebooks of Samuel Taylor Coleridge*. (Edited by Coburn, K.) New York: Pantheon.

—— (1983 [1815]) *Biographia Literaria*. 2 vols. (Edited by Engell, J. and Jackson Bate, W.) Princeton, NJ: Princeton University Press and London: Routledge.

—— (1985) *Poems and Prose* (selected by Raine, K.). London: Penguin Books.

Coltart, N. (1986) ' "Slouching towards Bethlehem" or Thinking the Unthinkable in Psychoanalysis', in Kohon, G. (ed.), *The British School of Psychoanalysis: The Independent Tradition.* London: Free Association Books.

Constantine, D. (1988) *Hölderlin.* Oxford: Clarendon Press.

—— (1996) Introduction to Hölderlin, F. (1996).

Corradi Fiumara, G. (1990) *The Other Side of Language: A Philosophy of Listening.* London: Routledge.

Cotton, T. and Loewenthal, D. (2011) 'Laing and the Treatment is the Way we Treat People', in *Post-Existentialism and the Psychological Therapies: Towards a Therapy without Foundations.* London: Karnac.

Crews, F. (1995) *The Memory Wars: Freud's Legacy in Dispute.* New York: The New York Review of Books.

Denis, P. (2006) 'Incontournable contre-transfert'. *Revue française de psychanalyse,* 70: 331–50.

Derrida, J. (1967) 'Cogito and the History of Madness', in Derrida (1978).

—— (1978) *Writing and Difference.* Chicago, IL: University of Chicago Press.

Desjardins, P. (1887) 'Charles Baudelaire'. *La Revue bleue.*

Dewhurst, K. and Reeves, N. (1978) *Friedrich Schiller: Medicine, Psychology and Literature.* Oxford: Sandford Publications.

Diderot, D. (1967 [1821]) *Le Neveu de Rameau.* Paris: Garnier-Flammarion.

—— (1970 [1796]) *Jacques le fataliste.* Paris: Garnier-Flammarion.

Dracoulides, N.N. (1953) 'Psychoanalytic Profile of Charles Baudelaire'. New York: *Psychoanalytic Quarterly,* 23: 461–85.

Eagle, M.N. (2009) 'Postmodern Influences on Contemporary Psychoanalysis', in Frie and Orange (2009).

Eichner, H. (ed.) (1972) *'Romantic' and Its Cognates: The European History of a Word.* Manchester: Manchester University Press.

Eigen, M. (1985) 'Towards Bion's Starting Point: Between Catastrophe and Faith'. *International Journal of Psychoanalysis,* 66: 321–30.

Eitner, L. (1972) *Géricault's 'Raft of the Medusa'.* New York: Phaidon.

—— (1982) *Géricault: His Life and Work.* London: Orbis.

Ellenberger, H. (1970) *The Discovery of the Unconscious: The History and Evolution of Dynamic Psychiatry.* New York: Basic Books.

Ellman, S. (1991) *Freud's Technique Papers: A Contemporary Perspective.* Northvale, NJ: Jason Aronson.

Enckell, M. (1981) 'Freud and Romanticism'. *The Scandinavian Psychoanalytic Review,* 4: 177–92.

Eng, E. (1984) 'Coleridge's "Psycho-analytical Understanding" and Freud's "Psycho-analysis"'. *International Review of Psycho-Analysis,* 11: 463–6.

Erikson, E.H. (1977) *Toys and Reasons: Stages in the Ritualization of Experience.* New York: W.W. Norton & Company.

Esquirol, E. (1838) *Des Maladies Mentales considérées sous les rapports médical, hygiénique et médico-légal.* Accompagnées de vingt-sept planches gravées. 2 vols. Brussels: Meline, Cans et Compagnie.

Evans, D. (1996) *An Introductory Dictionary of Lacanian Psychoanalysis.* London: Routledge.

Faflak, J. (2002) ' "On Her Own Couch". Keats's Wandering Psychoanalysis', in McDayter, G. (ed.), *Untrodden Regions of the Mind: Romanticism and Psycho-analysis. Bucknell Review* 45(2). Lewisburg, PA: Bucknell University Press.

—— (2008) *Romantic Psychoanalysis: The Burden of the Mystery*. Albany, NY: State University of New York Press.

Falzeder, E. and Brabant, E. (eds) (2000) *The Correspondence of Sigmund Freud and Sándor Ferenczi*, Vol. 3, *1920–33*. Cambridge, MA: Harvard University Press.

Fehervary, H. (1977) *Hölderlin and the Left: The Search for a Dialectic of Art and Life*. Heidelberg: Carl Winter Universitätsverlag.

Feldman, M. and Spillius (Bott), E. (eds) (1989) *Psychic Equilibrium and Psychic Change: Selected Papers of Betty Joseph*. London and New York: Routledge.

Ferenczi, S. (1995) *Clinical Diary*. London: Routledge.

Fink, B. (1996) *The Lacanian Subject*. Princeton, NJ: Princeton University Press.

—— (1997) *A Clinical Introduction to Lacanian Psychoanalysis: Theory and Technique*. Cambridge, MA: Harvard University Press.

Fitzgerald, P. (2002 [1995]) *The Blue Flower*. London: Flamingo.

Fordham, M. (1969) 'Technique and Counter-transference', in Fordham, Gordon, Hubback and Lambert (1974).

Fordham, M., Gordon, R., Hubback, J. and Lambert, K. (eds) (1974) *Technique in Jungian Analysis*. London: Heinemann.

Foucault, M. (1971 [1961]) *Madness and Civilization: A History of Insanity in the Age of Reason*. (Translated by Howard, R.) London: Tavistock Publications.

Frampton, S. (2011) 'Montaigne and the Macaques'. *Saturday Guardian, Review*, 2 January.

Fraser, R. (2008) *Napoleon's Cursed War: Popular Resistance in the Spanish Peninsular War*. London: Verso.

Frederickson, J. (2009) 'Multiplicity and Relational Psychoanalysis: A Heideggerian Response', in Frie and Orange (2009).

Freud, A. (1993 [1936]) *The Ego and the Mechanisms of Defence*. London: Karnac.

Freud, E.L. (1961) *Letters of Sigmund Freud 1873–1939*. London: The Hogarth Press.

Freud, S. (1900) *The Interpretation of Dreams: The Standard Edition of the Complete Psychological Works of Sigmund Freud*, Vol. IV. London: The Hogarth Press, 1953–64.

—— (1912) 'Recommendations to Physicians Practising Psycho-analyisis', *The Standard Edition of the Complete Psychological Works of Sigmund Freud*, Vol. XII, 109–20. London: The Hogarth Press, 1953–64.

—— (1913) 'The Claims of Psychoanalysis to the Interest of the Non-psychological Sciences. Part II. The Philological Interest of Psychoanalysis'. *The Standard Edition of the Complete Psychological Works of Sigmund Freud*, Vol. XIV, 176–8. London: The Hogarth Press, 1953–64.

—— (1915) 'The Unconscious', *The Standard Edition of the Complete Psychological Works of Sigmund Freud*, Vol XIV. London: The Hogarth Press, 1953–64.

—— (1916) Letter from Freud to Lou Andreas-Salomé, 25 May. *The International Psycho-Analytical Library*, 89.

—— (1920) 'A Note on the Prehistory of the Technique of Analysis'. *The Standard Edition of the Complete Psychological Works of Sigmund Freud*, Vol. XVIII. London: The Hogarth Press, 1953–64.

—— (1923) 'Two Encyclopaedia Articles'. *The Standard Edition of the Complete Psychological Works of Sigmund Freud*, Vol. XVIII. London: The Hogarth Press, 1953–64.

—— (1924) *A Short Account of Psycho-Analysis: The Standard Edition of the Complete Psychological Works of Sigmund Freud*, Vol. IX, 189–209. London: The Hogarth Press, 1953–64.

—— (1937) 'Analysis Terminable and Interminable'. *The Standard Edition of the Complete Psychological Works of Sigmund Freud*, Vol. XXIII, 209–54. London: The Hogarth Press, 1953–64.

Freud, E., Freud, L. and Grubrich-Simitis, I. (eds) (1985) *Sigmund Freud: His Life in Pictures and Words*. New York: Norton.

Frie, R. and Orange, D. (eds) (2009) *Beyond Postmodernism: New Dimensions in Clinical Theory and Practice*. London: Routledge.

Frosh, S. (1994) *Sexual Difference: Masculinity and Psychoanalysis*. London: Routledge.

Furst, L. (1980) *European Romanticism: Self-Definition*. London and New York: Methuen.

Garland, H. and M. (1976) *The Oxford Companion to German Literature*. Oxford: Clarendon Press.

Gasché, R. (1991) Foreword to Schlegel (1991).

Gautier, T. (1874) *Histoire du romantisme. Notices romantiques. Les progrès de la poésie française depuis 1830*. Paris: Charpentier.

—— (2008 [1837]) *My Fantoms*. (Translated with a new introduction by Holmes, R.) New York: New York Review Books.

Gay, P. (1988) *Freud: A Life for Our Time*. London and Melbourne: J.M. Dent & Sons.

—— (1995) *The Freud Reader*. New York: Vintage.

Georget, E. (1972 [1820]) *De la folie*. (Textes choisis et présentés par Postel, J.) Paris: Privat.

Gide, A. (1910) 'Baudelaire et M. Faguet'. *Nouvelle Revue Française*, 1 November.

Glendinning, N. (1977) *Goya and his Critics*. New Haven, CT and London: Yale University Press.

Glover, N. (2000) *Psychoanalytic Aesthetics: The British School*. London: Free Association Books.

Gode von Aesch, A. (1965) Foreword to Hölderlin, F. (1965 [1797 and 1799]).

Goethe, J.W. (1964) *Selected Verse: With Plain Prose Translations of Each Poem*. (Introduced and edited by Luke, D.) London: Penguin Classics.

Goldstein, J. (2001 [1987] *Console and Classify: The French Psychiatric Profession in the Nineteenth Century*. Chicago. IL: University of Chicago Press.

Goya, F. (1969 [1799]) *Los Caprichos* (Introduction by Hofer, P.) New York: Dover Publications.

Green, A. (1996 [1980]) 'The Dead Mother', in *On Private Madness*. London: Maresfield Library, Karnac.

—— (2005) *Key Ideas for a Contemporary Psychoanalysis: Misrecogntion and Recognition of the Unconscious*. (Translated by Weller, A.) London and New York: Routledge.

—— (2005 [2002]) *Psychoanalysis: A Paradigm for Clinical Thinking*. (Translated by Weller, A.) London: Free Association Books.

Greenson, R.R. (1991 [1967]) *The Technique and Practice of Psycho-Analysis*. London: The Hogarth Press and the Institute of Psycho-Analysis.

Grotstein, J.S. (2002) '"Love is Where it Finds You": The Caprices of the "Aleatory Object"', in Scalia, J. (ed.), *The Vitality of Objects*. London and New York: Continuum.

Habermas, J. (1972) *Knowledge and Human Interests*. London: Heinemann.

Hamburger, M. (1961) Introduction to Hölderlin (1961).

—— (2003) Introduction to Hölderlin (2007).

Harrison, R.P. (2011) 'The Faith of Harold Bloom'. *New York Review of Books*. 13 October. New York: New York Review of Books.

Haughton, H. (2003) Introduction to Freud, S., *The Uncanny*. (Translated by McLintock, D.) London: Penguin.

Hayter, A. (1971 [1969]) *Opium and the Romantic Imagination*. London: Faber & Faber.

Hazan, E. (2010) *The Invention of Paris: A History in Footsteps*. London: Verso.

Hazlitt, W. (1969 [1805]) *An Essay on the Principles of Human Action*. Gainsville, FL: Scholars' Facsimiles and Reprints.

Heaney, S. (2002) *Finders Keepers: Selected Prose, 1971–2001*. London: Faber.

Hegel, G.W.F. (1977) *Phenomenology of Spirit*. (Translated by Miller, A.V.). Oxford: Oxford University Press.

Heidegger, M. (1966) '*Der Spiegel*'s interview with Martin Heidegger', in Wolin (1993).

—— (1975a) 'What are Poets For?', in *Poetry, Language, Thought*. (Translated by Hofstadter, A.) New York: Harper Colophon Books.

—— (1975b) *Early Greek Thinking*. (Translated by Farrell Krell, D. and Capuzzui, F.A.) New York: Harper & Row.

—— (1976) *What is Called Thinking?* (Translated by Glenn Gray, J.) New York: Harper Perennial.

—— (1996 [1984]) *Hölderlin's Hymn 'The Ister'*. (Translated by McNeill, W. and Davis, J.) Bloomington and Indianapolis, IN: Indiana University Press.

Heimann, P. (1950) 'On Counter-Transference'. *International Journal of Psycho-Analysis*, 31: 81–4.

Hibbert, C. (1980) *The French Revolution*. London: Allen Lane.

Hildesheimer, W. (1982) *Mozart*. New York: Farrar Straus Giroux.

Hinshelwood, R.D. (1991) *A Dictionary of Kleinian Thought*. London: Free Association Books.

Hobsbawm, E.J. (1988) *The Age of Revolution: Europe, 1789–1848*. London: Abacus.

Hoffmann, E.T.A. (1979) *Contes. Fantaisies à la manière de Callot. Tirées du Journal d'un voyageur enthousiaste 1808–1815*. (Edited by Béguin, A., Preface by Roy, C.) Paris: Gallimard, Collection Folio.

Hofmann, M. (2004) Review of Hölderlin (2004a), *Guardian Review*, 20 November.

Hölderlin, F. (1965 [1797 and 1799]) *Hyperion or The Hermit in Greece*. (Translated by Trask, W.) New York, Toronto and London: Signet Classics.

—— (1996) *Selected Poems*. (Translated by Constantine, D.) Newcastle-upon-Tyne: Bloodaxe Books.

—— (2004a) *Poems and Fragments (Poetica)*. (Translated by Hamburger, M.) London: Anvil Press Poetry.

—— (2004b) *Poems of Friedrich Hölderlin*. (Translated by Mitchell, J.) San Francisco, CA: Ithuriel's Spear.

—— (2007) *Selected Poems and Fragments*. (Translated and edited by Hamburger, M., with a new preface by Hamburger, M., selected by Adler, J.) London: Penguin Books.

—— (2009) *Essays and Letters*. (Edited, translated and with an introduction by Adler, J. and Louth, C.) London: Penguin.

Holmes, R. (1998) *Coleridge: Early Visions*. London: HarperCollins.

—— (1999) *Coleridge: Darker Reflections*. London: Flamingo.

—— (2008) *The Age of Wonder: How the Romantic Generation Discovered the Beauty and Terror of Science*. London: Harper Press.

Holt, E. (1979) *The Triumph of Art for the Public 1785–1848: The Emerging Role of Exhibitions and Critics*. New York: Anchor Books.

Horner, A.J. (1987) 'The "Real" Relationship and Analytic Neutrality'. *Journal of the American Academy of Psychoanalysis and Dynamic Psychiatry* 15: 491–501.

House, J. (2004) *Impressionism: Paint and Politics*. New Haven, CT: Yale University Press.

Hughes, G. (1979) *Romantic German Literature*. London: Edward Arnold.

Hughes, R. (2002) Interview with Mick Brown. *The Telegraph*, 23 February.

—— (2003) *Goya*. London: The Harvill Press.

Ingleby, D. (1999) 'Being Peter Lomas: Social Change and the Ethics of Psychotherapy', in King (ed.) (1999).

Israelstam, K. (2007) 'Creativity and Dialectical Phenomena: From Dialectical Edge to Dialectical Space'. *International Journal of Psycho-Analysis* 88: 591–607.

Jiménez, J.P. (2008) 'Theoretical Plurality and Pluralism in Psychoanalytic Practice'. *International Journal of Psycho-Analysis* 89: 579–99.

Johnson, B. (1977) 'The Frame of Reference: Poe, Lacan, Derrida'. *Yale French Studies*, 55/6: 457–505.

Johns-Putra, A. (2011) 'Gender', in Chaplin and Faflak (2011).

Jones, E. (1953, 1955, 1957) *Sigmund Freud: Life and Work*. Vol. I, *The Young Freud 1856–1900*; Vol. II, *Years of Maturity 1901–1919*; Vol. III, *The Last Phase 1919–1939*. London: The Hogarth Press.

Jordan, L. (2002) 'The Analyst's Uncertainty and Fear'. *Journal of the American Psychoanalytic Association*, 50: 989–93.

Joseph, B. (1983) 'On Understanding and Not Understanding: Some Technical Issues', in Feldman and Spillius (Bott) (1989), 139–52.

—— (1985) 'Transference: The Total Situation'. In Spillius (Bott) (1988), Vol. 2, 61–72.

—— (1987) 'Projective Identification – Some Clinical Aspects', in Spillius (Bott) (1988), Vol. 1, 138–50.

Juana, J. de and Castro (1991) 'Apuntes Sobre la Guerra de Independencia en Galicia', *Boletín Auriense*, años XX–XXI. Ourense, cited in Fraser (2008).

Jung, C.G. (1963) *Memories, Dreams, Reflections*. (Translated by Winston, R. and C., recorded and edited by Jaffé, A.) London: Collins and Routledge Kegan Paul.

—— (1993) *The Practice of Psychotherapy: Essays on the Psychology of the Transference and other Subjects*. (Translated by Hull, R.F.C.) London: Routledge.

—— (1993 [1928]) 'The Therapeutic Value of Abreaction'. *The Practice of Psychotherapy*. London: Routledge.

—— (1993 [1946]) 'The Psychology of the Transference'. *The Practice of Psychotherapy*. London: Routledge.

Junquera, J.J. (1999) *The Black Paintings of Goya*. London: Scala.

Keats, J. (1958) *The Letters of John Keats*. 2 vols. (Edited by Rollins, H.E.) Cambridge, MA: Harvard University Press.

—— (1988) *The Complete Poems*. (Edited by Barnard, J.) London: Penguin.

Khair Badawi, M.-T. (2011) 'Being, Thinking, Creating: When War Attacks the Setting and the Transference Counter-attacks'. *International Journal of Psycho-Analysis* (2011) 92: 401–9.

Khan, M. (1983) *Hidden Selves: Between Theory and Practice in Psychoanalysis*. London: Karnac.

King, L. (ed.) (1999) *Committed Uncertainty in Psychotherapy: Essays in Honour of Peter Lomas*. London: Whurr Publishers.

Klein, M. (1946) 'Notes on some Schizoid Mechanisms'. *International Journal of Psychoanalysis*, 27: 99–110.

Kleist, H. von (1978) *The Marquise von O and Other Stories*. (Translated and with an introduction by Luke, D. and Reeves, N.) London: Penguin.

—— (2004) *On the Gradual Production of Thoughts Whilst Speaking*. (Edited and translated by Constantine, D.) Indianapolis, IN: Hackett Publishing.

Koselleck, R. (1988) *Critique and Crisis: Enlightenment and the Pathogenesis of Modern Society*. Cambridge, MA: The MIT Press.

Kristeva, J. (1982 [1980]) *Powers of Horror: An Essay on Abjection*. New York: Columbia University Press.

—— (1991 [1989]) *Strangers to Ourselves*. New York: Columbia University Press.

—— (1995 [1993]) *New Maladies of the Soul*. New York: Columbia University Press.

Kuhn, T.S. (1962) *The Structure of Scientific Revolutions*. Chicago, IL: Chicago University Press.

Kuzniar, A. (1987) *Delayed Endings: Nonclosure in Hölderlin and Novalis*. Athens, GA, and London: University of Georgia Press.

Lacan, J. (1973) 'Les non dupes errent'. Séminaire oral du mardi 13 novembre 1973. http://espace.freud.pagesperso-orange.fr/topos/psycha/psysem/nondup/nondup1.htm.

—— (1988a) *The Seminar of Jacques Lacan, Book II, The Ego in Freud's Theory and in the Technique of Psychoanalysis 1954–55*. (Translated by Tomaselli, S. and Forrester, J.) New York: W.W. Norton, and Cambridge: Cambridge University Press.

—— (1988b) *The Seminar of Jacques Lacan, Book XI, The Four Fundamental Concepts of Psychoanalysis*. (Translated by Sheridan, A.) New York: W.W. Norton.

—— (2007) *Ecrits: The First Complete Edition in English*. (Translated by Fink, B. in collaboration with Fink, H. and Grigg, R.) New York and London: W.W. Norton.

Laforgue, R. (1932) *The Defeat of Baudelaire* (International Psycho-Analytical Library no. 21). London: Hogarth Press and Institute of Psycho-Analysis.

Laplanche, J. (1961) *Hölderlin et la question du père*. Paris: Presses Universitaires de France.

—— (1989 [1987]) *New Foundations for Psychoanalysis*. Oxford: Blackwell.

—— (1992) *Seduction, Translation, Drives*. London: Institute of Contemporary Arts.

—— (1996) 'Psychoanalysis as Anti-hermeneutics'. *Radical Philosophy*, 79 (September/October).

—— (2006 [1980]) *Problématiques 1. L'Angoisse*. Paris: Quadrige/Presses Universitaires de France.

Laplanche, J. and Pontalis, J.-B. (1988) *The Language of Psychoanalysis*. London: Karnac, Maresfield Library.

Lefebvre, G. (2001 [1957]) *The French Revolution*. (Translated by Evanson, E.M.) London and New York: Routledge.

Leader, D. (2009) *The New Black: Mourning, Melancholia and Depression*. London: Penguin Books.

LeBon, G. (1905 [1895]) *La Psycholgie des foules*. Paris: Edition Félix Alcan, and (1896) *The Crowd: A Study of the Popular Mind*. London: Ernest Benn.

Leclaire, S. (1998 [1968]) *Psychoanalysing: On the Order of the Unconscious and the Practice of the Letter*. Stanford, CA: Stanford University Press.

Levinas, E. (1947) 'Time and the Other', in Hand, S. (1989) (ed.), *The Levinas Reader*. Oxford: Blackwell.

—— (1985 [1982]) *Ethics and Infinity: Conversations with Philippe Nemo*. (Translated by Cohen, R.A.) Pittsburgh, PA: Duquesne University Press.

Lloyd, R. (2002) *Baudelaire's World*. Ithaca, NY and London: Cornell University Press.

Loewenthal, D. and Snell, R. (2003) *Postmodernism for Psychotherapists: A Critical Reader*. Hove and New York: Brunner-Routledge.

Lubbock, T. (2001) 'Holding their Ground', in Wilson-Bareau (2001).

Lukács, G. (1968 [1934]) 'Hölderlin's *Hyperion*', in *Goethe and his Age*. (Translated by Anchor, R.) London: Merlin Press.

Luke, D. and Reeves, N. (1978) see Kleist (1978).

McCabe J.D. (1869) *Paris by Sunlight and Gaslight: A Work Descriptive of the Mysteries and Miseries, the Virtues, the Vices, the Splendors, and the Crimes of the City of Paris*. Philadelphia, PA: The National Publishing Company.

MacCarthy, F. (2003) *Byron: Life and Legend*. London: Faber & Faber.

McDayter, G. (ed.) (2002) *Untrodden Regions of the Mind: Romanticism and Psychoanalysis*. (With contributions by Batten, G., Faflak, J., McDayter, G., Moi, T., Redfield, M. and Wilson, S.) *Bucknell Review*, 45(2). Lewisburg, PA: Bucknell University Press.

Magraw, R. (1983) *France 1815–1914: The Bourgeois Century*. Oxford: Fontana.

Malcolm, J. (2004 [1981]), *Psychoanalysis: The Impossible Profession*. London: Granta

Mann, T (1970 [1929]) *Freud et la pensée moderne*. Paris: Aubier.

—— (1956 [1936]) 'Freud and the Future'. *International Journal of Psycho-Analysis*, 37: 106–15.

Mansel, P. (2003) *Paris between Empires 1814–1852: Monarchy and Revolution*. London: Phoenix.

Marx, K. and Engels, F. (2004 [1848]) *The Communist Manifesto*. London: Penguin Classics.

Masson, J.M. (1984) *The Assault on Truth: Freud's Suppression of the Seduction Theory*. New York: Farrar Straus & Giroux.

—— (1985) (ed.) *The Complete Letters of Sigmund Freud to Wilhelm Fliess*. Cambridge, MA: Harvard University Press.

—— (1989) *Against Therapy*. New York: HarperCollins.

Matte-Blanco, I. (1975) *The Unconscious as Infinite Sets: An Essay in Bi-Logic.* London: Duckworth.

Meltzer, D. and Williams, M.H. (1988) *The Apprehension of Beauty: The Role of Aesthetic Conflict in Development, Violence and Art.* Strath Tay: The Clunie Press.

Merleau-Ponty, M. (1979 [1945]) *Phénoménologie de la perception.* Paris: Gallimard.

Miller, J.-A. (ed.) (2006) *L'Anti-Livre noir de la psychanalyse.* Paris: Editions du Seuil; see also Snell (2007).

Milner, M. [Field, J.] (1986 [1937]) *An Experiment in Leisure.* London: Virago.

—— (1987a) *Eternity's Sunrise: A Way of Keeping a Diary.* London: Virago.

—— (1987b) *The Suppressed Madness of Sane Men: Forty-four Years of Exploring Psychoanalysis.* London and New York: Routledge.

Milton, J. (2004) *Paradise Lost.* (Edited with an Introduction and Notes by Orgel, S. and Goldberg, J.) Oxford: Oxford University Press.

Mitchell, S.A. (1996) 'Gender and Sexual Orientation in the Age of Postmodernism: The Plight of the Perplexed Clinician'. *Gender Psychoanalysis* 1: 45–74.

—— (1997) *Influence and Autonomy in Psychoanalysis.* Hillside, NJ, and London: The Analytic Press.

Moi, T. (1989) 'Patriarchal Thought and the Drive for Knowledge', in Brennan, T. (ed.), *Between Feminism and Psychoanalysis.* London: Routledge.

Molino, A. (ed.) (1997) *Freely Associated: Encounters in Psychoanalysis with Christopher Bollas, Joyce McDougall, Michael Eigen, Adam Phillips, Nina Coltart.* London and New York: Free Association Books.

Montaigne, M. de (1991) *The Complete Essays.* (Translated and edited with an Introduction and Notes by Screech, M.A.) London: Penguin Books.

Moran, D. (2000) *Introduction to Phenomenology.* London: Routledge.

Motion, A. (1998) *Keats.* London: Faber & Faber.

Murat, L. (2001) *La Maison du docteur Blanche. Histoire d'un asile et de ses pensionnaires de Nerval à Maupassant.* Paris: J.C. Lattès.

Murray, L. (2010) Interview with Nicholas Wroe. *Saturday Guardian Review,* 20 November.

Myrone, M. (2006) *Gothic Nightmares: Fuseli, Blake, and the Romantic Imagination.* (With essays by Frayling, C. and Warner, M.) London: Tate Publishing.

Nerval, G. (1972) *Promenades et souvenirs: Lettres à Jenny. Pandora. Aurélia.* Paris: Garnier Flammarion.

Nietzsche, F. (1967) *The Birth of Tragedy and The Case of Wagner.* (Translated by Kaufmann, W.) New York: Vintage Books.

Novalis (1989) *Pollen and Fragments: Selected Poetry and Prose of Novalis.* (Translation and Introduction by Versluis, A.) Grand Rapids, MI: Phanes Press.

Ogden, T.H. (1998) 'A Question of Voice in Poetry and Psychoanalysis'. *Psychoanalytic Quarterly,* 67: 426–48.

—— (2001a) *Conversations at the Frontier of Dreaming.* London: Karnac

—— (2001b) 'Reading Winnicott'. *Psychoanalytic Quarterly,* 70: 299–323.

Orange, D. (2009) 'Towards the Art of the Living Dialogue: Between Constructivism and Hermeneutics in Psychoanalytic Thinking', in Frie and Orange (2009).

Orbach, S. (2007) 'Democratising Psychoanalysis'. *European Journal of Psychotherapy and Counselling,* 9(1), March 2007. (Special issue on Relational Psychology in Europe, guest editors Hargaden, H. and Schwartz, J.) London: Routledge.

Orgel, S. and Goldberg, J. (2004) Introduction to Milton (2004).

Ortega y Gasset (1972) *Velazquez, Goya and The Dehumanization of Art.* (Translated by Brown, A., Introduction by Troutman, P.) London: Studio Vista.

Parsons, M. (2007) 'Raiding the Inarticulate: The Internal Analytic Setting and Listening Beyond Countertransference'. *International Journal of Psycho-Analysis*, 88: 1441–56.

Paulin, T. (2003) 'Spirit of the Age'. *Guardian*, 5 April.

Peckham, M. (1981 [1962]) *Beyond the Tragic Vision: The Quest for Identity in the Nineteenth Century.* Cambridge: Cambridge University Press.

Pernoud, G. and Flaissier, S. (1965) *The French Revolution.* (Translated by Graves, R., Preface by Maurois, A.) London: Mercury Books.

Phillips, A. (2002) *Equals.* London: Faber & Faber.

—— (2005) *Going Sane.* London: Hamish Hamilton.

Pichois, C. and Ziegler, J. (1991) *Baudelaire* (Translated by Robb, G.) London: Vintage.

Pieper, J. (1964 [1952]) *Leisure, the Basis of Culture.* New York: Pantheon Books.

Pinel, P. (1980 [1800]) *Traité médico-philosophique sur l'aliénation mentale ou la manie.* Présentation par F. Azouvi. Geneva and Paris: Editions Slatkine.

Plann, S. (2007) *The Spanish National Deaf School: Portraits from the Nineteenth Century.* Washington, DC: Gallaudet University Press.

Plumly, S. (2008) *Posthumous Keats: A Personal Biography.* New York: W.W. Norton.

Poe, E.A. (1984) *Essays and Reviews: Theory of Poetry, Reviews of British and Continental Authors, Reviews of American Authors and American Literature.* New York: Library of America.

—— (2008) *Tales of Mystery and Imagination.* (With essays by Hayes, K.J., Peeples, S. and Renza, L.A.) Cambridge: Worth Press.

Pontalis, J.-B. (1990) *La force d'attraction.* Paris: Editions du Seuil.

—— (2002) *En marge des jours.* Paris: Gallimard.

Porter, R. (2003) *Madness: A Brief History.* Oxford: Oxford University Press.

Power, M. (1997) *The Audit Society: Rituals of Verification.* Oxford: Oxford University Press.

Praz, M. (1970) *The Romantic Agony.* (Foreword by Kermode, F.) Oxford: Oxford University Press.

Quetel, C. and Morel, P. (1979) *Les fous et leurs médecines. De la Renaissance au XXe siècle.* Paris: Hachette.

Quinidoz, D. (2003) *Words that Touch: A Psychoanalyst Learns to Speak.* London: Karnac.

Racker, H. (1982 [1968]) *Transference and Counter-Transference.* London: Karnac, Maresfield Library.

Rayner, E. and Tuckett, D. (1988) 'An Introduction to Matte-Blanco's Reformulation of the Freudian Unconscious and his Conceptualization of the Internal World', in Matte-Blanco, I. (1988) *Thinking, Feeling, and Being: Clinical Reflections on the Fundamental Antinomy of Human Beings and World.* London and New York: Tavistock/Routledge.

Reik, T. (1948) *Listening with the Third Ear: The Inner Experience of a Psychoanalyst.* New York: Grove.

Renza, L.A. (2008) 'Poe and Identity', in Poe (2008).

Rexroth, K. (1986 [1968]) *Classics Revisited.* New York: New Directions.

Reynaud, E. (1922) *Charles Baudelaire*. Paris: Librairie Garnier Frères.

Rivière, J. (1911) *Etudes*. Paris: Editions de la Nouvelle Revue.

Rizq, R. (2011) 'IAPT, Anxiety and Envy: A Psychoanalytic View of NHS Primary Care Mental Health Services Today'. *British Journal of Psychotherapy*, 27(1), February 2007, 37–55.

Rogers, C. (1967 [1961]) *On Becoming a Person: A Therapist's View of Psychotherapy*. London: Constable.

Rolland, J.-C. (2006) *Avant d'être celui qui parle*. Paris: Gallimard.

Rosen, C. (1998) *Romantic Poets, Critics, and Other Madmen*. Cambridge, MA and London: Harvard University Press.

Rosen, C. (2010) 'Happy Birthday, Robert Schumann!' *The New York Review of Books*, 23 December 2010–12 January 2011, LVII(20).

Rosen, C. and Zerner, H. (1984 [1979]) 'Romanticism: The Permanent Revolution', in *Romanticism and Realism: The Mythology of Nineteenth-Century Art*. New York: The Viking Press.

Rosenblum, R. (1970) *Transformations in Late Eighteenth-Century Art*. Princeton, NJ: Princeton University Press.

—— (1988) *The Romantic Child: From Runge to Sendak*. London: Thames & Hudson.

Rosenfeld, H. (1987) *Impasse and Interpretation*. London: Routledge.

Roudinesco, E. (1989) *Théoroïgne de Méricourt: Une femme mélancolique sous la Révolution*. Paris: Editions du Seuil.

—— (1993) *Jacques Lacan: Esquisse d'une vie, histoire d'un système de pensée*. Paris: Librairie Arthème Fayard.

Roudinesco, E. and Plon, M. (1997) *Dictionnaire de la psychanalyse*. Paris: Fayard.

Rousseau, J.-J. (1979 [1782]) *Reveries of the Solitary Walker*. London: Penguin.

Roustang, F. (2006 [2001]) *Le Thérapeute et son patient: Entretiens avec Pierre Babin*. La Tour d'Aigues: Editions de l'Aube.

Roy, C. (1969) 'Préface', in Hoffmann (1979).

Sachs, H. (2010) *The Ninth: Beethoven and the World in 1824*. London: Faber & Faber.

Sacks, O. (2000 [1989]) *Seeing Voices: A Journey into the World of the Deaf*. New York: Vintage Books.

St Augustine (2007) *Essential Sermons*. (Introduction and notes by Doyle, D.E., translated by Hill, E.) New York: New City Press.

St Benedict (1998) *The Rule of St Benedict*. (Preface by Moore, T., edited by Fry, T.) New York: Random House.

Schafer, R. (1983) *The Analytic Attitude*. London: The Hogarth Press and the Institute of Psychoanalysis.

Schlegel, K.W.F. (1991) *Philosophical Fragments*. (Translated by Firchow, P., Foreword by Gasché, R.) Minneapolis, MN and London: University of Minnesota Press.

Schulz, A. (2005) *Goya's Caprichos: Aesthetics, Perception, and the Body*. Cambridge: Cambridge University Press.

Searles, H.F. (1986) *Collected Papers on Schizophrenia and Related Subjects*. London: Maresfield Library.

Séché, A. (1928) *La Vie des Fleurs du mal*. Paris: publisher unknown.

Sharpe, E.F. (1932) 'The Defeat of Baudelaire'. London: *International Journal of Psycho-Analysis*, 13: 375–78.

—— (1988 [1937]) *Dream Analysis: A Practical Handbook for Psycho-Analysts.* London: Maresfield Library, Karnac.

Shelley, P.B. (1994) *The Selected Poetry and Prose of Shelley.* Ware, Hertforshire: Wordsworth Editions.

—— (2002) *Shelley's Poetry and Prose.* (Edited by Reiman, D.H. and Fraistat, N.) New York: Norton.

Singer, P. (2001) *Hegel. A Very Short Introduction.* Oxford: Oxford University Press

Snell, R. (1982) *Théophile Gautier: A Romantic Critic of the Visual Arts.* Oxford: Oxford University Press.

—— (2007) review of Miller 2006, *European Journal of Psychotherapy and Counselling,* June 2007, 9(2): 231–9.

Spillius (Bott), E. (1988) *Melanie Klein Today: Developments in Theory and Practice.* Vol. 1: *Mainly Theory*; Vol. 2: *Mainly Practice.* London and New York: Routledge.

Spinelli, E. (1989) *The Interpreted World: An Introduction to Phenomenological Psychology.* London: Sage.

Starobinski, J. (1979) *1789: Les emblèmes de la raison.* Paris: Flammarion.

—— (1989) 'La mélancolie au miroir', in *Conférences, essais et leçons du Collège de France.* Paris: Juillard.

Steadman, R. (1982) *Sigmund Freud.* London: Penguin Books.

Stendhal (1949 [1892]) *Memoirs of an Egotist.* London: Turnstile Press.

—— (1970 [1825]) *Racine et Shakespeare: Etudes sur le romantisme.* Paris: Garnier-Flammarion.

—— (1973) *Stendhal and the Arts.* (Selected and edited by Wakefield, D.) London: Phaidon.

—— (1973 [1890]) *The Life of Henry Brulard.* London: Penguin Books.

Stephens, S. (1999) *Baudelaire's Prose Poems: The Practice and Politics of Irony.* Oxford: Oxford University Press.

Stoichita, V.I. and Coderch, A.M. (1999) *Goya: The Last Carnival.* London: Reaktion Books.

Stolorow, R.D. (2009) 'Trauma and Human Existence: The Mutual Enrichment of Heidegger's Existential Analytic and a Psychoanalytic Understanding of Trauma'. In Frie and Orange (2009).

—— (2011) *World, Affectivity, Trauma: Heidegger and Post-Cartesian Psycho-analysis.* New York and London: Routledge.

Strathern, M. (2000) *Audit Cultures: Anthropological Studies in Accounting, Ethics and the Academy.* London: Routledge.

Streeck, W. (2011) 'The Crises of Democratic Capitalism'. *New Left Review,* 71, September/October.

Symington, N. (1986a) *The Analytic Experience: Lectures from the Tavistock.* London: Free Association Books.

—— (1986b) 'The Analyst's Act of Freedom as Agent of Therapeutic Change', in Kohon, G. (ed.) *The British School of Psychoanalysis: The Independent Tradition.* London: Free Association Books.

—— (2008) 'Generosity of Heart: Source of Sanity'. *British Journal of Psychotherapy,* 24(4), November.

Symmons, S. (2004) *Goya: A Life in Letters.* London: Pimlico.

Sulloway, F.J. (1979) *Freud, Biologist of the Mind: Beyond the Psychoanalytic Legend.* New York: Basic Books.

Thirlwell, A. (2008) 'Author, Author'. *Saturday Guardian (Review section)*, 26 July 2008.

Thomson, D. (1966) *Europe Since Napoleon*. Harmondsworth: Penguin.

Thomson, R. (2004) *The Troubled Republic: Visual Culture and Social Debate in France 1889–1900*. New Haven, CT and London: Yale University Press.

Thornes, J.E. (1999) *John Constable's Skies: A Fusion of Art and Science*. Birmingham: University of Birmingham Press.

Tomlinson, J.A. (1989) *Francisco Goya: The Tapestry Cartoons and Early Career at the Court of Madrid*. Cambridge: Cambridge University Press.

—— (1992) *Goya in the Twilight of Enlightenment*. New Haven, CT and London: Yale University Press.

Trilling, L. (1979[1950]) 'Freud and Literature', in *The Liberal Imagination: Essays on Literature and Society*. New York and London: Harcourt Brace Jovanovich.

Tucker, R.C. (ed.) (1978) *The Marx-Engels Reader* (2nd edition). New York: Norton.

Van Rillaer, J., Pleux, D., Cottraux, J., Borch-Jacobsen, M. and Meyer, C. (eds) (2005) *Le Livre noir de la psychanalyse: Vivre, penser et aller mieux sans Freud*. Paris: Les Arènes.

Vermorel, M. and Vermorel, H. (1986) 'Was Freud a Romantic?' *The International Review of Psycho-Analysis*, 13: 15–37

Vernière, P. (1970) Preface to Diderot, D. (1970 [1796]).

Versluis, A. (1989) Introduction to Novalis (1989).

Villiers de l'Isle-Adam, P.-A. (1980) *Contes cruels. Nouveaux Contes cruels* (Edition de Castex, P.-G.). Paris: Garnier.

Vigny, A. de (1963 [1832]) *Stello: A Session with Dr Noir*. (Translated by Massey, I.) Montreal: McGill University Press.

White, J. (2006) *Generation: Preoccupations and Conflicts in Contemporary Psycho-analysis*. London: Routledge.

Whyte, L.L. (1960) *The Unconscious Before Freud*. New York: Basic Books.

Williams, G.A. (1976) *Goya and the Impossible Revolution*. London: Allen Lane.

Williams, M.H. and Waddell, M. (1991) *The Chamber of Maiden Thought: Literary Origins of the Psychoanalytic Model of the Mind*. London and New York: Tavistock/Routledge.

Williams, R. (1976) *Keywords: A Vocabulary of Culture and Society*. London: Fontana.

Williams, R.L. (1980) *The Horror of Life*. Chicago, IL, and London: Chicago University Press.

Wilson-Bareau, J. (2001) *Goya: Drawings from his Private Albums*. London: Hayward Gallery.

Winnicott, D.W. (1985 [1971]) *Playing and Reality*. London: Penguin Books.

—— (1992 [1947]) 'Hate in the Countertransference', in *Through Paediatrics to Psycho-Analysis: Collected Papers*. London: Institute of Psycho-Analysis and Karnac.

Wolfenstein, M. (1966) 'Goya's Dining Room'. New York: *Psychoanalytic Quarterly*, 35: 47–83.

Wolff, R. (1981) 'Castration Symbolism in Baudelaire's *Fleurs du Mal*: An Essay in Psychoanalytic Content Analysis of Literary Texts'. Amsterdam: *Poetics*, 10: 409–56, October.

Wolfson, S. (1995) 'Keats and the Manhood of the Poet'. *European Romantic Review*, 6 (Summer).

Wolin, R. (ed.) (1993) *The Heidegger Controversy: A Critical Reader*. Cambridge, MA: MIT Press.

Wordsworth, W. (2000) *The Major Works: Including The Prelude*. Oxford: Oxford University Press.

Wroe, A. (2007a) *Being Shelley*. London: Jonathan Cape.

—— (2007b) 'Spirit for our Age'. *Saturday Guardian (Review section)*, 7 July.

Zinkin, L. (1969) 'Flexibility in Analytic Technique', in Fordham, Gordon, Hubback and Lambert (1974).

Žižek, S. (1998) 'The Cartesian Subject versus the Cartesian Theatre', in Žižek, S., *Cogito and the Unconscious*. Durham, NC: Duke University Press.

—— (2006) *How to Read Lacan*. London: Granta Books.

Index

Please note: page numbers relating to notes have the letter 'n' following the page number; references to figures are in *italics*.